By the same author:

In French:

Moissons d'Enfance, Editions De Borée, hard cover 2006
Moissons d'Enfance, Editions De Borée, paperback 2011
La Ferme aux Ecrevisses, Editions De Borée, hard cover 2008
La Ferme aux Ecrevisses, Editions De Borée, paperback 2015
De Michelin au Nouveau Monde, Editions des Monts d'Auvergne, 2011
Les Gamins de la Rue St. Quentin, Editions De Borée, hard cover 2014
La Course des Erables, Editions L'Harmattan, 2017. This book received
    the award *Prix de la Francophonie* in April 2018.

In English:

A Summer in Eden, Linden Press, 2010
Vernon Howe Bailey's America, Linden Press, 2014
Elvis, the Gospel Singer, Linden Press, 2016
Precisionism, An American Celebration, Linden Press, 2016
Elvis in Hawaii November 1957, Linden Press, 2017
Elvis in Las Vegas April May 1956, Linden Press, 2017
Elvis Black & White to Technicolor, Linden Press, 2017. This book
    was selected Best Book of the Year in 2018 by the Elvis Information Network, Australia.
The Messages of America, The Golden Age of Printmaking, Linden
    Press, 2018
Elvis April 1956, Linden Press, 2018
Elvis Seven Days in March 1960, Linden Press, 2018
The Messages of New York, The Golden Age of Printmaking, Linden
    Press, 2019
Kathe Kollwitz, Mothers and Children, To be published

Copper, Fiber & Lean Times

A Memoir of my years with a Telecommunications Giant

COPYRIGHT © 2018 BY PAUL F. BÉLARD

ALL RIGHTS RESERVED

LIBRARY OF CONGRESS CONTROL NUMBER: 2018907088

ISBN: 978-0-9998939-2-0

FIRST EDITION: 0 9 8 7 6 5 4 3 2 1

PRINTED IN THE UNITED STATES OF AMERICA

Picture front cover © Paul Bélard
Picture back cover © Alice Bélard Biais
Cover design by Paul Bélard
Cover set up by Walter Sargent, sargentwebservices. com

PAUL BÉLARD

COPPER, FIBER & AND LEAN TIMES

A MEMOIR OF MY YEARS WITH A TELECOMMUNICATIONS GIANT

The work of an unknown good man is like a vein of water flowing hidden in the underground, secretly making the ground greener.
Thomas Carlyle

There are many good men and women working for Verizon, whose names are seldom acknowledged. They all contribute to making the company successful, some even more than others.

This book is dedicated to:

> The memory of Gary Shumway who gave of his time, energy and talent well beyond what is expected of an employee. He made the Telephone Company a better place.

> George Famulare who was instrumental in the recovery of the Telephone Building heavily damaged on September 11, 2001. He was recognized by New York City Mayor as one of ten heroes of 9/11.

Prologue

Wednesday, March 19, 2003.

An eight-page card was displayed on our assigned table. The cover was horizontally traversed by a slanted yellow band on black background. Three pictures stood above this yellow strip: a bouquet of pink flowers, an array of golden pistils erupting from the inside of curled petals, and a butterfly alighting on a blossom. Underneath, "Verizon Excellence Awards" was printed. Further down, starting across the yellow band and ending on the black background was written: "An extraordinary person is sitting here." Would you believe I was the "extraordinary person?"

I was not the only one, being a member of a team that had been nominated for this award ceremony. There were dozens of other teams made of "extraordinary persons" scattered throughout the room. This was a big night for all invited. For a time, we were "la crème de la crème", the Verizon elite, the select few. It was like the Oscars, the Emmys, and a high school honor roll ceremony all rolled into one. Inside the cover of the card, held in place by a red cord punctuated by an attractive knot, was a vellum page on which was printed: "Verizon Excellence Awards, Network Services Group, Regent Wall Street, New York City, New York." Below was a menu touting salad as New York State field greens and dessert mousse as a Wall Street pyramid of bittersweet chocolate. The filet mignon, however, was qualified as *petit*. I would have preferred a large one, but let's not quibble. After all, the accompanying jumbo shrimp would surely make up for the puny size of the filet mignon.

The organizers did an outstanding job. A long black limousine had been rented by the company for my wife and me so that we could travel in style, as befitted an "extraordinary person". We were dropped off in front of a grand building with a granite facade fronted by two levels of twelve tall columns each that my boss, who was an architect, would have recognized as Greek revival style. Indeed, it was an imposing colonnade. The interior leaned more toward classical Roman. The place was stylish on a grand scale. For a second, I, who was born on a farm in the middle of nowhere in France, felt out of place and as conspicuous as a black fly in a glass of milk. Thankfully, I adjusted quickly to the life of the rich and famous. We entered an imposing room which extended under a sixty-foot-high central gilt dome. Monumental Corinthian columns supported an elegant circular lintel trimmed with cornices and friezes. Barrel vaults and high windows were adorned with graceful details. The use of luxurious gray marble on the floors and walls, coffered ceiling, and elegant mezzanine railings, contributed to the grandeur and dignity of the room.

The original structure had been constructed in the mid-1800s. Built for the Merchants' Exchange, it later housed the Stock Exchange, then the United State Custom House. When this later institution outgrew these quarters and moved to Bowling Green, the building became the headquarters of the National City Bank. At the beginning of the 20th century, the building was remodeled and more stories and columns added. In January 2000, the building became The Regent Wall Street, the first luxury hotel in New York's financial district.

The ceremony was a brilliant success. All participants behaved well. The introduction of the winners was eloquently made by some of the Verizon brass, peppered by a few well-received humoristic anecdotes.

Our team did not win. Most of the awards were given to teams involved in the restoration of the West Street building, following the damages it had suffered during the tragic events of September 11, 2001. This was as it should have been, as these individuals did a terrific job to bring the building back on line in record time and under great pressure. At any rate, as so many also-rans at the Oscars are fond of saying: "the important thing is to be nominated."

We had no regrets. We still received a commemorating

plaque inscribed with the word "Finalist" and the salad, aka New York State field greens, tossed with balsamic vinaigrette had been a real treat for sophisticated palates. The filet mignon melted on the tongue, the shrimp were firm, and the pyramid of bittersweet chocolate mousse with passion fruit crème and exotic coulis collapsed exquisitely in the mouth. The wine was decent and plentiful.

On the way back, the radio in the limousine announced in surround sound that the "decider" and his team of reputable advisers had decided to go for another round of Gulf Wars. Young men and women were to be sent to Iraq to destroy the Weapons of Mass Destruction that allegedly hung over the free world like the sword of Damocles.

Monday, March 1st, 2004.

The card posed on the table read on one of the quadrants that divided the colorful cover: "You hold the key to the extraordinary." This sentence was flanked by a key entering a key hole. It was above another picture depicting a golden key resting on two opened hands. The symbolism was clear: The beneficiaries of the card were the keepers of the key to success. On the last quadrant was the now familiar "Verizon Excellence Awards".

Following the dictum "If at first you don't succeed, try again," our team, once again, put forward a project to the judges. In fact, it was technologically identical to the one submitted the year before. The only difference was that it was installed in a building with a different address. Would the judges be fooled? Against all odds, we were nominated again.

This year, the ceremony was taking place at Gotham Hall in New York City, a grand building that ate up quite a few yards along Broadway. According to the venue's brochure, this was where "style met sophistication". To be sure, the reception hall was impressive. We entered a room with a magnificent inlaid marble floor and an exquisitely gilded domed ceiling with a stained-glass skylight in its center. Solid limestone Corinthian columns adorned each end of the hall's oval shape. This former Greenwich Savings Bank headquarters proved, like Regent Wall Street, that bankers indeed knew how to take care of themselves in a grand manner. Recent events have once again proven that they have not lost the Midas touch. They still know how to recompense themselves with panache and other people's money, and apparently with little consequence as evidenced by their latest shenanigans in 2008.

Inside the card was a vellum page on which was printed: "Verizon Excellence Awards, Network Services Group, Regent Wall Street, New York City, New York". The menu was less refined than the one from the previous year. The salad was simply called "salad." Wild striped bass, charred filet of beef and white chocolate bread pudding followed. All in all, a rather pedestrian menu, but still nothing to sneeze at.

Our table became a little tense when our team category was announced. The accomplishments of the teams in competition for the Excellence Award were read aloud. As "the-envelope-please" moment arrived, my wife squeezed my hand for good luck.

When our team's name was read and its members invited to the stage, I felt almost as giddy as I had been on my first date. A Verizon Officer, whose name I did not get, flooded as I was by waves of emotion that affected my information intake, shook hands with each of us. This was a moment to be counted among the best Verizon had to offer. What a validation of all of the hard work and dedication that so often went unrecognized. That moment near the top, even though it would be brief, was savored, relished, and valued. It was a parent's moment, very exhilarating, when you wish they were still around to see that, after all, they had done a pretty good job with their kids.

Later on, we went to receive the trophy that commemorated this achievement. No wonder it was not given on the stage. The darn thing weighed close to a ton. It was not very classy, making up in mass what it lacked in grace. A chunky marble Verizon logo "V" rested on an equally thick marble base. Between the branches of the "V" was imbedded a glass circle in which was etched: "Verizon Excellence Awards".

The award also included a monetary component. I opened the envelope, expecting that being an "extraordinary person holding the key to the extraordinary" would rate a few thousand dollars, maybe more. What a letdown to find a check which, after taxes, would not even cover a decent meal at an equally decent restaurant. The amount was not even enough to buy a nice bottle of Sauternes or Chateauneuf-du-Pape. Oh well, it seemed that a free meal, a statuette and a limousine ride was enough reward as far as the company was concerned.

Thursday, October 30th, 2008.

In my modest office in the Huntington central office, a thick white envelope was gingerly handed to me by my immediate supervisor. In my hand, it seemed as heavy as the Ten Commandments tablets. Above the cellophane window was printed an attractive "confidential", in capital red letters. Through this opening, a ominous warning enjoined: "To be opened by addressee only." Had I not been aware of what it foreshadowed, it would have been very threatening indeed. At least, it did not add: "Destroy after reading!" In the left top corner, an address indicated that this envelope originated from Human Resources.

I knew only too well what it contained. For weeks a forboding of bad things to come had been hovering over me. It was as if I had a glimpse around the curve of my future. So I opened it with a calm I did not have to feign. It was time to face the music which I knew would sound more like a funeral dirge than Beethoven's *Ode to Joy*.

The stack of paper I extracted was made up of several dozen pages. Lord, that thing was longer than a Russian novel. What happened to the simple pink slip!

It started with a notification letter. The first paragraph read: "This is to advise you that, due to reductions, re-staffing or reorganization of the work force, you are now in the redeployment period of a Reduction in Force (RIF)…" Great, now I can add that to my business card: Paul F. Belard, MME, PE, CEM[1], RIF.

It continued: Your last active day at work will be November 6th and your last day on payroll will be November 28th, 2008." Hmm, laid-off just before Thanksgiving, how considerate! Indeed, it was going to be something to be thankful for to be discussed around the dinner table. The selfless and gallant actions of the corporate world never cease to overwhelm.

What followed was a table of contents longer than a day without bread. Here are some of the highlights:

- Notification letter
- Separation agreement and release
- Explanation of severance calculations
- Verizon management severance program Q&A

There were another fourteen sections to digest. I decided to read them before going to bed because they would certainly be more effective than a sleeping pill.

---

1   MME: Master in Mechanical Engineering
       PE: Professional Engineer
       CEM: Certified Energy Manager

What had happened to a once proud recipient of the "Verizon Excellence Award"? Was it simply that what the Romans had discovered a long time ago had caught up with him? *Sic transit gloria Mundi*, they said, "Thus passes the glory of the world".

In the old days, the newly elected pope proceeded from Saint Peter's Basilica sitting in his richly-adorned, silk-covered portable throne. On his way to his adoring flock waiting in the piazza, a papal master of ceremonies would fall to his knees before him. Three times, he would say in a thunderous, yet mournful voice: "Holy Father so passes worldly glory!"
These words served as a reminder to the infallible pontiff of the transitory nature of life's earthly honors.

I must say that they did not bring me any comfort. Also, I call your attention to the fact that in view of my height that is on the short side, I did not cotton to being downsized again all that happily. My boss took his leave, tapping my shoulder in an appreciated gesture of empathy. I was now left with my own thoughts.

What happened to the "extraordinary person"? How did "the key to the extraordinary" become the key that would fatefully unlock the company exit door?

CHAPTER 1

First Contact

Since my move to the United States from France at the end of 1978, I had been working for several consulting engineering firms. I can still recall answering a want ad from *The New York Times* in early January 1979, following my arrival. Two days later, I received a phone call. The company that placed the want ad asked me to come for an interview in New York City. Following a dialogue of about thirty minutes, I was hired. I was amazed.

In France, it would have taken multiple meetings in no particular order. It is likely that several tests would have been scheduled to interpret my reactions to the shape of a few ink blots to help the company get an insight into some hidden trait of my personality. In other words before a final decision would be made, several weeks, sometimes even months, would go by.

I marveled at this country, where you could get a job following a half-hour interview. Little did I know then that this same job could be lost in an even shorter period of time. Twelve years of engineering work taught me that employment in these companies was tightly wed to active projects one could charge one's time to. When these projects dried up, the weekly hours had to be shifted to overhead on the weekly time sheet. It was the kiss of death. Those with no billable hours would become undesirable and quickly disposed of.

The bad news was characteristically conveyed on a Friday afternoon. You were told that there was no need to come back to the office on Monday, due to lack of work. The only consolation was the promise of a telephone call as soon as a new project was under contract and a half-hearted "Fate and fortune be your friend." I had been in this situation three times in a ten year period. Do I need to add that benefits were also terminated?
So, well aware of the precariousness of the positions in these consulting firms, my résumé was always up-to-date and floating in several of the employment agencies that dotted the New York City and Long Island landscape. I had made the Boy Scout motto "Be prepared" mine.

In 1982, I worked for Crawford & Russell, an engineering firm located in Stanford, Connecticut. From where I lived, it was a long and tedious commute, too often close to two hours each way. Luckily, there were four employees also living on Long Island. We decided to car pool to spread the stress of driving on I-95. We met in a parking lot situated in Christopher Morley Park, off exit 36 on the Long Island Expressway. There, in turn, one car picked up the other drivers and we all proceeded to Stanford.

The radio was always on to keep track of the locations of accidents, or of which bridge was the less clogged. We adjusted our route accordingly. One morning in January, we heard of the breakup of AT&T. It was big news, although I did not really understand why. Frankly, I did not know much about this company, except that its initials were on the telephone sets and its bell symbol was on the phone booths that dotted the American landscape. Since its inception in the late 1800s, AT&T had been the most important provider of telephone service throughout the United States. There were also several small companies which served rural America, Continental Telephone and GTE are notable examples. They were not part of the "Bell System" and were not owned by AT&T. I later learned that, in addition to being a power-house, most of AT&T telephonic equipment was produced by its subsidiary, Western Electric. Consequently, in 1974, the United States Department of Justice filed an antitrust lawsuit against AT&T.

One of the commuters was a company's vice-president. I remembered him deploring this breakup. For days, he fumed about the interference of the government into the business world. Personally, I did not have an opinion. But in one of these twists of fate that life plays on you at times, little did I know that, eight years later, I would be a beneficiary of this ruling.

Early in 1990, one of the employment agencies I had sent my résumé to contacted me regarding a potential job. The agent informed me that New York Telephone was looking for engineers with my technical background.

"Would I be interested?" he asked. Would I like to work for a company that had, to my knowledge, not laid off a single employee for the past hundred years? My goodness, it was like asking a French politician if he had a mistress! Of course, yes, yes, I would be very much interested; when can I start? "Well", he said, "You have a little obstacle in your way that needs to be cleared first. It is called an interview."

Promptly, one was set up at an office building at 111 Livingston Street in Brooklyn. I went there dressed in my best suit, set my tie properly looking at the mirror-like shine of my shoes and entered. My potential boss, Bill Drum, met me in the lobby. He took me upstairs to a small conference room. A no-nonsense man, he did not beat around the bush with existentialist questions such as, "Why you and not somebody else?", or pedestrian ones like "What do you feel makes you an asset for the phone company?", "Where do you see yourself in five years," or "What are your hobbies?" His questions were straightforward and highly technical, as the following suggest:

> "Please tell me what is the amount of water lost by evaporation and drift in cooling towers?"
>
> "And what is the velocity of the air stream in a building air conditioning system's distribution shafts?"
>
> "Can you tell me what is the net positive suction head of a centrifugal pump?"
>
> "You know that the power factor is the ratio of work-

ing power to apparent power and that it measures how effectively electrical power is being used in a building. What would you propose to improve the power factor?

All these years as a consulting engineer had not been for naught. These questions came up regularly in construction or renovation project calculations. I answered all of them easily and without hesitation.

The interview did not last more than a half hour, but it went well, I thought, as I left the building.

CHAPTER 2

First Days

Soon after, the agency informed me things were indeed looking good. I was advised to go to the Company's headquarters, located behind the New York Public Library on the Avenue of the Americas. This was an impressive building, with walls clad in white and black marble, about forty stories high. It befitted the reputation of the Telephone Company and I was thoroughly impressed.

There, a manager in the Personnel Department welcomed me. That was before they were called Human Resources managers. In my opinion, the removal of the word "Personnel" from the department appellation put the employees squarely in the capitalistic system where they belonged. After all, had not Karl Marx, prescient about the excesses of capitalism, said: "In the capitalist age, we began to treat one another as commodities." Employees had been reduced from individuals to resources, to the same levels as air conditioning machines, writing pads and light bulbs. It would not be long before they could be bought or rented from the likes of Office Depot or Staples. Indeed, in some companies, a pound of flesh was not more valuable than a pound of copy paper.

Philosophical musing aside, that morning the manager was very cordial and offered me a position in the Standards Group without really explaining what it entailed. I would be reporting to a building in Brooklyn, the one in which the initial interview had taken place. Although the salary would be $10,000 less that I was currently earning, I gladly accepted without asking any questions. Avoiding an eventual nervous breakdown was worth that kind of money. The fact that I was not offered a contract in writing was not even raised. I was too happy to finally leave consulting engineering behind. I did it without an ounce of regret.

The first days were spent in becoming acquainted with my new colleagues and new surroundings, notably the men's room and the cafeteria. They also entailed signing a few forms, learning about the benefits that filled a three-ring binder as thick as a brick standing on its side, and reading about the company Code of Conduct, an opus with slightly fewer pages than *War and Peace*.

These blissful days were like the best dreams one could have. After the grueling years in the trenches of engineering fields of battle, where sixty to seventy hours a week had been the norm, I felt as if I had been admitted to an exclusive country club. Now, the work week took a drastic drop to an unheard of and steady thirty-five hours. It was, in addition, sweetened by coffee or tea breaks in the second floor cafeteria. Copies could be printed and telephone calls made without having to first enter a project code number to which they would be charged. No time sheet to keep track of how the hours were spent were handed to me. In brief, it was the Garden of Eden without the snake! There was a relaxed atmosphere in the office. One of Bill's first welcoming sentences astonished me. He said that it would probably take a year for me to learn everything I needed to know to do my job efficiently. A year! When I started in a consulting firm, if I had one hour to become adjusted before I was expected to put some productive lines on a drawing board, I was lucky.

I learned a lot about the history of New York Telephone. It was an offspring of American Telephone and Telegraph Company. The beginnings of this famed company went back to the company founded by Alexander Graham Bell, the inventor of the telephone. It was named Bell Telephone Company. For some legal reasons, it morphed into AT&T which soon established a network across the entire United States. In doing so, it became for a century a huge monopoly, affectionately known by the nickname Ma Bell. It was the world's largest phone company.
In 1982, the Department of Justice broke up this mo-

nopoly. The company was forced to divest its regional subsidiaries. These new companies became known as Regional Bell Operating Companies. They were soon dubbed, Baby Bells and operated locally without competition. New York Telephone, which had been created as a subsidiary of AT&T in 1896 to provide services to New York City and Long Island, was now an independent entity. AT&T, on the other hand, retained the long distance call services, but now, it faced competition from rivals such as MCI and Sprint.

The pace of work was no more stressful than a leisurely stroll on a sunny lunch break along the Promenade in Brooklyn Heights, only a few minutes away from the office. My hiring occurred because quite a few people were retiring in the coming weeks. Consequently, there were untold numbers of farewell parties still being paid for at the time by the department for the retirees. They started around 2:00 p.m. and lasted until quitting time, 4:00 p.m. The quality of the catered food was so-so, but it was plentiful. The audience was laid-back and funny. So were most of the tributes and the jokes told at the expense of those leaving.
After the pressure that had been my constant companion during the previous decade, stress disappeared. I became so relaxed that I even used my new found free time to paint. Watercolor mostly, to save time on cleaning the brushes. Churchill was right when he said "To paint is to love again". Indeed, I felt born again, professionally.

Our office was on the seventh floor. We were seven employees in the Standards Group, a sub division of Corporate Real Estate. Including our boss, there were three Bills. One had been working for Western Electric and was having a sort of second career before finally hanging up his slide rule for good. I could not tell his age but he was still pissed off at Franklin D. Roosevelt for some reason so he must have been around quite a long time.

Then there was Bill who was in charge of everything that involved Fire Protection. This was an odd choice because, if there was a spot in the entire building that was a fire hazard, it was his area. His filing system was extremely simple. Everything was right there on his desk, or in piles beside it. A mountainous clutter of paper at least two inches thick covered the top, loose sheets hanging from the sides bent like palm tree fronds. Notwithstanding, it was he who kept the company abreast of all aspects of Fire Protection. Still, there was logic to this mess. When his boss asked him for a document from, let's say, five years ago, he plunged into the pile with the ardor of a fox terrier running after a ferret and always came up with the proper piece of paper in a decent amount of time.

The remaining members were Ari, a quiet Iranian expatriate who was an electrical engineer; Terry, another electrical engineer who gave me the best recipe for pizza dough I had ever tasted, and Mark, a young engineer who was also coming from the consulting world. He was hired at the same time as I was.

The third Bill, our boss, was the man who interviewed me and gave me a new lease on my professional career so to speak. For this, I will be ever grateful to him.

The new colleagues were a nice bunch, pleasant and easy to be with. The work was not very demanding. It mostly consisted of reviewing new regulations or Code changes enacted by different nation-wide, state-wide or county-wide organizations. We selected the ones that concerned the telephone company and disseminated them to the right department. In addition, since the group was comprised of technical experts, we were at time consulted about design problems that fell into our area of expertise. It was an interesting job, rewarding and without any smidgen of stress. I loved it.

One afternoon, Bill Drum took me to New York City to visit a telephone central office (CO), also known as a telephone exchange. It was on the eighth floor of 140 West Street telephone building, in the shadows of the two towers of the World Trade Center. A central office contains the equipment or switches that allow the subscribers to call any number within the area served by this CO. Bill explained that two copper wires which he called tip and ring ran between the subscriber's location and the local telephone exchange. The calls are dialed using a seven digit number. To place a call in a location served by another CO, a three digit area code identifying this CO must be dialed before the regular telephone number.

Presently, I was shown the only remaining electromechanical switching equipment in the New York area, known as a cross bar 5. The equipment covered half of the floor. The space was alive with the incessant clicking of the relays which sounded like a thousand dogs with uncut nails walking on ceramic tiles. The peeling paint on the vertical steel frames bespoke decades of operation. Two years later, a new digital switch, enclosed and almost silent would replace it, taking only one quarter of its space.

As the general manager for real estate at New York Telephone said to the *New York Times:* "The new digital switching systems have caused our need for space to diminish precipitously, because the new devices are one-fifth the size of the old devices." Of 140 West Street, he added the company was "going to take advantage of that transition and put people back in that building."[1] Indeed over the next three years, much of New York Telephone's engineering department had moved into the spaces freed by the diminishing equipment.

Later, we went to have a drink in the cafeteria of the telephone building located on seventh Avenue. It was about 3:30 p.m. I would have preferred to head to Penn Station to catch an early train home rather than nursing a coke, but Bill insisted on staying until our working day officially ended, that is 4:00 o'clock. He was a representative of the old guard, a nine-to-four loyal employee who gave the company every minute it was due.

---

1   Source: http://www.nytimes.com/1991/10/20/realestate/commercial-property-communications-landmarks-new-technology-old-architecture.html?

CHAPTER 3

Slippery Slope

Two unrelated things became apparent after a few weeks at New York Telephone. Firstly, the numerous retirement parties were in fact the prelude to a long period of reduction in personnel, although nobody was aware of it at the time. Secondly, there was a purge going on in the Design and Construction department, of which the Standard Group was a component.

An investigation had started to review the shenanigans of one or two employees. It seemed that these enterprising and creative, albeit not too honest workers, had found a way to increase their earnings by requesting kick-backs from contractors. In short, they had turned the department into their own ATM. This investigation soon expanded to other departments, most of which were in direct contact with contractors, such as the Maintenance Group. The inquiry seemed to turn into an inquisition directed against all employees suspected of having received gifts from undesirable sources.

One day, entire departments were asked to gather in a conference room at 140 West Street. It was my second visit to this building in just a few weeks. We were all going to be given our marching orders regarding the ways to deal with suppliers.

The bearer of this news barged into the theater-like conference room as if he was imbued with some celestial powers, the left hand of God personified. He strutted on the stage, a cross between a "taking-no-prisoners" General Patton and one of those mad clerics threatening the sinners with the fires of hell and eternal damnation for good measure.

Those who expected a Dale Carnegie moment were going to be disappointed. Obviously, he was not here to make friends and this was no morale booster. He had been sent to clean out this den of thieves and "by golly", this is exactly what he was going to do. His eyes surveyed his audience with the intensity of a machine gunner sighting his next victims. His message was clear, ready to be imparted to the bunch of shady individuals running on a hamster wheel of which he would from now on control the speed. The enforcer had come to town, with instructions from on high to make the trouble go away and make the people causing the trouble go away as well.

"The investigation is still going on, more heads are

going to fall," he sneered, his eyes corruption-seeking missiles homing in on his captive audience. "In the meantime, do not even think about accepting anything from a contractor, not even an Altoïd because it will bring you closer to the slippery slope of bribery. Beware of the contractor bearing gifts! He would own your soul instantly and expect all those padded change orders of his to sail across your desk with your seal of approval."

You had to give it to him; he exuded an undeniable taste for the theatrical. His oratory flair would have made a southern preacher blanch with jealousy. At times, he was so "holier than thou" that one thought about sending his name to the Vatican so that they could have a head start on his canonization process. The verbal cataract continued unabated for a while, a torrent of words that flowed, inundating the entire room. At times they tumbled out of his mouth like soda cans from a vending machine. He seemed to enjoy himself so much that when he finished, he must have gone out to the loading docks to smoke a post-coital cigarette, convinced that he had righted everything that was wrong in the world.

It was plain to see that he felt he was one of the self anointed lords of the universe, with an inflated opinion of himself and the assurance that, without him, the company would not survive. Yet, like so many irreplaceable employees, what would happen if he were killed by a wayward bus the next morning? How great a ripple would it cause in the company? How many days would it take for his name to be forgotten?

As my father used to wisely say: "The cemeteries are full of irreplaceable people." I often thought about him; I missed his wisdom and prudence in navigating life's treacherous paths.

After the performance, somebody who knew this bombastic gentleman was telling his small audience that, yes, he was a sanctimonious, patronizing bastard, but he was also strongly connected within the company. He had a powerful rabbi. In other words, he was someone to be wary of.

He was right on one point though; an investigation was in the works. Accepting gifts in any company had always been frowned upon, an offense against which swift corporate action was required.

Yes, receiving gifts might greatly reduce the odds of doing one's job with impartiality and fairness. As there is a big difference between a little white lie and a whopper, there is a huge disparity between asking for bribes on the cost of a contract in the form of cash under the table and receiving an unasked for bottle of wine at Christmas. One is a felony; the other a peccadillo compounded by bad judgment, at the very most. Still, the company seemed to paint any transgression with the same broad brush, making it difficult to separate the wheat from the chaff.

Consequently, a wide net was cast by the Security Department. Many employees were captured in its tiny mesh. Like in any inquisition, some employees were found guilty by association and a few innocents must have been punished.

For weeks, people were called in, sometimes called again. The small fry, defined as having received a $50 gift certificate or a couple of bottles, had their salaries red lined, capped for a few years and no bonuses. Above this threshold, firing appeared to be the rule. Quite a few employees came back only to clean their desks; their careers at New York Telephone abruptly ended.

Were they all guilty? The contractors were often in the office. They had access to the internal telephone directories and the names they contained. Those who were most unscrupulous could use any name on the back of a restaurant receipt to justify an expensive dinner to impress a girlfriend. A few employees had a hard time disproving the incriminating but fabricated evidence.

The investigation continued for a while. New hires were brought in to plug the holes. Some careers were even launched into an ascendant trajectory, proving once again that the misfortune of some is the luck of others.

The Standard Group was not touched and we remained whole. It would only exist for another year though.

CHAPTER 4

Strikes

A phone company comprises all types of employees. There are splicers, engineers, secretaries, linemen, accountants, installers, lawyers, technicians, supervisors to name a few. More simply though, these people are divided in two classes: the union employees and the managers. The members of a union are protected by labor contracts. The managers are non-unionized. Consequently, they serve at the whims of the company officers and board without any organization to represent and defend them.

At New York Telephone, the contract cycle is every three years, however that can change due to the occasional extension. A few months before the expiration of the current contract, preliminary talks take place. More often than not, they do not lead to an agreement and the unions flex their muscles the only way they know how: by going on strike! This occurs when a new contract is not in place on the day the previous one expires, usually right after midnight.

When there is a strike, picket lines form at the entrances of most buildings and the managers that have been "volunteered" to fulfill the strikers' functions are forced to walk a heckling gauntlet before entering their assigned building. Per company instructions, management is not allowed any confrontation, not even to flip them the finger. I can confirm that this humiliating walk is not a pleasant experience, having gone through quite a few. This is even worse when some of the union members take it upon themselves to improve their harassment skills.

Have you ever heard of "the goon squad"? In Manhattan there was a motivated group of twelve or so union members that hopped into a passenger van and went from building to building to pester managers with a few choice words and explicit epithets. They were hurled at their victims via a megaphone. Every so often, they picked on an employee who looked meek. Courage has never been a trait of bullies who come in a group to victimize an innocent target. The "squad" would follow the poor manager as he or she was leaving the building to go to lunch or for a stroll and harass him or her as he or she was eating or walking, shouting "scab" and other not-so-nice names. In short, these things made the poor prey feel terrible. The group's actions were probably not even sanctioned by the union locals, hence the derisive name.

Once, a woman came back in tears, telling between sobs

what had happened to her. She had been one of their harmless victims. The picket line was more often than not behind police barriers because they had to remain at a certain distance from the telephone buildings. The picketers came well prepared: they sat in lounging chairs, coolers well filled with cold ones, close at hand; and boom boxes churning out belligerent music. In short, they were picketing in style and a jolly good time was had by all. A colleague who had a few friends in the police contacted them. He explained the situation and the police decided to teach the strikers a lesson.

Several officers came and explained that the law was very explicit regarding picket lines: loitering was not permitted; they had to walk at all times. Then, they proceeded to enforce said law, at times at the point of their truncheons. Reluctantly, the picketers got up and started marching back and forth, no longer a happy group. The strikers could not even stop to grab a beer can from the coolers. Half an hour later, three quarters of them had retired to their homes or the next bar. After two days of this treatment, the building entrance was free of picketers. "The goon squad" also got the message loud and clear. What a relief it was! Strikes were hard enough on managers without having to suffer the insults of the strikers.

Do not mistake the contempt I feel towards the poor attitude of the strikers on the picket lines for a dislike of unions. On the contrary, I feel they are a necessary counterweight to the excesses of the other side.

In 1989, the company had just experienced one of its longest and most embittered confrontations. The issue had been health care costs. The phone company had wanted to shift some of these costs to the union members. To these company proposed give-backs, the major unions, including the Communication Workers of America (CWA) and the International Brotherhood of Electrical Workers (IBEW) responded "health care for all," which translated to "no cut in medical benefits" for union workers. They went on strike to parry this threat.

NYNEX, the holding company, owned New York Telephone and New England Telephone and provided local telephone service to seven Northeastern states. Although strikes at other regional telephone companies throughout the country had been settled over the summer, NYNEX claimed it needed to take a harder line because it faced a more difficult operating environment. It is a fact that NYNEX had significantly higher operating costs than other Baby Bells because the older telephone equipment and switches in its network were expensive to maintain and replace. In addition, it operated in areas that required more labor to provide services, at higher costs than in the rest of the country.

The company promised it would not budge on its demands. For months, it had been clear that a major showdown loomed between NYNEX and the unionized employees. More than forty locals had banded together, prepared for it, and organized the troops. When the contract negotiations broke down, they were ready and willing. In excess of 60,000 telephone workers in New England and New York went on strike on August 6, 1989. The union leadership had formed valuable alliances with a number of organizations, such as the National Organization for Women (NOW) and community associations. All this preparation insured that the strike would last a long time. And indeed it did.

Of course, there had been strikes before. Among the longest in recent years were:

> 1955: The strike was in answer to management's effort to prohibit workers from striking. It lasted ten weeks and, as the following strikes were to prove, it was successful.
> 1971: Strike over wages. While the rest of the country settled after three months, the New York locals held out for another four months, resulting in slight salary increases.
> 1983: This one involved the last contract with the Bell System before its breakup. 600,000 employees went on strike during three weeks. While ATT sought givebacks, the contract resulted in wage increases, employment security, as well as pension and health improvements.
> 1986: The COLA (Cost Of Living Allowance) won during the strike of 1971 is suspended. Also, the contracts for the Baby Bells and ATT started to differ substantially.

No one could have predicted the 1989 strike would last

as long as it did. When it entered its third month, the corporation started to feel the pain. The number of telephone lines in service had declined drastically because new ones could not be installed fast enough. That, in turn, took a bite out of revenues and profits. Even so, NYNEX claimed it could hold out for many more months before the strike began to have a financially devastating effect. Still, a telecommunications analyst with Paine Webber reduced his earnings estimate to $5.85 a share from $6.00, for 1989, and to $6.20 from $6.50, for 1990. This was confirmed by the vice chairman of NYNEX: "The strike is having a negative impact on revenues because we have a continuing backlog of new installations, because our focus during the strike is keeping those folks who are already in service in service. In terms of the general question, "Are we losing money in the strike?" the answer is nobody makes money in a strike. While we in the short term have some expense reductions, we also have increased costs from folks doing security and overtime. Put it all together, and the strike is close to an aggregate financial neutral." Neutral impact, maybe, but both sides hurt. First-time-ever visits to food banks were recorded by union members; dismissal, suspension, or arrest of hundreds fell on union activists in New York and New England. Pressure was coming from multiple directions to end this work stoppage.

The turning point came when a CWA picket captain was hit by a car driven by what the unions labelled a scab. The victim died of brain injuries in a garage in Greenburgh, NY. The "scab" was a nineteen-year-old girl who was trying to cross the picket line to fulfill her duties. The fact that for her it was a choice between going to work or losing her job, did not soften the picketers. What gave a bunch of union members the right to hurl insults and misogynist comments at colleagues? They could take lessons from French workers. When they have problems, they go to the source to seek retribution. To illustrate this point, here is an article that appeared in a French paper in 2008.

PITHIVIERS, France (AFP) – Angry French workers are holding the boss of their factory hostage to try to make their U. S. employers improve their redundancy package, police and union officials said on Wednesday. The detention came less than two weeks after workers held the boss of Sony France hostage overnight before freeing him after he agreed to re-open talks on their pay-off when the factory closed. The latest case was in the central town of Pithiviers where employees of the US industrial conglomerate 3M detained their boss late Tuesday to force him to renegotiate pay-offs and compensations for workers moved to other plants. "This action (hostage-taking) is our only currency. But there is no aggression," union representative *name withheld* told AFP. "Talks were held overnight but they led nowhere." There have been several cases of executives being held hostage over the past year by French workers outraged at learning that their jobs were being slashed. Last week, angry tire factory workers burst into a management meeting and pelted their bosses with eggs to protest the closure of their plant.

Doesn't the last sentence have a nice ring to it? Haven't you honestly felt the same way sometimes? In truth, it might have been a little excessive: after all, why waste a good omelet? You know that a Frenchman must have been pushed to extremes to squander food this way!

Anyway, it is indeed the safe and spineless way to abuse management colleagues with nobody to defend them rather than taking the fight directly to the company officers. Go to the upper-crust part of town, park yourselves next to the manicured lawns and insult anybody who drives in and out of the sprawling mansions. Of course, the owners would not have any qualms about calling the police and having all the protesters thrown in jail for disturbing their peace.

What would the union members who took arms to gain rights and were killed in the Herrin Massacre and the Ludlow slaughter think of these picketers insulting their fellow workers instead of picketing NYNEX upper management where they lived?

Back to the incident: hit by a "scab'" was the union version of what happened. Witnesses offer a different explanation. Both sides accused the other of reckless behavior.

For the union, this day would henceforth be known as "Bloody Thursday." Since then, members wear red on Thursdays, not to show communist leanings as some think, but to commemorate this heartrending occurrence. Through the years, this garage has remained a hot bed of activities. In the mind of quite a few employees, it should have been razed to the ground. Instead it has been turned into an impromptu shrine. Following this sad event, Governor Mario Cuomo became actively involved and the strike was soon settled. NYNEX had lost the bravado of the early days and simply caved in on all fronts. After nearly four months of conflict, the company agreed to drop its demand for weekly payroll deductions to cover the cost of medical coverage. Most dismissed employees were reinstated.

How did the company make up for this financial retreat? By increasing the portion managers paid for their health care. For all intents and purposes, management and union employees were now working for two different companies with respect to their benefits and job security. The latter were feared and placated at the expense of the former.

CHAPTER 5

First Projects

Following the forced departure of a few engineers in the Design and Construction (D&C) group, the Standard Group was dissolved and integrated into the D&C group in 1993. We all became involved with Network projects. Corporate Real Estate was a support organization. Network was the real thing, the bread and butter of the company. They installed and maintained the switches through which all telephone conversation passed. The D&C was responsible for preparing the physical spaces required by providing power, air conditioning, smoke and fire protection, and whatever else was needed to complete the project. Projects came from the Planning Group in green folders. They contained the name of the internal customer, the nature of the project, its location, the crucial dates and other pertinent information. The next step was to hire a consultant to perform the design work. When the design and construction documents were ready, they were checked; first with the designer, then with the customer to get his OK. Next, they went out to bid. When a contractor was selected it was time to request funding. An estimate case, the name that the company gave to the document requesting funding, was put together. It included all the costs associated with the project, and critical dates. A projection of what might go wrong if it were not approved was often cited. It was then sent up the line for several signatures, the number of levels depending on the cost. If this cost was substantial, it could go up as high as a vice president. Once the estimate case was approved, construction started.

The design documents had to be very clear about the precautions to be taken and the protection necessary to insure that no disturbances would be caused to the adjacent existing installations. Before any construction started, an MOP, or Method of Procedure, had to be presented by a representative of all groups involved in the construction. It was a crucial document and no project could proceed until it had been signed by all parties. It detailed all the steps that had to be taken, as well as starting dates, and potential power shut downs that might be required, such as installing new electrical panels. If a breakdown in telephone lines resulting in loss of revenue occurred because one of these rules had been breached, the culprit was in big trouble.

I liked this job. As much as I had enjoyed my stint with the Standard Group, now I was doing real engineer's work. I was involved in the design, checked drawings and calculations, recommended modifications, coordinated the work between the architect, and the mechanical and electrical designers. I was in my element.

Self-development was an important part of our yearly evaluations. In addition to seminars or courses prescribed by the company, such as "Teaming up With the Customer" and "The Sexual Awareness" course in 1993, we were required to choose our own ways to develop our skills. That year, I applied to become a Certified Energy Manager. The application was complex. Eligibility was determined by balancing education against experience. Since I had a Master's Degree in Mechanical Engineering, what was needed were 3 years of energy engineering or management experience. Not a problem! Selected candidates were also to attend a training seminar in Washington for a few days. Not a bad place to be! The final exam was long and difficult. An instructor told us that, although the exam was allocated five hours, we should be out in three. He must have been high on something because on the day of the exam, nobody left before the five hours had elapsed, and quite a few did it against their will. The questions were tough:

- In an Orsat apparatus, what is the remaining gas after its introduction in the stack?
- Of methanol, ammonia and water, which of these heat-transfer fluids has the highest temperature range?
- Identify the equation for net heat to process in a cogeneration system.
- Which lighting system is affected the least by a 10

percent reduction in voltage?

In the end, I passed the grueling five hour exam and became the first Certified Energy Manager throughout the NYNEX footprint.

So my boss made me the czar of the field of energy savings. Czar - it has a nice ring to it, doesn't it? Yes, but it did not come with any autocratic authority. I could not use the knout (a whip-like instrument of torture used within the Imperial Russian penal system) to force people to turn off the light switches at the end of the day. Still, it was a fine title as long as I did not end up like the Romanovs.

One morning, in April 1993, my boss told me he was sending me to Colorado for two weeks to take a course in Basic Building Engineering. I told him that I was a professional engineer, that I had worked on projects that involved buildings most of my career. I wondered what I might learn over there. He was honest: "Probably not too much", he said, "but this is a company requirement. Look at it like a refresher course."
The company had not yet entered its frugal phase. If I was given a two-week vacation to visit a city I had never seen, who was I to complain?

I took the plane from La Guardia sometime in May, landed on the mile-high tarmac of the Denver airport, and rented a car to drive to the school. The facility was beautifully located. From the cafeteria, one could see a plain that extended to the foothills of the Rockies, still covered with snow. A magnificent view indeed. Plus, the food was very good.

As expected, I did not acquire a lot of new knowledge during those two weeks. I did, however, experience some nose bleeds due to the altitude and the dryness of the air. A large contingent of my fellow students must have had some hint of the Midwestern relaxed ways of doing things, because they all came with their golf clubs. The courses started at eight in the morning, ending around two. There were some exercises after each class. Soon, I was giving the answers to my compadres, allowing the golfers to hit the course by three. Mostly, I spent my free time reading a book, lying on a lawn outside the campus, and working on a Colorado tan.

During the weekend, a couple of us toured the area. On Saturday, we went to the U.S. Air Force Academy in Colorado Springs, and visited some Anasazi Indian ruins. On Sunday, we took the cog railway to Pikes Peak. When we reached the summit, it was like the train had taken us back in time. It was a clear day. The sky was Delft blue and has hard as porcelain. We had to shade our eyes from the sunlight bouncing off the snow that still covered the summit. Here it was winter again. The wind formed eddies of snow scurrying about the summit. Stupidly, having left the base of the mountain in spring we had not dressed for that kind of harsh weather. We enjoyed the panoramic view for a while. The scale of it all was difficult to fathom. The endless sweeping country stretched for what looked like hundreds of miles; so far that it erased the horizon and one could not tell were the land ended and the sky started. The human impact on the land was almost invisible. The panorama was a work of art, majestic and timeless. It was easy to imagine dinosaurs roaming this land, pterodactyls flying above it. To take in the magnificence of it all was almost incomprehensible. Sometimes, distance allowed you to see things more clearly. If it was God's intent to show us humans how small and inconsequential we were, He succeeded. How could not one have a feeling of insignificance at the heart of this sublime part of the country. Still, we were so high that for once, one could feel God was looking up at us.

I asked a colleague if he had seen the pictures of the earth taken from satellites.

> "Why, you're not going on one of your philosophical tangents, are you?" he replied.
> "You see this orb marbled with white and blue shades, it's marvelous, but you cannot see any sign of life and, beautiful as it is, it doesn't give you the same humbling feeling as this view. Look, you can see roads winding through the countryside, so thin, make out cities that appear so tiny it makes you feel small, insignificant, doesn't it?
> "Well you know what, Aristotle, it's getting hard to breathe, so let's go."

He was right. Our breath had become shallow and the

subzero sting of the air hurt the lungs, so we went for hot chocolates in the small restaurant.

Later in the evening at dinner in a Denver restaurant, he asked me why I came to the States from France. I followed *la femme,* my wife being American, born in Brooklyn, I said. We talked about other things, about what I like about America. Had I not fallen in love with my future wife, it would have been the music that would have brought me to America. This caught him by surprise. I told him that music was the greatest gift that America had given to the world, not these McDonalds and Burger Kings with their mass produced hamburgers and fries (not that I do not enjoy them every once in a while). I went on, enthusing about jazz (although I am not a true connoisseur), rock-and-roll, the music of my youth, Elvis, Chuck Berry, Little Richard, Jerry Lee Lewis, country-and-western, Gospel music, Dixieland, the inimitable blues still alive with the sweat and pain of slaves toiling in the sun-drenched cotton fields.

"Yes," I emphasized in my best local accent, "the greatest contribution of this here country to mankind is music, bar none. Music; it is a unifier, it brings people together."
"But what about the last two wars when we came to save your hide?" he said.
"Yes, true enough," I replied, "although some think that France was liberated in 1944 mainly because it was on the shortest way to Berlin. You know, wars come and go. The Russians were camping on the

Champs-Elysees in Paris in 1815, and eventually they left. The Germans had Paris surrounded in the winter of 1870-71; they left too. Look at our best friends since the end of World War Two: the Germans and the Japanese. Consider what happened to our Russian ally during the same war, it is now our worst enemy. What does it tell you? That politics makes for strange bedfellows. The nature of political and diplomatic intrigues and wars is transitory. There is nothing fleeting or short-lived about music. It stays with us, it brings us peace and pleasure. OK, maybe this is not the case of *The Marseillaise* and other military patriotic tunes, but they are the exception that confirm the rule. Enfolded in music is what the world would be like if it was perfect."

So I spent two weeks under the Colorado blue sky and its pure air. Professionally, I did not learn a thing, but I discovered a beautiful part of America, and made several friends so, all in all, it was a worthwhile trip.

CHAPTER 6

First Tremors

The roof of the central office at Seventy-Seventh Street in Brooklyn was being replaced. I was picking up where an expelled victim of the purge had left off. During visits to this site, I met the architect who was making sure the roof was properly installed. He was a condescending individual, particularly to the foreman, mostly because all the other workers, who were South American, could not understand a word he said to them and therefore, did not care. Under the constant carping of the architect, the face of the foreman grew even redder than the heat rising from the hot tar used on the roof caused it to be. He held his tongue with more and more difficulty. One of my last visits took place when the roof was 99.99 percent completed. All that was left to do was the punch list, a final inspection to ensure that everything in the construction documents had been adhered to.

The architect was walking across the roof, writing a few

things on his clipboard. At one point, he summoned the foreman in a patronizing tone accompanied by a snotty gesture: "Hey you there". The foreman approached, listened for a few seconds, and exploded. "You little pompous prick. If you don't get off this roof this second, I'm going to throw you over the guard rail and watch you splash on the side walk." I approached the architect, whose face had lost some of its color and told him to leave the site immediately. I went to the foreman to find out what happened. He was in such a huff that he did not even want to talk to me.

Back at the office, I related this episode to my boss Bob. I thought it was kind of funny, in my opinion. I made sure to add that the project would not be affected since the roof was completed and I would complete the punch list myself. Bob did not say anything. Case close I believed.

However, it was not. When I got a copy of my appraisal at the end of the year, I could not believe my eyes. I glanced toward Bob's office. He was in and the door was open. I barged in, waving the appraisal:

"I don't want to be impertinent, but really!" I said.
"What are you taking about?" He looked at me, perplexed, as if I had said something in tongues.
"Poor decision skills, suggest Paul takes a course on decision making", I read, my voice not concealing my outrage
"Oh that!" he said in a dismissive tone. "Well, uh, yes, in retrospect, I may have been a little harsh," he admitted with a millisecond smirk.

"I thought so too," I agreed.
"You know, sometimes, it doesn't hurt to inject a little anxiety into one's life. That's a way to keep everybody on their toes, no?"

Funny really, I liked this boss! I smiled, an effort to stay on his good side rather than a signal that I was in agreement with his assertion. Was he becoming a philosopher of sorts? Was it supposed to make me feel better?

"Thanks, but no thanks, there is enough unease created by all these re-engineering maneuvers that always end up in layoff, without you adding to it."
"Granted! I guess I could have found a better reason."

You may think I was a little chummy with him. He was younger than I was and I kind of liked him despite his sometimes aloof way. He told me once that he enjoyed fly-fishing for trout. I did not know much about this activity, except for the fact that it required real talent. In addition, one had to be an excessively patient man to practice it. It made me think of my uncle on his farm amidst the old volcanoes of Auvergne where he taught me fishing. The only difference was that my uncle caught them by hand. It required patience too to look for the spots where they might be hiding, skills to catch them when a tail drifted from under a rock for a millisecond. He was a maven at it. In the middle of the afternoon, my Grandmother would ask him to bring six trout for supper. In the evening, he would arrive with enough time to prepare them as he pulled them out from various pockets of his jacket.

"All right, Paul, don't worry, you're a core contributor" he said, "I'll make it up to you one day."

Then he flicked his hand like a general sending his commanders back where they belonged in order to do what they were supposed to do. True to his promise, a couple of years later, he may well have saved me during one of those periodic forced migrations from the company.

At times, his actions were difficult to interpret. One day, I saw a piece of paper on my desk, an indecipherable column of numbers with one circled and some scrawling. It was a list of calls placed from my phone. The circled number was a call to Washington, D.C. and the writing was "Big brother is watching you!"

What the heck, I work for the phone company and I cannot use the phone to call whomever I want. It's not like I placed a call to Papua New Guinea for God's sake. I did not even remember what the call was about; maybe I called my brother, a military doctor who was stationed at the French embassy; then again, I may have called the Environmental Protection Agency to get some information on their Green Light Initiative, a project I was working on. Or somebody used my phone to place a call he did not want traced back to him. In any case, my boss had a lot of free time on his hands if he could afford to check every call made by each member of his team. I did not confront him on the matter. I tore apart the piece of paper and filed it in the waste basket. In the end, he did not even raise the question himself.

During those years, we were under the constant threat of involuntary separation, a euphemism for being let go. I had chosen to switch careers from consulting engineering to the phone company for two reasons. The first: if I had stayed, I was closely courting a heart attack induced by a high level of stress which was also threatening my mental health. The second: the phone company was stable and, as already mentioned, had not to my knowledge, laid off anybody in the past hundred years.

Of course, the break up of the AT&T monopoly in the early 1980s had unleashed fierce competition between the newly created phone companies. It was therefore obvious that this safe environment could not last. What was unexpected was that the chicken would come to roost only three years after I was hired. The first tremors that worrying changes were in the air came with the "banding" system. It was a consequence of the Force Management Plan, soon to be known as the dreaded FMP. It was a name that barely disguised its purpose: Reducing the number of employees on the payroll.

All employees were required to fill out a private document called "Individual Employee Banding Feedback Form". The name sounded like a punishment already. In it, you had to define your work, your background, your assets, your weak points - an odd request because who wanted to advertise their shortcomings in those troubled times? My results came back in the following form:

Band: 2
Status: EVS – Eligible.

You have been assessed against criteria that were established for your banding entity. You are designated "Eligible for Voluntary Separation" under the NYNEX Force Management Plan. If you choose to separate voluntarily, you are eligible for FMP benefits.

The last sentence implied that if you did not opt for a voluntary separation, an involuntary one would be without benefits. A few questions here and there throughout the office confirmed that everybody had been given the same status. That banding drill had turned out to be a branding session. We all had an invisible 2 marked on our foreheads that was a ticket to leave the company at any time. It hurt one's self esteem to find out that the company had accepted that a few departures would not create the tiniest hiccup in its operations.

CHAPTER 7

Energy Conservation Meeting

Raven haired, high cheek boned, the Corporate Real Estate general manager's secretary was wonderfully good-looking; a real pleasure for our underlings' eyes. She always wore expensive and tastefully elegant ensembles that gave away more than an inkling of her attractive silhouette. Her legs were gorgeous and it was a terrible shame indeed they were most of the time hidden under a desk. If there ever was a Miss Verizon contest, she would have won it hands down, but for her personality. The vibes she emitted did not encourage any compliments. Because she was not married, a few pushy employees had tried to whittle away at her personality, but they would have had better luck chipping at Siberia's permafrost layer with #60 sand paper. Talking to her was akin to having a conversation with an ice cube. She had a way of looking at you with the detached interest of a tired housewife watching a millipede scampering under some kitchen cabinet. You complimented her at your own risk. At least in France, when you congratulate a woman on how good she looks, she thanks you with an appreciative smile rather than reporting you to the sexual harassment police. This lady was about as warm as an icicle, an approach she must have acquired by osmosis from her boss.

The office of the department general manager was huge, larger than the square footage stipulated in the rule book which allocates space according to level of responsibilities. It was plush, paneled in highly polished exotic wood, regally decorated. Well, it was so impressive that I wondered if I should curtsy or genuflect in front of his highness. There were no diplomas hanging. Instead, a large portion of one wall was dedicated to pictures of him golfing with various people. It may have been a little shrine to some individuals who undoubtedly helped him along as he climbed the ranks leading to his present position. His desk was outsized, but almost devoid of any documents. To paraphrase Einstein's quip, "If a cluttered desk is a sign of a cluttered mind, what does an empty desk suggest?" His clothing matched his office, a sartorial style he wore well.

It was a well-known fact that he ruled his department like a vain monarch, at times imperial, at times simply insufferable. He was the type who never returned phone calls to inferiors and barged into elevators without even acknowledging anybody sharing the space with him, with a very "Kiss up, kick down" attitude. Clearly, his department was not run as a democracy. Of course, there is nothing inherently wrong with that as long as it runs well. When one gives some thought to it, all the organizations that have been put in place to defend our republic are less than democratic. Neither the armed forces, the FBI, nor the police departments are known to be egalitarian institutions.

My supervisor had requested an audience to present a report outlining plans to decrease the energy consumption across the company footprint, with the intent of asking for the budget to implement them. I had spent quite some time putting it together. It was a well-considered proposal; well composed. It had been vetted by my supervisor as well as by several colleagues. The GM who took us into a conference room adjoining his office, sat at a table large enough to handle a square dance contest. Resting his chin on the back of his left hand in a Rodin's *The Thinker* pose, he started leafing through the report. The next fifteen minutes were an exercise in self-discipline. My boss began to explain in his best sunny voice what the report was all about, the impact that the prescribed measures would have on the company financial bottom line. My philosophy in meetings is that if I am accompanied by a supervisor, I keep my mouth shut and let him do the talking unless I am asked a question. It must have been a leftover from my tender years when children were told to be seen but not heard. Also, there is always more to learn listening than speaking.

However my boss could have been whistling Dixie as far as the GM's ears were concerned. As he was looking at the charts with the frustrated look of a monk dissatisfied with his latest illuminated page, he did not seem to pay much attention to what was said to him. The rustle of the turning pages was accompanied by low mumbling. It was hard not to notice his interest faltering like a toy whose battery is dying.

We gathered from his clarifications that he was disappointed because the graphs on the presentation lacked color. His tone was patronizing, his smile, when it graced his lips, perfunctory. This did not escape my boss who was surreptitiously rolling his eyes. If what bothered the GM was the lack of primary colors in the report as opposed to its content, we were not going to commit professional suicide trying to change his mind. My boss had warned me that this person was not an individual to brook dissent from his own subjects.

The fact that he was not fond of others casting doubts on his opinions had also been confirmed by others, so none of us bothered to bring him back to the important things outlined in the report: the mind-boggling amounts of electrical energy wasted in the company buildings. It was clear that his mind did not want to be encumbered by such technical and economical details. He made clear the meeting was concluded, but did not stand up until we did; it was the gesture of a regent acknowledging that we were his minions. At the door, he did not offer his hand. We noticed he did not turn off the lights in the room. Was it a last dig at his interest in energy conservation? We never heard more on the subject. On our way out, I glanced at the secretary, regally sitting at her desk. Isn't it startling how beauty can brighten one's mood? I felt better just looking at her. The trip to the city was not a total loss.

The person we had just met was a bona fide member of a caste whose forte resides in the fact that none were ever bothered by illusions of incompetence. Always carried along by an ambition that knows no bounds, these individuals eventually reach a level of ineptitude. If they still have a smidgen of unprejudiced judgment left in them, it is certainly not for admitting that they are in above their heads. He did not inspire any loyalty, no esprit de corps. Nobody who worked under him, sycophants not included, derived any pride from it.

Unbeknownst to him, we had the last word. We outflanked him, implementing some of our recommended measures by tacking them to existing projects which he had signed off on. That is the beauty of having a boss that does not really read the estimate cases which he is approving.
Later I wrote an article based on the results that was published in a couple of national energy magazines, one of them being the monthly *Energy User News*. The full article appears in Appendix 1. After the publication, I spent several days talking to engineers across the country interested in energy conservation, sharing experiences with them.

Meanwhile, the company was going through different molting stages as it periodically attempted to re-engineer itself. Re-engineering was a euphemism for downsizing. As it was the beginning of lean times, this word was considered less blunt and unsettling. Since the company had not had a layoff for quite a few decades, it was hesitant as to how to proceed. Being new at this, it was tackling the first few with kid gloves. Nevertheless, all proposed measures had something in common; they all would lead to cost cutting which inevitably led to painful people cutting.

Oftentimes as a new boss shows up, he starts to make superficial, quick changes. To paraphrase Hemingway, "one should not confuse movement with action". More often than not, that's all it was, a display of smoke and mirrors that resulted in a relatively simple rearrangement of chairs, except of course for the poor guy left standing up when the music stopped. The concept of massive layoffs had not yet been implemented and those which happened to be let go were yet few and far between.

One of the first victims of deeper changes was competence. We had come to the point where the experts in the Real Estate department were no longer deemed to be experts. The general manager would declare during a conference on the state of the company that diplomas obtained more than five years ago were not worth a "rat's behind". Was he joining the anti-education crowd? Diplomas are not symbols of elitism, they are testimonies of seriousness. They are not found in cereal or happy meal boxes; they have been painstakingly earned with long hours of rigorous work, over years of hard slog. The knowledge acquired during these years of study remains with you all your life. Michael Specter, the author of the book *Denialism: How irrational thinking hinders scientific progress, harms the planet and threatens our lives* quoted: "It is appalling that we are a country that has descended into a complete disregard for expertise."[1] Why

---

1 Published October 29th 2009 by Penguin Press

has self-congratulatory ignorance and smugness in having never read a book become such a source of pride for too many individuals? How can one be so full of oneself to reject the sum of human knowledge and imagination books bring? Hearing somebody saying proudly he never opened one makes you cringe. It makes you wonder where he got stuck on the arc of evolution.

To dismiss diplomas in such a cavalier way showed how little regard this general manager had for the know-how of his employees. The company did not need engineers, architects, designers. How did we come to be held in such low esteem? Now I felt a certain kinship with all the victims of "reeducation" purges that happened at one time or another under certain regimes.
Interestingly enough, the diplomas outside the company were still valuable. More and more studies were given to outfits of experts whose main asset appeared to be the fact that they were not Verizon's employees.

Until now, the curriculum of the Design and Construction group had been very precise regarding the qualifications of the applicants, specifying that it must be composed of engineers and architects, professional or licensed preferred. This was no longer the case. Individuals with no relevant background were hired as project engineers. Welcome to the age of Generic Managers. It did not stop in our group. Employees with no experience of building operations were brought in as property managers. And all were lumped into the same category. Of course, the tactic was to dump the maximum of personnel in the same gene pool and salary category, resulting in lower wages for qualified people. But not to worry, the company had done its homework. The salaries had been benchmarked with those of other companies, so everything was copacetic. What parameters were used to benchmark was anyone's guess. They were never divulged, lest one find out that apples were compared to oranges.

All those changes fell under the label "paradigm shift", a new expression en vogue in the business world. It has been used, overused and abused to the point of turning into a meaningless expression.

A real paradigm shift is going from a propeller plane to a jet plane, or from an electro-mechanical switch to a digital one. What was happening in the corporation was merely a "company culture" change characterized by a slow but steady retreat to the halcyon days of the late 1800s and early 1900s. Its aims: shrink the work force and get rid of the gains painfully acquired by those pesky Unions.

We met again with this general manager several times during speeches he gave about the current state of the company. God only knows who was in charge of the corporate clichés' library, but he had been unloading most of its stock during these presentations: "paradigm change", "time to step to the plate", "be a leader", "lead by example", "be proactive, not reactive". Inescapably, he would say that we were living in exciting times. Exciting for whom? What is so exciting about working on borrowed time? This is a word that every worker eventually came to hate. It was too close to the Chinese curse "May you live in interesting times."

As employees, we were told to be diligent, to follow through, to be "self-starters," to have a good attitude, to be flexible and patient and dependable and loyal and respectful and efficient and this and that. "Most of you he declared, at least among those who would stay after the dead wood had been removed, were the cornerstone of the company". Right! Being cynical, I can take any compliment, especially the phony ones, quite well.

Regarding the "dead wood", it was undeniable that the company was a little bloated, personnel wise. Protected by its monopoly status, it had become a bureaucracy. Too many employees had been around for so long that they were cruising along towards their retirement without contributing much. The dead wood was mostly gathering moss on its limbs.

We were told there is no "I" in "team", meaning we had to be team players, to which one smart aleck counterattacked by saying that there is no "WE" either. Ironically, this old saw was often stated by people that knew there was also an "M" and a "E", as in "me" and took thorough advantage of it.

In the end, the message of these sentences, laden with insincerity, was that an ill wind was sweeping throughout the company and quite a few of us would be blown away outside the job safety of its walls.

CHAPTER 8

Secondment

In 1994 New York Telephone merged with New England Telephone and the newly formed company became known as NYNEX. One of its first actions was to implement an aggressive move to reduce the number of its managers. To do so, a tailored offer was put in place. It would prove difficult to pass up by many. This buyout consisted of a plan shaped to encourage a massive employee departure in order to cut costs. The plan was christened the Six & Six offer. In simple terms, the company added six years to the employee's time of service and six years to his or her age. For some older employees, it was nothing less than manna falling from the Heavens. Many of these old timers had become complacent over the years, working no more than dead men on vacation; there was no denying it. These veterans seemed to be RIP, not for Rest In Peace, but for "Retired In Place", an expression used for aged pieces of equipment that had reached the end of their usefulness. They were retired from the books for tax purposes. Sometimes too big to remove, they remained where they stood, hence the expression "Retired In Place".

The result of this generous offer, as intended, would result in a huge migration of personnel. The buyout was indeed truly a gift. What led the company to offer such liberal terms remains a mystery to this day. In all probability, it was the first incentive to incite the employees to leave en masse and it was just testing the waters. Maybe the potential reaction of the unions, although they were not affected, encouraged caution. Needless to say, if the same conditions had still been in effect when some of us were "volunteered" to retire in 2008, we would have jumped on such a lavish deal. Unfortunately, it did not take long for the company to realize that they did not need such tempting offers to get rid of people. Each subsequent reduction in personnel became less and less attractive.

In order to compensate for the expected massive exodus that would occur once the offer was put on the table, the first major attempt at outsourcing was put into effect. A construction managing company, or CM, for Construction Manager as it came to be called, was hired to help in the handling of the construction projects. A NYNEX leadership team was put in place to handle the transition. One of the overt characteristics of this team was its aversion to all specialists, engineers and architects included. It followed a pattern that had been hard not to notice since my hiring; the unremitting and systematic disparaging of the technical personnel in the Real Estate group.
Toward the end of the year, the design and construction

group was summoned to a conference room. It was to be one of those meetings during which the latest paradigm shift - a favorite expression of these "exciting" times - was presented to us. It did not go well. The head of the NYNEX transition team explained the plan. His disdain for our technical expertise was immediately apparent. At one point, he even went as far as saying that "anyone can be an engineer". With this expression, we had been marginalized.

A profound and long silence followed that demeaning assertion. Looking across the room at my colleagues, I saw quite a group of smart individuals. My neighbor said: "Man, this guy is having a terminal case of assholitis!"
When my gaze returned to "this guy", the head of the transition team, it could be said, without a shred of a doubt that, not only was he not the cleverest man in the room, but also that the sensitivity training seminars we all had to endure had not left a lasting impact on his manners. Condescending and conceited, he was befitting perfectly the Samuel Butler quip: "The truest characters of ignorance are vanity and pride and arrogance."

Still talking, comfortable in his bespoke suit, smelling of pretense and self-satisfaction, he was at times scathing, at others caustic; never for a second was he the least bit sympathetic. No doubt about it, his professional etiquette left a lot to be desired. His tepid smile was that of a salesman trying to sell a used car not even worth half the price he was proposing. He seethed with a contempt for us that was difficult to fathom, taking an infinite pleasure in igniting fires of anxiety in us, stoking the coals with unbecoming delight. One had to wonder whether he already knew how many in his audience would be carted toward the guillotine in order for him to bring in the new regime. Probably not. He did not know any of us, so he would leave that dirty task to one of his henchmen. His insolent words could sap a proud engineer's will to live! So I took some solace from the words of Mark Twain: "The trouble ain't that there is too many fools, but that the lightning ain't distributed right."

One might wonder if he would have the guts to allege that anybody could be a physician in front of an assembly of doctors; or anybody could be an attorney in front of a group of lawyers. In his defense, this gentleman probably knew little about construction, or maintenance for that matter. After all, like so many managers, he had bounced through company positions like an out-of-bound basketball, gathering just enough expertise along the way to make it risky for others, as in the idiom "a little knowledge is a dangerous thing."

Still, it did not prevent him from uttering ludicrous comments, indifferent to the sensibilities of others. But what else can be expected from these company nomads, who some like to refer to as corporate butterflies? This moniker is apt. They flutter from one position to another, never staying too long in any of them, for fear that the time will come when they have to explain what they really do or justify their actions. Their background is somewhat elusive, which in their minds makes them ideal candidates for any position. There is some logic in this approach.

Not knowing exactly what your next destination will be is not a problem for them. Isn't it well known that, when you do not know where you are going, any road you take will lead you there?

These anointed demigods have mastered the A-to-Z of the "How to Climb the Corporate Ladder" manual. A is for Aping the boss, B for Brown nosing or blaming others for one's own mistake, C for Crushing anybody who might get in the way, D is for Drinking with the "Powers that be", E is for Echoing the opinions of his or her boss of the moment, F can equally apply to Flattering, Following the leader (even to the bathroom if it allows for a private conversation), or F…ing everybody who might be in the way. Further down the alphabet, P is for Playing golf with the right threesome. Well, you get the picture! Along the way, they surround themselves with trusted sycophants, yes-men with enough brains to keep them out of trouble. Since they are cunning, they make sure these aides do not have too much ambition, lest they have their eyes on their superior's position. They climb through the echelons of the food chain where politics and patronage matter more than expertise and intelligence. From positions of restrained authority to flashier ones, they continue their ascent until, eventually, the fact that they have finally exceeded their level of competence cannot be hidden any longer and the abrupt fall comes.

The smear "everyone can be an engineer" stuck in our throats, but mostly, we endured this indignity in silence, although I heard somebody mumbling "What a jerk!"

Memories of events in my early career came to mind. Fresh out of engineering school, I went to work for Michelin Tire Corporation, in the Research and Development group. There I devised an apparatus to cool the rubber products as they exited the extruding machines, so that they did not vulcanize[1] during the storage process. These various strips of rubber were subsequently used in the confection of tires. Following successful experiments in a pilot plan in Clermont-Ferrand, France, tests in a real environment took place in a Michelin factory in Italy. Why Italy? Simple! The Italians had proven time and time again that they were more interested in trying new things than the French, who were too often satisfied with proven ways. As somebody who embraces any opportunity for change, I am always amazed that, as Tocqueville lamented, "people fear new theory as a danger, every innovation as a toilsome trouble". I still recall stepping into the Michelin Falcon jet. Michelin was very democratic. If the company plane was flying to where you were going, and seats were available, you could hop in and travel in style, ensconced in leather seats that had required the sacrifice of an entire herd of cattle. For those few hours, I felt like a member of the rich and famous.

When the plane landed in Milan, I was welcomed by a chauffeur who would spare me all the pesky annoyances of customs and take me to the Michelin plant. What never left my mind is that he called me *Dottore Belard*.

---

[1] Vulcanization is the process of hardening rubber with heat. The word originates from the Roman deity Vulcan, the god of fire and of skills that used fire.

This is the respect granted to engineers in Italy. That is also how they are treated in the rest of the world. It was a nice feeling to hear this mark of respect. If this was not honor enough, the machine I had designed had been baptized "Tunnel Tipo Belard". How many people can claim that a machine had been named after them?

More recently, in 1983, I had been detached to Newport News, Virginia, to work on designing the primary cooling system for a Continuous Electron Beam Accelerator Facility (CEBAF) built for the Department of Energy. CEBAF is a linear accelerator, in which the electron is accelerated between steering magnets. Liquid helium is used to cool these magnets to reduce their electrical resistance to almost zero in order to allow the most efficient transfer of energy to the electron. I was involved in the primary cooling of the liquid helium and, in doing so, came in contact with some of the sharpest minds in the country at the vanguard of science.
Some of my colleagues could also have listed similar achievements which would have made this conceited gas-bag turn red with envy.

The speaker did belong to this exalted category, hence that utter nonsense: "anyone can be an engineer". At no time in his soliloquy was there a hint that we might feel insulted. In his eyes, he saw an audience having reached the bottom of the professional food chain.

I guess that, in a country where garbage collectors are called sanitation engineers, where train conductors are named engineers, where maintenance mechanics are watch engineers, the significance of the title has been diluted and lost some of its aura. No wonder that, when Japanese engineers come to this country, they alter their business cards to read "manager of something!" Where is the American Society of Professional Engineers when you need them? What do they do to protect the name of a brotherhood that has been associated with every progress made in society? Compared to the associations which defend the rights of doctors and lawyers, they are woeful amateurs.

Anyway, slur or no slur, the CM was hired to perform what had been entitled "Secondment." Since none of us had ever heard of that term, we went to the dictionary.

> Definition: Secondment is the detachment or transfer of a person from their regular organization for temporary assignment elsewhere. Secondment offers different work situations, which is valuable for staff development. Specific required experience/skills, which do not exist, can be brought into the organization.
> Secondments offer everyone concerned a number of benefits:
> - Secondees gain specialist skills, knowledge and experience.
> - Secondees return to their employer or clients with valuable skills, knowledge and experience.
> - The organisation where the secondment is taking place benefits from a different set of skills and expertise.

From this definition, it appeared that it was more a takeover of the department, although it was also referred to as an alliance or as the Program Management Design/Build concept. When I dug a little deeper into the history of the word, I found out it originated from the French *en second*. It meant "second in rank". There you have it. It was evident that the remaining NYNEX employees, if there were any, which was unclear at the time, would be demoted and relegated to an assisting function, rather than a commanding position. Their role would be to pass from one of engineer or architect to one of mere paper pusher.

Here is how this new organization was supposed to work. When a new project was selected, the leadership team passed it to the CM. Following some preliminary work, the CM came back with the cost of the project. It was in the form of a so called Gross Maximum Price (GMP), which is a price that would not be exceeded if unforeseen conditions did not lead to costly revisions. If this GMP was not reached, the "savings" would be split between the phone company and the CM. Already, this raised questions from the group, the most obvious one being:

> "What is in place to prevent the CM from aiming for a high number in his GMP in order to generate artificial savings he would later enjoy when he claimed he had come in under budget?"

No satisfactory answers were given to us, except that the

"secondment" train had left the station and nothing was going to stop it. Other questions and answers followed:

"Who will hire the design consultants and the contractors?"
"This is a Design/Build concept, akin to turnkey projects for those who are familiar with it. The CM will hire his own consultants and contractors."

"Who will check and pay the bills?"
"Some of you who will survive the next FMP (the term Reduction in Force was not yet in use at that time. It was still called Force Management Plan) will be kept and form a cadre that will take care of the invoices.

The most important questions were glossed over, sometimes with a dismissive tone conveying that this new concept was all too complicated for us peons to understand. Something crucial was missing. It was like a kid at the science fair talking about the solar system without once mentioning the sun.

Finally it dawned on us that the role of the survivors of this disguised FMP would be more or less relegated to pay the bills. No more engineering work for the engineers.

"Anybody else?"
"Since you believe anyone can be an engineer, can you tell us how to calculate the size of an I-beam that spans ten feet and must withstand a bearing load

of…", asked a colleague who still retained a sense of humor after this wretched news.

He was quickly cut off.

"Since there are no more relevant questions, this meeting is adjourned."

To rub the salt in the wound, he dismissed us with a wave as though he was chasing away a cloud of pesky gnats.

I did not open my mouth. Nothing to be gained in being singled out as uncooperative, except to get bounced out of the program before it even started.

A few weeks later, the entire Design and Construction group was taken on a field trip. We met at the headquarters of the CM, in what used to be the Pan Am building in midtown Manhattan, on the northern side of Grand Central Station. In a huge conference room with great views of the city, we all sat around a table on which we could have played a game of softball without stepping on each other. While we were sitting, the takeover team was standing up. The symbolism was inescapable: they were already showing who was in charge. Their chief proposed that we introduce ourselves, adding some personal information, such as hobbies, likes and dislikes.

Were we signing up for one of those online dating web sites? So we all hemmed and hawed, probably inventing a few facts for the sake of appearing compliant.

If the outcome of this meeting would not have been the end the professional life in the phone company for quite a few of us, it may have been looked at as a circus act circus.

Indeed, what was clear was that professionally we were in a boat rocking on a sea crested with waves of uncertainty. The Six & Six offer was imminent. It would indeed be great for some. For those who did not have the right age and years of employment in the company, the possibility of being summarily dismissed without much to show for it was real and feared.

CHAPTER 9

Survival

With the coming of a Construction Manager, I did not want to be one of the eliminated project managers. I was still fifteen years or so away from retirement age; it was time to think of self-preservation. Despite the fact it was changing its spots more often than a molting leopard, I liked working for this company. Plus, the thought of going back to work for a consulting engineering firm gave me hives. It became clear that swallowing a little bit of pride was the smart thing to do. Also, there was the famous saying: "If you don't ask, you don't get." So I wrote a memo to one of the leaders, who happened to be a former boss of mine. In the letter, after unashamedly praising the merits of this alliance, I expressed my interest in a position between NYNEX and the new CM.

It was polite, short and to the point, sprinkled here and there with careful hints of flattery. A condensed version follows:

Dear Bob,

During our meeting with, *name withheld*, on November 7, 1994, your supervisor mentioned that he would welcome any comments and suggestions regarding the Program Management Design/Build concept. I am following up on this opportunity.

During the years before I came to NYNEX, I had the opportunity to work for Design/Build companies such as Gilbane, Brown & Root, CRS Sirrine, Halliburton. Invariably, these companies would get involved in the design, but only inasmuch as the design choices had an impact on the schedule of the project. They often lacked the expertise to make pure engineering resolutions. Such decisions were always left to the Owner and/or the Engineering/Architectural firm hired to design the project. Also because of this dearth of expertise, they did not get involved in checking drawings and specifications.

You are well aware of the errors and omissions that invariably appear in design documents. They are subsequently the cause of multiple and costly change orders. As Director of Operations, you took corrective measures and successfully created a team of Subject Matter Experts (SME's) to review the drawings and specs. The immediate result was a not inconsequential reduction in the amount of change orders.

I think that your concept was an excellent idea and that, should it be applied to the Design/Build concept, it would be instrumental in insuring its success from the start. However, in keeping with the first law of quality control that states that no effective control can be carried out efficiently by someone having stakes in the process, a team of NYNEX SME's should be retained to handle these duties. They would include:

- Review design and construction documents. - Perform Value Engineering when necessary.
- Visit construction sites to insure quality of workmanship, adherence to NYNEX methods and procedures, act as advisors during shut-downs or other activities impacting telephone services.
- Assess validity of CM's claims regarding change orders.
- Participate in punch-list inspections and insure timely and competent follow-up.
- Collect up-to-date as-built drawings and maintain usable archives.

I strongly feel that a small team of NYNEX SME'S with the responsibilities outlined above would be instrumental in the success of the Program Management Design/Build concept.

Should you agree, I would put forward my services for your consideration. As my former supervisor, you know I have the technical expertise, the organization skills, the computer literacy and the team player approach to make it happen.

At the time, I was a Subject Matter Expert in "HVAC (Heating, Ventilating & Air Conditioning) systems", as well as in "Energy Conservation", technical skills of which I unashamedly reminded him. Moreover, the expression "Make it happen" was a favorite of his. Indeed, anytime we had a question regarding a problem that required his input, his answer had been a terse "Make it happen." As a matter of fact, he repeated it so often that we toyed with the idea, at least for a short while, of presenting him, on his birthday, with a piece of marble engraved with these three words.

Was it necessary to write this letter? Did it tip the balance in my favor? Did he remember the promise he had made a few years ago? Would my technical qualifications have been enough? The good news was that I was retained as one of the four employees selected to act as liaison between NYNEX and the CM. I had dodged the bullet once more.

A few weeks later, the plan was put in place. Once again, I was under Bob's command. My inclusion in his group was alluded to in my 1995 yearly appraisal:

"In February 1995, on the strength of his past performances, I personally selected Mr. Belard to be part of the Program Management team and participate in the implementation of the Design/build concept. While carrying out the responsibilities that the new position required, he also pursued the management of several projects he was handling as a project manager."

Not unexpectedly, being described as incompetents had created friction from the very first days of working closely with these newcomers. They had fallen hook, line and sinker for the fabrication that we were a group of bungling boobs. They came in as God's gift to Verizon, anointed with the mission to save it from the likes of us, a bunch of pitiful amateurs. Step aside Spiderman, make way for the new breed of super heroes! For a while they seemed to have their own opinion of who worked for whom. As professionals we kept our feelings to ourselves. However, my goodwill and that of my NYNEX colleagues did not last. The major open conflict occurred with the arrival of the first invoices. To say that the CM was front loading the projects was an understatement. Construction had not even started, and already, they were charging more than 25 percent of the GMP. We protested to our leaders, explaining that it was not the right way to operate, that the amount of the invoice should match the amount of work performed, not be an arbitrary amount. Moreover it was against company policy which stated that the invoices should accurately reflect the amount of work performed till the date of the invoice.

Still, these sound arguments fell on deaf ears. The answer to all of them was consistently the same: "Pay the bills."

So pay the bills, under duress, we did. It seemed for a while we had entered a maze with no exit.

Although we scarcely realized it at the time, this "Pay the bills" diktat would prove to be the first misstep that eventually would lead to the sinking of the entire first-sortie of the outsourcing ship. Quite a few members of the managing crew went down with it too.

CHAPTER 10

The Headquarters Chillers

The project managers who had been selected to be members of the Program Management team were transferred to Manhattan. I bid my good-byes to our Brooklyn office and entered the grandeur of the company's headquarters at 1095 Avenue of the Americas. It was a forty-one-story skyscraper. It has been said that its design mirrored the relays which were found inside telephone switches in the seventies. The only remark that could be made was that relays were not very attractive. The design translated into a rather dull flat rectangular frontage clad with black and white marble. Inside, it was more inviting, starting with an eye catching lobby. One of the most impressive floors was the thirty-third where the cafeteria was housed. The view was spectacular. You could have lunch sitting at a table against a window and take in Bryant Park directly across Sixth Avenue, or look at northern Manhattan. It did not beat the 360-degree panorama I had when I worked for a while on the ninety-ninth floor of one of the twin towers of the World Trade Center. Nonetheless, it was lovely to quit one's claustrophobic cubicle and see Manhattan open in front of one's eyes.

A few years ago, I worked for a consulting firm located in Port Washington. It was a small outfit, a dozen or so employees, with interesting projects. Several took me to the Naval Academy in Annapolis. The trips to this historic institution, with its campus dotted with stately buildings, monuments and memorials along the Severn River and the Chesapeake Bay were enjoyable.
Back in the office, a couple of the employees were very colorful. One was a young designer who liked to predict the weather and who, at times, recited passages of Martin Luther King's "I have a dream" speech. He also regaled us with stories of his stint on the design team of the doomed Shoreham nuclear power plant on Long Island. For him, it had been a golden era, particularly because of the extravagant salaries that were paid to members of the design team. The other individual was a draftsman. He was so talented that you could not tell if a drawing had been done by him or generated by a Computer Aid Design program. He was also an intense born again Christian. At times, he dropped his pencil to enter into a silent prayer. One day, these two got into an argument that quickly escalated. In order to diffuse it, I started to whistle the hymn "How Great Thou Art". I do not really know why I did it, but it was as if a switch had been turned. The spat abruptly ended when the devoted servant of God uttered "Praise the Lord" and went back to his drawing board.

My brother Antoine, a successful banker in Paris, came to visit regularly, either on business or as a tourist. I had once brought him to this office before he went on a shopping spree to the Miracle Mile in Manhasset to shore up the Long Island economy. We entered the office through a dingy parking lot. It was a modest office, really a low ceilinged, plain space with a few cubicles on one side and drawing boards on the other. I could see the disappointed look on my brother's face. He expected more from me.

But let's jump back to 1095, as the headquarter building was familiarly known. The day I invited Antoine in, a board meeting was taking place. The cafeteria had put, as we say in France, *les petits plats dans les grands*, loosely translated as placing small dishes in larger ones. It basically meant that the host was doing his very best to please his guests. If there was a Michelin Guide for cafeterias, ours would have rated the coveted stars. My brother's astonishment was all I needed to erase that disenchanted look of a few years back. We were light years away from the cheerless office in Port Washington.
The space was immense, attractive, with a magnificent view on one side of the Hudson River and the northern part of New Jersey. There were islands throughout serving salads, breakfast items, burgers, omelets, fruits and other goodies that would not have been out of place in a five star restaurant.

In 1993, because of my proven expertise in mechanical engineering and as a HVAC (Heating, Ventilating & Air Conditioning) Subject Matter Expert, I was put in charge of the replacement of several refrigeration machines, also known as chillers, in Manhattan, to meet the Montreal Protocol schedule pertaining to the chlorofluorocarbons (CFC) phase-out. Not only did I know how to design refrigeration installation, I also had a strong knowledge of how they worked, since I had successfully passed the exam (albeit on my second try!) that granted the license to operate refrigeration units in New York City. It would prove a dubious blessing as it was an asset that was put to good use by the company during strikes.

Refrigerants make air conditioning and refrigeration possible, both allowing us to enjoy cool drinks in a comfortable setting during the dog days of summer. However, it has been suspected for a while that refrigerants containing chlorine, mainly CFCs and hydrochlorofluorocarbons (HCFC), when released into the atmosphere, pose a danger to the ozone layer which absorbs 93–99 percent of the sun's high frequency ultraviolet light, which is potentially damaging to life on earth. They also increase the greenhouse effect and both impacted global warming.

The "Montreal Protocol on Substances that deplete the Ozone Layer" is an international treaty designed to protect the ozone layer by phasing out the production of a number of substances believed to be responsible for the ozone depletion. It was ratified in 1987. It spelled out the worldwide phase-out of CFC by 1996 and HCFC compounds by 2004. In response to this agreement, the United States amended the Clean Air Act, adding provisions to establish a schedule to phase out the use of CFC and HCFC compounds in the USA.

This project was wide-ranging, the time to implement it short. Nonetheless, in less than two years, more than ten chillers located at Varick Street, Manhattan Avenue, Third Avenue, Pearl Street, 1095 Avenue of the Americas had been replaced or retrofitted.

The project that made me most proud was the replacement of two mega chillers in the company headquarters located at Avenue of the Americas. The building was served by two 2,700-ton steam turbine driven chillers, as well as a smaller unit for operation at partial loads when the building did not require full cooling.[1] A 2,700-ton unit is a huge piece of machinery. Imagine that a one-ton unit is often required to cool a fairly large room in a house and it will give you an idea of what is needed to air condition a forty-one story skyscraper.

These confusing units prompted one of these technical newbies affected to our group to ask: "What has the weight of the chiller to do with anything?" This reminded some of us of Lincoln's precept: "Better to remain silent and be thought of fool than to speak out and remove all doubt."

This project came at the time the secondment was in the process of being rolled out. It was therefore on the

---

1   Large refrigeration systems in the US are rated in tons of refrigeration units. In the rest of the world, cooling systems are specified in BTU/h or calories. A refrigeration ton is equivalent to 12,000 BTU/h. One ton of refrigeration capacity can freeze 1,000 kilograms (one ton) of water at 0°C (32°F) in 24 hours.

list to be immediately handed on to the Construction Manager. I did not want to let it go. In order to keep it, I approached my boss and convinced him that the project was too well advanced to pass it along to people unfamiliar with the building.

I artfully added that if they screwed up, the company officers on the forty-first floor would not be too thrilled to have to work without the comfort of air conditioning; that it would not reflect too well on this secondment thing and its instigators.
Whether he believed me or not, he left me in charge of the project, adding his famous expression: "Then, make it happen." I think what swayed him in the end was the fact that the funds had already been allocated for this project and they did not include the hefty fee that the Construction Manager would have demanded.

It was the type of project where I felt like a fish in water. It was highly technical, fraught with risks and on a tight schedule. However, more than the challenges it presented, what I liked was the fact that nobody wanted to be near it, just in case something went wrong. Imagine for an instant the department head being called upstairs to explain to sweating head honchos that they would not have air conditioning for the foreseeable future because of unforeseen problems with the chiller replacement project. Not the best career move; not something you want on your record when the raises and promotions are being discussed. In fact, if you want to commit professional suicide, you report to the highest placed people on the company chart that you have failed at something, especially if it affects their daily comfort. Retribution will not be long in coming and it will be swift and without recourse, be it in the form of a pink slip or a demotion to collector of the coins in the Bronx public telephones. These young lions were no strangers to cover-your-ass politics. They had long ago determined that the best way to cover it was not to expose it in the first place. Consequently they stayed away from any project that may impact their climb to the next level in the corporate hierarchy.

So I was left alone; the perfect scapegoat if anything went wrong. If all turned out all right, it would add a nice feather in my cap, but I would no longer be lonely. As my good friend Dan likes to say: "Failure is an orphan, but success has many fathers."
Still I was not overly worried. I had handled very sensitive projects at Verizon and other companies. The most recent included the air conditioning design for the new Atlantic City railroad station that will serve the new convention center, as well as the cooling system for the electron accelerator in Newport News for the Department of Energy. My last project with my former company was the air conditioning of a high security prison in Valhalla, New York. It included the installation of two 900-ton centrifugal chillers. My in-laws lived in a plain, but cozy brick house. Honest as they were, they did not have central air conditioning. A bunch of hardened criminals, on the other hand, would live in an environment where temperatures and humidity would be monitored to insure a maximum of comfort.

I had the experience but more importantly, one of my

most precious assets has always been that I was smart enough to know what I did not know. My lack of knowledge in certain areas would be dealt with by the expertise of members of the team I would gather. I contacted the New York representative of the manufacturer of the machines. We had worked together several times before on some engineering projects. He brought in the best engineers of his company. We were talking the same language; we understood each other; we did not inundate ourselves with paper work; we grasped what did not need to be spelled out. Nobody was trying to hog the blanket. We all know the type: the assertive kind, which is more often than not derived from an inferiority complex. The sort that barges into a conference room, grabs the best seat and that you half expect to take a leak right then and there to claim his territory.

None of these characters on our team, just people intent on the goals, with no egos involved. We determined what had to be done to convert the existing units within the tight schedule. Following these meetings, with their input when needed, I wrote the scope of work and the entire specifications. It included replacing the compressors, as well as the tubes of evaporators and condensers which had reached the end of their useful life, made obvious by developing multiple leaks that had to be fixed before every spring start-up. Since these tubes are made out of copper, an expensive material, the manufacturer took them back and gave us a generous credit. We went out to bid. Luckily, the low bidder was a contractor we had worked with before, very competent, with a skilled work force. All was now in place to start the work. The equipment to be replaced was large and heavy. It had to be broken down in pieces to remove it. However, the new equipment would come in larger parts and would require a substantial crane to unload it. It would necessitate closing a street to lift it from the trucks. Therefore permits were required from the city. The unloading would in all probability occur during the weekend.

Construction started and went fairly smoothly. The project was completed before the cooling season was in full swing and upper management did not have to break a sweat, at least from lack of air conditioning.
Every once in a while, I ventured into the Holy of Holies, the *inner sanctum* of the company, to make sure the air was not corrupted. You could tell right away that you had left the ordinary land of the peons behind. The building metamorphosed from painted sheetrock walls, steel desks, and ordinary posters or cheap reproductions into a grand club. Coming from the steerage levels, I had entered stately rooms. Everything was elegantly panelled with highly polished mahogany, teak or cherry wood. Genuine paintings adorned the walls and you could vanish in the deep-pile of the carpeting. A lush silence reigned. At this level, the faint hearted visitors not accustomed to this rarefied air might have to bring an oxygen bottle to live to tell the story.
So this was how the bigwigs lived! I was duly impressed. Do not think I felt like an intruder. I could have easily adapted to these lavish quarters.

Erroneously I had assumed that if the project was completed successfully, it would add another feather to my cap. This turned out not to be the case. At the time of this project, Con-Edison was giving generous rebates to reduce electricity consumption throughout the footprint of their electrical network. The use of energy efficient equipment qualified us for such rebate. I filled out all the necessary forms.

Upon review of the project, Con-Edison agreed to issue a rebate to NYNEX of nearly $1 million. It was a big deal, so much so that, when Con Ed came to the building to hand over the check, a ceremony was organized on the twenty-third floor of the building. A large crowd of people attended. Our department general manager was present to do the honors. A sharp dresser, he sported light pants and a blue blazer that nicely set off a deep tan acquired on some golf course in Florida unless it was up and down some ski slopes in Colorado. Then again, maybe he merely took naps in a tanning bed. All that was lacking was a captain's cap and he could have stepped off some rich friend's yacht. The press may even have been present too. When the Con-Ed representative handed the check to the general manager, a roar of applause erupted. Then our big wheel made the predictable speech. He lauded the relationship between the two companies, and of course, did not fail to take the credit attached to this project successfully conducted. At no time did he mention the names of any of the personnel who, in the words of my boss "made it happen." We remained insignificant cogs in the department's well-oiled machine. He did not even ask to meet the team members.

It would be a lie if I said it did not hurt a bit. By handling the project without a design consultant, an amount close to $200,000.00 had been saved, the usual Architect's fee on a project worth $2,400,000.00 In addition, since the Construction Manager was not involved either, an equivalent sum had also been saved. Weren't $400,000.00 savings worth mentioning my name at some point? I think so! After all, they would cover several years of my salary. Was it as a minimum worth a pat on the back? It would have been deserved.

What hurt most though is the fact that I knew it was my fault. I did not toot my own horn. I was given a beautiful hand, one only receives once in a blue moon and I did not play the cards right. What I should have done was gone to the upper floor during the construction phase and visited every executive office. There, I should have introduced myself to the occupant, asked him politely if I could have a minute of his precious time and explained what was being done. I should have gone regularly, keeping him abreast of the progress, inquiring if everything was OK, shoot the breeze with his secretary. Maybe, one day, a short but to the point *Power Point* presentation would have kept them up to date on the project's progress. But I did not and I could kick myself for not doing so.

At the very least, at the end of the project, I should have written a memo to the company chairman. It should have described this venture, its ramifications, the lack of disruptions, the savings gained and the advantages of using in-house talent to lead projects. In line with the attention span of the reader, all this in no more than one page that could be read in less than five seconds of course. The wheel that does not squeak rarely gets attention, and this is what happened. Why blame others when I was the one who missed his chance.

My aversion to being in the limelight did not serve me well this time. I missed the opportunity to invaluable exposure, to rub elbows with the company VIPs. It would have done wonders for my reputation.

On the other hand, aware of what was going on, some executive could have made my life miserable, calling me at any time to request progress reports. A French proverb says: *Pour vivre heureux, vivons cache*. It means *to live happy, stay in the shadows*. There is some truth to this. It was echoed by a Japanese adage that warned that *the nail that sticks out gets hammered down*. So, what's one to do?

In the end I did not dwell too long on the road not taken, I just braced myself for the next challenge.

My 1995 yearly appraisal recognized my efforts. It read:

> "Paul is a Subject Matter Expert in the building engineering field and in energy management and is relied upon for technical assistance. His expertise was particularly apparent in the replacement of the chillers at 1095 Avenue of the Americas. On this project, he developed the design documents, wrote the specifications, reviewed the shop drawings and performed construction supervision. The project was completed within budget, on schedule and without any service

interruption in a highly sensitive building."

Further, it added:

> "Paul was also nominated three times for the NYC 1995 Energy Conservation Award. For Paul's energy conservation undertakings, Con-Edison rebate approval for a total amount of $1,000,000 was obtained. He was invited to an award ceremony during which *name withheld* received a rebate check from Con-Edison."

Apart from the assertion that "he was invited" (I did not received any invitation card, I just showed up) to the ceremony celebrating the project that I had led from start to finish, my only objection was that my supervisor did not push for an EMA (Excellence Merit Award) which consisted of a certain amount of money. Oh well, one can't have it all!

Somehow, this project came to the attention of BOMA, the Building Owner and Managers Association[2].

They asked me to write an article for their yearly publication which touts atypical and successful projects. The article was published in the 1995 issue.

---

2   Founded in 1907, BOMA represents the owners and managers of all commercial property types including nearly 10.5 billion square feet of U.S. office space that supports 1.7 million jobs and contributes $234.9 billion to the U.S. GDP. 2017 figures.

CHAPTER 11

Program Management

Subsequent to another restructuring and the advent of secondment, the project engineer title disappeared for a while. The scythes of reorganization, coupled with those of the Six & Six offer, had cut a wide swath through the staff of the engineering department. Understandably, the number of projects had not been reduced in proportion to the cutback in personnel. To pick up the slack a Construction Manager (CM) had been hired. The survivors in the Design/Construction group were renamed Program Managers (PMs). They all reported to a Program Management Executive (PME). The primary role of the PMs would now be to oversee a Construction Program, in other words, a list of projects assigned to them, more numerous than before. More balls had to be juggled in the air, but this was not deemed a reason to worry. Since there was no time left to review every individual project on a technical and accuracy basis, these tasks were relegated to the CM. PM's responsibilities included managing their budget, insuring that the associated projects were completed in a timely manner and to the satisfaction of the customers, negotiating change orders, approving invoices among other administrative duties. In effect, since considerably less emphasis was dedicated to the technical aspects of the projects, it was thought they would put aside their engineer's cap and don the one of an administrator.

However, by definition, secondment would bring to new organization experience and skills. The problem, though, was that the CM had no telephonic experience. So instead of just administering and paying bills, we first had to train the CM personnel in the ways and means of working in telephone buildings. It took time. Consequently, our work load was not reduced as we had initially believed it would be. As my 1995 appraisal, previously cited, recognized:

> "As Program Management was implemented, Paul had to assume a greater leadership role in guiding and advising the CM personnel. He has used his skills to motivate the CM project managers."

One had to wonder who was helping who? We had entered T. S. Eliot's "Wilderness of mirrors."

To fulfill these new duties in a more efficient manner, several training courses and seminars had been put into place to facilitate the transition Project to Program Management. Most took place in Shenectady. It was at a time a booming city, humming General Electric plants keeping everybody employed. Now it is the too typical American town. Industry has defected to more welcoming places for unbridled capitalism. Old shops in empty streets, when they are not boarded, sell the same wares you can find in so many places across the land. Local handicrafts come from China or some other Asian country.

The telephone building had plenty of empty rooms to run these seminars.
One of them was "Coaching the Coaches." This course had been devised by Paul L. Brown, Ph.D. It was a useful and extremely well run seminar. It was built around the movie *Hoosiers* which, as you will remember, depicts a fairly classic tale of redemption prized by Hollywood. In the film a coach takes over a wretched basketball team and turns it into an unstoppable winning cohesive unit. Segments of the film were selected to study relationships, analyze individual attitudes and appraise their impact on the team's performance. How the coach solved the many hurdles he encountered in his path were independently scrutinized and discussed. Then, these coaching skills were applied to our jobs, translating them into practical tools for improving suppliers' performance, in effect, teaching us how to become coaches to our suppliers. We were in turn asked to develop a Program Management Action Plan for "Coaching the Suppliers."

My plan was peppered with all the buzzwords *du jour* that would make it look attractive as well as literate. The corporate gobbledygook included: meet and exceed expectations, review of program strategy, customer laser-focused performances, thinking out of the box, top performers' rewards, commendation letters, proactive identification of roadblocks, accountability and lessons learned, meeting with peers, expected behavior, leading by example, on-time delivery, conflict resolution, and a few more. In brief, it was a sound report that should please the initiators of "Coaching the Coaches." I was afraid that I laid it on too thick, but no, it was well received and I got some accolades. I guess flattery works well.

Truth is, this inspirational seminar and the action plans resulted in more positive meetings with design professionals (DPs), contractors, and construction managers. Money was getting tight, so a special emphasis was put on the accuracy of the Cost of Construction estimates put together by the DPs. Our budgets were established based on them. Low estimates led later on to either reduction of project scope or request for more dollars from the customer, never an appreciated move. High estimates led to the immobilization of capital that could have been used for other projects. Discussing these matters had a positive effect and, all in all, it worked pretty well for ensuing estimates.

Another training tool *en vogue* at the time covered the concept of "value engineering," also known as "value analysis" or "value management." It originated during World War II in General Electric when resources were scarce and getting the biggest bang for the buck (aptly named for those troubled times!) was required. Value is defined as the ratio of function to cost. Value can therefore be increased by either improving the function or reducing the cost. In most of our projects, it meant reducing cost. That it involved walking on a tight rope to rein in the costs without displeasing the customer was the challenge. When I was working for consulting engineers, I had participated in value engineering studies a couple of times. One of them involved looking at a project for five water treatment plants in New York City. For a week, engineers from my company and others had pored over hundreds of drawings, discussing the pluses and minuses of concepts, coming up with ways of accomplishing the intended goals for less capital. These professionals from various companies had been brought in because one of the requirements for any objective value engineering study is to bring in independent specialists who can look at the project with unbiased eyes. Naturally, to hire these nonpartisan professionals costs money. Thus was the conundrum we found ourselves in: to save money, one had to spend money. This is of course possible in the case of a huge project where the budget is so large that the cost of value engineering can be offset by the savings. Not too many of our projects rose to that level. Most of the value engineering studies were therefore performed by the design engineer or the construction manager. The first was asked to criticize his own work and the second to reduce costs when his fee depended on the final cost of the project. King Solomon himself would have been at pains to judge evenhandedly. Consequently, this concept never gained much traction.

As you may have gathered, these courses had only one goal: to find ways to save on all fronts. Frugality became the new order. It involved trimming what were deemed to be unnecessary expenses; finding cheaper ways of doing things, "doing more with less" to use the company catchphrase. Here we were, a few decades later, joining Mies van der Rohe, the German-American architect pioneer of the modern architecture movement, famous for his minimalist dictum "less is more."

We all got a kick out of these new and sometimes whimsical rules. It led to the following humorous parable that made its way through the office.

Unable to attend a concert, a Bell Atlantic chief engineer gave his ticket to one of his Program Management Executives. The next morning, the officer asked this PME how he enjoyed the performance. Instead of the expected usual polite remarks, such as: "Thank you very much for thinking of me, I thoroughly took pleasure in this concert," the PME handed him the following memo:

> The undersigned respectfully submits his report and recommendations for your review and comments relative to the performance of Shubert's Unfinished Symphony, as observed under actual performing conditions. You will note that this memo incorporates observations in line with the new Coaching the Coaches concept outlined in the seminar we attended in Marlboro, Mass. It includes as well what I believe to be improvements in total sync with Value Engineering tenets.
>
> 1. The undersigned feels that the attendance of the orchestra conductor is unnecessary for public performances. The orchestra has obviously practiced and been properly coached. It should be empowered

to play the symphony at a predetermined and agreed level of quality. A considerable amount of money could be saved by merely having the conductor critique the orchestra's performance during post-performance review meetings during which report cards and "lessons learned" sheets would be handed out. Also, instead of conducting only one orchestra, the conductor would be freed to handle many of them during the same time period, via something akin to conference calls, should the needs arise.

2. The undersigned noted that for considerable lengths of time, the five oboe players had nothing to do but sit idle. Their numbers should be reduced and their work spread over the whole orchestra, thus eliminating peak-and-valley activities in the performance. Consequently, the reduction of oboist numbers would eliminate payroll checks.

3. The undersigned also noted that all fourteen violins were playing identical motions. This is a preventable duplication: the staff of this section should be drastically cut, which would in turn lead again to important savings. If a large volume of sound is required at times, this could be obtained through electronic amplification or hiring temporary players, such as the fired oboists possibly (for which, it goes without saying, no benefits would have to be paid).

4. The undersigned observed as well that much effort was expended playing 16th notes or semi-quavers.

This seems an excessive refinement as the average listener's ears are unable to distinguish or appreciate such rapid and efficient playing. It is therefore recommended that all notes be rounded to the nearest 8th. Were this to be implemented, it would be possible to use less experienced and/or lower grade musicians with no apparent loss of quality, but non negligible gains in salary cuts and benefits.

5. The undersigned noticed that no useful purpose appeared to be served by repeating similar passages. If all such redundant passages were eliminated, as determined by the recommendation of a review committee, the concert could have been reduced from two hours to less than twenty minutes, with corresponding savings in the concert room booking fees and overhead.

It is the undersigned's conclusion that, if Shubert had attended such courses as Coaching the Coaches and Value Engineering, the title for this piece, which is presently Unfinished Symphony would have become inappropriate because he would have had plenty of time to bring it to completion.

Amusing, yes, in the ways it carries to the extreme the needs to save. Still, applied within reason to our projects, some tenets advanced in "Coaching the Coaches" resulted in successful achievements. Being a good coach, I distributed commendation letters to the members of my teams, as recommended. One example follows in connection with the collocation projects.

But first, some background on this frenzied period. In the mid-1990s, the Public Service Commission had allowed well established competing phone companies, as well as smaller start-ups to build small switches in Verizon's central offices. These undertakings, which had been dubbed collocation projects, were numerous and always due yesterday! What followed was a period of one closely following another or concurrent collocation projects. The equipment was located in cages, protected with heavy wire mesh used for walls and ceilings of the cages. The demand at one point was so high that it became extremely difficult to find this wire mesh.

In the end, it was mostly for naught. Most of these start-ups with names such as Rythms, HarvardNet, Broadview, Covad, had borrowed heavily to fund their fledgling companies. Plagued by debt during both the dot-com bubble and Telecom crashes around 2000, the bulk of them ended belly up during this "tech meltdown". Only the strongest ones did not perish. One of these survivors after this debacle was AT&T. Before its monopoly break-up in 1982, all buildings had been owned by AT&T. At last, more than twelve years later, they had reclaimed a little bit of their former stature. They must have exulted like France after it recovered its long lost Alsace-Lorraine at the end of World War One[1].

---

1   The provinces of Alsace-Lorraine were taken from France by the Germans after the end of the 1870 war. They remained in German hands for close to fifty years.

For years after this debacle, one could walk in central offices and see empty cages one next to the other. It was like visiting a zoo that had gone out of business.

What follows are passages of one of the commendations letters sent to members of the team.

"To the Long Island CRE collocation team,

Congratulations have been recently extended to Corporate Real Estate with regard to the way the collocation requests were handled in the past eight months. It is an honor to extend these thanks to all of you. I do not have any doubt that without your help, Bell Atlantic would not have achieved its goal. We have been on the front line, more often than not taking the blame for any perceived delays incurred by other trades and only with exemplary team work, dedication and a good dose of resilience did we carry out the projects successfully."

It was followed by more personalized thanks to team members; in no particular order because everybody listed had at one point or another played a crucial role. However, I chose this moment to single out a friend and former ATT, New York Telephone, NYNEX employee without whose help, my tenure on Long Island would not have been as pleasant and successful as it was. Here it is, excerpted from this very letter and which still reflects my enduring respect for him.

"There is one individual, however, without whom it can be said that it is highly improbable the success achieved would have been met. His knowledge of Long Island central offices, his capacity to work long after most of us have already collapsed, his ability to supply on Monday morning answers to requests, which for some unknown reason, always seem to come Friday at 5:07 p.m., were assets that allowed us to maintain an uninterrupted flow of work. Here I salute you Gary Shumway[2], because without you, none of this would have happened and you should be proud of it. This being said, more cages are coming, so do not plan any vacation in the near future!"

The final paragraph was:

"Once again, thank you for all your help. These projects were a real test (and still are!) We had our share of crises to resolve and moments of doubts, but in the end, we met Bell Atlantic's goals and that is what counts."

These were rousing words that indeed pleased the troops. This lasted only a couple of hours, until the next crisis loomed, of course.

---

2   Sadly, untimely, Gary passed away in August 2017. See Appendix III.

CHAPTER 12

Long Island Here I Come

On December 23, 1995, in our office at 1095 Avenue of the Americas cheerfully decked with Christmas decorations, one of the supervisors, Rick Winner approached me out of the blue. "Paul, how would you like to work on Long Island?" he asked.

I knew Christmas time "'tis the season to be jolly," but I was in no mood to be the butt of a joke played at my expense on such an important subject. Since 1978, I had been working in the city, suffering through the Long Island Rail Road's shortcomings, from signal problems to trains stuck in the tunnel under the East river or cancelled from Penn station forcing commuters to go to Flatbush Avenue or King's Point stations which became mobbed. Like Moses parting the waters, one had to push oneself through the swells of a human sea to reach a car that was often "standing room only", not to mention lack of heat in the winter, with passengers copiously sharing their coughs, and failed air conditioning in the summer in cars that reeked with human sweat. There were even a couple of strikes which caused me to find temporary shelter in the city. So, yes, working on Long Island would be a God send.

"What do you mean?" I asked him in a guarded voice.
"Exactly what I said. Would you like to be responsible for Long Island from now on?"
"Of course, but you're serious?" I questioned him, still incredulous at this turn of good fortune, trying to control my voice so that it did not convey too much hope.
"Yes, the person we sent there a few weeks ago is not working out. So, do you want it?"

Did I want it? Does a Frenchman speak French? You bet I wanted it. It would be a dream come true. No longer any reason to spend more than two hours a day on the Long Island Railroad to New York City after eighteen long years, to freeze on the platform in the winter, to sweat in the bowels of Penn Station in the summer. No travel in subway cars packed as tightly as sardines in a tin can. If it was a genuine offer, it would be my best Christmas gift in a long time.

"Yes, I'll take it," I said, being careful not to sound too excited.
"Good! Call George in the Long Island office. He'll fill you in."
"When do I start?"

"Officially, January 1st. But get there right away, you'll have a lot to cover in just a few days."

It was rather short notice and I thought of saying: "How do you expect me to do that in two days?" But I was not going to quibble. I wanted badly to immigrate to Long Island so, damn the torpedoes, I was going full speed ahead. Just like that, without having a single clue that morning when I woke up that my life was to change for the better, I had a new assignment before lunch. When I told my wife that evening, she shared my delight.

George Josberger was the last of the Long Islanders, the lone survivor of the most recent forced separations. After playing telephone tag for a couple of days, we decided to meet in the Hempstead building, in the 4th floor office, the headquarters of the Long Island Design and Construction team. I had been there a few times in the past. It had been a lively office then. A happy buzz of activities had permeated a room nicely decorated with beautiful reproductions of a few paintings by Andrew Wyeth.

It was different that morning. I walked into the elevator, as happy as if I were ascending to heaven. But as I entered the office, my cheerful mood was brought down a few notches. It looked as if a neutron bomb had hit the office: all the furniture appeared to be intact, but not a single human being was in sight. Cuts had decimated the troops. Of the ten engineers and assistants who had worked there, all were gone. They had either taken the Six & Six offer or had been transferred to other locations.

All that remained, stacked precariously on top of the desks, were piles of files, project binders, unanswered letters and some unpaid bills.

I was going to have this huge empty space for myself. Obviously, there would not be any socializing or spreading of gossip near the water cooler on this floor, unless loneliness forced me to have a conversation with myself.

I selected a cozy corner far from the entrance door, but with an excellent view of it. It would give me time to awaken should I succumb to a little siesta after lunch and look busy before any potential visitors reached my desk. From this spot, I had a nice view of the roofs of Hempstead covering a hodgepodge of buildings including a post office, an Abraham and Strauss store now boarded up and some other nondescript structures. To say the area was economically depressed was not stretching the truth. I soon discovered that the rules of driving did not seem to apply here. When I entered the area, I had to grow another pair of eyes in the back of my head to anticipate any move by the reckless drivers that proliferated.

When George entered, he overloaded me with information about my new responsibilities. Several projects were ongoing, two of them which, as the days wore on, would soon become the bane of my existence. But I did not know it at the time, so I dutifully listened to George's long list of things to do.

Taking over Long Island was a trying time. George's swift passing of the baton left plenty of areas of quick sand.

Now looking at the piles of documents spread helter-skelter on the desks and the floor nearby, it seemed to be a mammoth undertaking. Would I be up to the task? I spent days delving through paperwork, practicing a sort of triage to take care of the more urgent matters first. They would be the unpaid bills. Then, this being done, little by little, I cleared, filed, discarded, and eventually, most desks were cleared.

Long Island did not fall under the authority of the Team leaders in New York City. It was overseen by Albany. In other words, I had a new boss. Since I had started, it was my fifth direct supervisor and my fourth director. After a week, I had not heard from my new supervisor, so I gave him a call to introduce myself. The only drawback of my transfer to Long Island was that this boss insisted on monthly staff meetings. Based in Albany, it made sense that these meetings would take place there. So I developed an intimate knowledge of the Taconic Parkway, and on one occasion, of the State troopers that patrolled it.

There were two major projects involving buildings undergoing extensive renovations. One was in Garden City, the other in Port Jefferson. They were both heavily unionized and this was bad news. Now, don't get me wrong. I believe unions are necessary, and as set forth in Newton's Third Law of motion, action requires reaction. Unions must react in order to clip the wings of those powers who take from the many to profit the few, who are never satiated and can never be trusted to make decisions that benefit the majority of the workers. It is nonetheless indisputable that too many of the members of the unionized workforce have come to believe that they are a privileged class with certain entitlements. So much so that any perceived indignity visited upon their territory was always the cause of an immediate walk-out with corresponding loss of working hours for the company, but not forfeiture of wages for the union members. Knowing this, I was fully aware that they would colonize the parking lots the days the walls of their offices would be repainted because the odors were intolerable to their delicate nostrils. The same would happen when carpet or floor tiles would be replaced, the smell of the glue being too aggressive. If this leads you to wonder how they could renovated their own homes without anyone to blame for the smells, dust and noise, you are not alone! Quite a few of them were operators. Their skills were impressive. They pecked away at their keyboards with the tempo of concert pianists playing the intro to the *Emperor's Concerto*.

The Garden City Central Office and Administration building was located on Zeckendorf Boulevard, not too far from Roosevelt Field. It was smaller than Lichtenstein, but not by much! Because of this vast size, the guard gave visitors a plan of the premises in the hope that he would not have to send out a search party if anyone had not come back after three days. A maze of corridors crisscrossed the interior. In them, one could often see three or four ladies on their break, walking fast, even running at a slow pace, possibly training for the New

York Marathon or intent only on losing a few pounds. The building was mostly a one floor construction, save for a mezzanine on the south side. It was about 300,000 square feet, roughly the equivalent of three football fields. It was a leased building which had been an ammunition plant, which would explain floors so thick that they could support the passage of tanks without uttering the slightest complaint. My first visit to what would become a dreaded building had to do with its roof replacement. It had reached the end of its useful life and let it be known by weeping all over the interior of the building every time it rained. The Construction Manager had been assigned the replacement project. To say that it had not started very well was an understatement. The new roof was a three-ply asphalt type system where each individual ply is welded to the others by hot tar. The tar was melted in a huge kettle that sat next to a wall. This kettle had caught fire twice in the previous fall, prompting the Nassau County Fire Marshall to issue a warrant to stop the project. Since the snow had been falling every few days during this winter, I mercifully would not have to deal with the problem until the spring thaw.

The other building was located on Route 114 in Port Jefferson. While the Zeckendorf building was one-third telephone equipment and two-thirds administration, this one was 100 percent personnel, most of them operators and union members, spread out over two stories. The project consisted of the renovation of one full floor. It involved replacement of duct work, new carpeting, lighting, painting, etc. In addition, four new gas-fired air conditioning units were installed on the roof. The problems began with the removal of sections of the old duct work which took place on a weekend, when the customer service operations were moved to another building. The contractors had covered the desks and put cheese cloth on the diffusers to prevent dust from entering the spaces. They had done a good job, but not good enough for the union stewards. In the early hours of Monday morning, they called for a meeting to complain about the lack of protection that affected their performance. Listening to them, it was no less than a plot to take away labor protection. Suddenly we had gone from protecting furniture and equipment to stripping away their rights as union employees. Most of these union reps were female, and apparently, they had not been chosen for their tact.

What followed was one of the more acrimonious meetings I had the bad luck to attend. The contractor was accused of trying to do harm to their operations, preposterous allegations, but made nonetheless. These accusations were made in an aggressive tone, at times bordering on the confrontational. The contractor was Smith McCord and the on-site supervisor was Willie Koch, a veteran who had years of experience working on phone company projects. It was my first contact with him, but I learned quickly to rely on his vast experience. He did not deserve to be at the receiving end of these ludicrous assertions. We had a few of these surreal meetings during the remainder of the project. Honestly, it would have been safer to run with the bulls in Pamplona than to face these furies.

This was, however, nothing but the appetizer. The main course, the real *piece de resistance*, was brought in when the units on the roof were put into operation. The heating fuel being natural gas, extreme precautions had of course been taken to check for leaks in the piping. We were all confident that there would not be any problem in this area. By we, I mean the contractor and myself. The first night the units were on, a burning smell seeped into the building. The fire and smoke alarms sounded. The personnel, rightly so in these circumstances, vacated the premises. Calls were sent out by the guard: one to me, one to the contractors and one to the Fire Department. The latter was very dramatic, something like: "We have an emergency here. Fire and smoke alarms are on. I have people out in the parking lot. We need help fast!" So, like many others, I got up a little before midnight, wiped the sleep out of my eyes and drove to Port Jefferson.

When I arrived, I was welcomed by police car and ambulance sirens which were still cutting through the night, the frozen ground amplifying their sounds. They wailed like a cat whose tail has been set on fire by a precocious arsonist. The swooshing of the blades of a medevac helicopter hovering over the site did not instill confidence and my heart started beating faster. Looking on the positive side, if I had an heart attack, the helicopter could take me to a hospital in record time! Emergency lights had dispelled the darkness: orange, blue and red strobes could have illuminated Time Square on New Years' Eve. These lights were reflected on the low clouds. It was as if an Aurora Borealis was floating over the lot. "My God,"

I thought, "what is going on?" It was complete pandemonium!

There was no reason to panic as it became clear soon after. The fireman receiving the call about people out in the parking lot had assumed the worst. For him, "out" meant unconscious. He reacted by sending a small relief army to revive all the comatose victims. For the Verizon manager, "out" had meant that the people were outside in the parking lot, some placidly smoking, pounding the black top with their feet to keep warm, waiting patiently for the emergency to be over. It was a classic failure to communicate. Was I glad that the cost of the rescue operation was not charged to my budget? Yes, absolutely! I entered the building with Tim Moore and Willie Koch from Smith McCord. It was empty but for a few firemen, safety persons and the guard. A quick investigation determined that the odors did not come from a gas leak, but from the oil that coated the heating equipment inside the units to prevent them from rusting during storage and transportation. As the first flames licked the coating, it burned and generated the harmless smell that had caused the panic.

Three days after, strange odors, again akin to gas, permeated the building. As expected, everybody walked out into the parking lot until the situation was investigated. Nothing was found inside the building, or on the roof, leaving the inspecting crew rather perplexed. It was later discovered that a truck had been delivering gasoline to a nearby gas station up the road. As luck would have it, the wind was blowing towards the building, carrying with it the odor of gasoline. At least, thank God for small favors, it did not happen in the middle of the night.

One week later on a cold morning, a similar scenario occurred. Smoke had penetrated inside the building for a third time. Following a now familiar drill, everybody proceeded to the parking lot. This time, it turned out that the neighbor across the street, probably feeling the effects of this endless and cold winter, had decided to start a wood stove. It was some of the smoke generated that had migrated into the building, via the air intakes of the air conditioning units.

It was such a relief when this job was complete and the personnel stopped walking out under any pretext. The heavy weight borne by my shoulders for so many weeks disappeared. It was also a relief that this project was completed before the roof replacement at Zeckendorf began again. I did not think I could have survived two concurrent jobs in these two "plagued-by-problems" locations.

The year in my new Eden had not started too well, but thankfully, my new boss had recognized the challenges I was facing. In my year-end review, his conclusion echoed my own take on the situation I inherited. Here are some of his assessments:

> "In January 1996, Mr. Belard was transferred to Long Island. While carrying the responsibilities that the 1996 budget required, he also pursued the manage-

ment of several projects in progress. Because of a lack of continuity and only five days of training in this new location, an inordinate amount of time was spent looking through a maze of documents left in a deserted office… In this period of dramatic changes in the ways NYNEX is doing business, Paul has shown a great degree of flexibility and integration. He has been at ease and efficient in a changing environment. He is effective in dealing with his customers and demonstrates major strengths in the area of team work."

Nice and to the point. I'd like to thank Bob Keyser for his support at this critical juncture of my career.

Meanwhile, the company itself had gone through another name change. As you know, in the early eighties, AT&T's monopoly had been broken up; one of the local companies the break-up spawned in our neck of the woods became known as New York Telephone. Later on, it merged with New England Telephone and was renamed NYNEX. More recently, the consolidation moved south and an aggrandized entity called Bell Atlantic was about to emerge. In a not too distant future, it would incorporate GTE and, under the name Verizon, the AT&T Humpty Dumpty was almost put together again.

CHAPTER 13

Zeckendorf Roof

The winter of 1996 had been pretty miserable with endless snow falls and persistent freeze and thaw cycles. Driving was hard on cars and drivers. Streets were dotted with potholes so huge they could have swallowed half my car. Still, these difficulties paled in the face of the welcomed fact that, thanks to this wretched weather, the Zeckendorf building roof had been covered by close to two feet of a mixture of snow and ice. I ventured out on the roof a couple of times. As soon as the door from the stairway was opened, the wind stung like a handful of sand thrown in my face. Its coldness stole my breath. Under an oppressive sky, this Siberian expanse, white as a bone, was gleaming lightly from the glow of a jaundiced sun. The shrieks of seagulls reassured me. It was the sweetest sound. Their coming so far inland often announced another snow storm.

The thin crust of ice on top of the snow cracked under my shoes as if I was stepping on five day old bread. I wished the roof would stay buried like this another ten years. When my eye lashes started to get heavy with frost, I went back inside, and the door, pushed by a burst of wind, banged loudly on its steel frame.

Alas, soon, this coat of snow would disappear and the removal and replacement of the old roof would resume. It was not an activity I was looking forward to. Yes, I deplored the end of this miserable winter.

But nature could not care less about my hopes. Too soon, the innocent blush of the new spring arrived, right on schedule. The robins pulled the worms off wet lawns, the rhododendrons unfurled their leaves, the green spears of the daffodils and the crocuses nosed out of the ground. The Zeckendorf's roof truce was over. Before long, it would again turn into a hive in full hum. The project in Port Jefferson had had its share of negative occurrences, most of them time-wasting and stress-inducing, but rather amusing after the fact. I had a hunch that the roof replacement project here would not be as droll.

The two instances when the kettle melting the tar that is used to join the plies that went into the construction of the new roof had caught fire have already been mentioned. Kettle fires are not rare. The tar comes in 100-pound cylindrical blocs that are loaded in the kettle for melting. The heat necessary to do this is provided by propane containers. Three critical tar temperatures are very close to each other:

- The application temperatures of the tar on the roof surfaces are between 300 and 400 degrees Fahrenheit (F).

- The flash point of a material is the lowest temperature at which its vapors will ignite, when given an ignition source.
- The auto-ignition temperature is around 600 degrees F. At this temperature, the tar ignites by itself without any outside ignition source.

Consequently, the kettle operator must carefully watch the temperature to prevent tar from overheating and igniting, particularly when the machinery is not equipped with thermometers, which is the case more often than not. Once ignited, it is very difficult to extinguish the fire; it can also start again when it is thought to have been stopped. Typically, the kettles are placed close to the building to avoid the tar losing heat during its transport to the roof. Therefore, a kettle fire which is not quickly controlled may set the building on fire.

Following the second fire, the Fire Marshal of Nassau County had issued a stop work order. My first move would be to meet with him and have this order rescinded. The Marshall carried a gun at his side. Whatever the reason, he was armed and not somebody one would want to upset.

However, even before the work on the roof resumed, another problem surfaced. You will remember that in the chapter "Secondment", a few of us took issue with paying invoices from the Construction Manager; invoices that we thought were inflated and did not reflect the work accomplished up to the date of the invoice. It seems the problem went beyond this.

Every year, a budget was allocated for construction projects. This capital was expected to be spent in its entirety. If that was not the case, it reflected badly on the project director.

It seemed that, since a lot of projects were not as advanced as they should have been, the CM had been asked to submit invoices that were inaccurate. The sum of these invoices would be taken into account to meet the annual construction budget. On paper, the budget had been spent. However, in order not to compound this accounting trick with more severe violations, the doctored invoices would not be paid to the CM until the work was completed. So, in the meantime, these invoices were being kept in a drawer. This was, alas, in contradiction with another company rule stipulating that an invoice must be paid within a certain number of days after receipt.

Somehow, this misbehavior became known. An investigation was opened by the Legal Department. Several project managers and their supervisors had already been called to its offices in Boston to answer questions from corporate attorneys. The Zeckendorf roof project was on the list. I received a request to send the entire project binder to the New England legal office. To be prudent, I made a copy of all the documents since the project had gone unfinished. As I pored through them, it became quite obvious that the amount on some of the approved invoices did not mirror the amount of work done-to-date on the invoice. So, I figured that a trip to Boston was in my future. I had never been to Boston, but this was not the best reason to visit this historical city. Although I was not at this stage involved with the project, this is a trip that I would not relish more than the one to the Fire Marshall. The odds that the questions would require replies implicating colleagues were high. After some amount of soul searching, I decided to remove the incriminating invoices from the documents sent to Boston. In order not to add trouble to the person who had requested and signed these optimistic invoices, I did not mention his name, nor the invoices to anybody. Let the Bostonian attorneys delve through a ton of project binders. Maybe, the fact that some invoices were missing would escape their due diligence. If it did not, in the tradition I adhered to of "better to ask for forgiveness than permission", I would say "oops, they must have been misfiled." It happened that the lack of some invoices did not raise an eyebrow, because, contrary to my belief, a summons failed to appear.

I had protected a colleague who would eventually climb the corporate ranks, but he did not even know about it. This was not the case for everybody involved in this secondment fiasco. It would not be long now before this first attempt at outsourcing was scrapped. A few of its proponents were encouraged to find another career, outside the company for some.

One of the major technical difficulties of the roof replacement was that the air handling units distributing the conditioned air throughout the building were on the roof. Consequently, so were the fresh air intakes. In any air conditioning system involving personnel, a certain amount of outside air must be introduced to avoid recirculating air that would soon become as rancid as the one in an aircraft after a ten hour flight. As a result, the fans would suck in some of the fumes generated by the hot tar and carry them right to the occupants' noses. Rightfully, the CM decided to close the intake louvers. This was a move in the right direction but not thought through. Soon, the law of unintended consequences reared its pesky head. Two things happened:

- After a while, the recirculated air became indeed stale and people started complaining. In order to combat the sullied atmosphere which reigned indoors, the doors of the buildings were propped open to create some cross ventilation.
- While closing the air intakes on the roof was a logical idea, something had been forgotten. There were multiple bathrooms in the building; each one was equipped with several exhaust fans. Since no more air was introduced inside the building, where was the air expelled from the bathrooms to come from? Right, through the open doors! With the draft hence created around the building came the tar fumes once again. Fed up, the employees walked out.

It was Port Jefferson all over again, or more precisely Port Jefferson squared! Where the former had involved hundreds of workers, here we dealt with one thousand. Also, someone appeared to have a direct connection at Channel 12, the regional television station, because a

TV truck and a reporter soon showed up to interview the displaced workers. The number of lost work hours was huge. Two pregnant women threatened to sue the company and requested MSD sheets[1] for the products used on the roof, probably in anticipation of a future law suit.

The direct consequence of this debacle was that it was decided that no work on the roof was to proceed during the day. This created more logistics problems. The CM now needed to provide adequate lighting, safety barriers around the perimeter of the roof to avoid accidental falls, and overtime pay. The project would also be lengthened. Replacing a roof is a tough job. Almost all the workers are immigrants from Mexico and South America. The removal of the old roofing system is dirty, generating lots of dust. Installing the new one is back breaking, uncomfortable and dangerous. To facilitate the mopping of the tar on the roof surfaces, it must be heated to 300 or 400 degrees F. On a hot summer day, it is like working on a griddle surrounded by the noxious smell of hot tar.

The worker's silhouettes were deformed by the rippling

---

1   A Material Safety Data Sheet (MSDS) is a form which details the properties of a particular substance. It includes physical data on this substance, its toxicity if any, potential health effects, first aid actions and other information. Its intent is to provide workers and emergency personnel with procedures for handling and/or working with that substance in a safe manner. The Occupational Safety and Health Administration (OSHA) requires that MSDS must be available to employees for potentially harmful substances used in the work place.

currents of hot air rising. The air was filled with humidity, as though the atmosphere above the roof was sweating.

One had to admire their grit. There was not an able-bodied American among them; the work was too demanding. During my inspections, I was welcomed by foreign chatter and exotic music coming from radios.

If I had a question, finding somebody who spoke English was a problem. So much so that, in future specifications for roof replacement, it was stated that a member of the crew must speak English. You would be right to ask "why the construction manager's representative was not on the job to supervise the operations and answer questions?" Although the CM had mentioned during the negotiations that every job would be overseen by a supervisor, it did not specify "at all times". So the poor fellow was given several projects to manage at once and had to split his time between them.

The job lasted a lot longer than anticipated. It was apparent that the CM was losing a substantial amount of money on this project and was trying to reduce the losses by submitting as many change orders as possible. Of course, each of them needed to be reviewed. Negotiations touched on the ones which were valid and their amount, and on the ones that I felt were inappropriate and should be rejected. Very often, there are penalties noted in contracts should the work not reach completion in a timely manner. This is not a clause that is customarily included in roof replacements given the fact that the work is heavily dependent on the weather, an important and uncontrollable element. In fact, the forecasts were monitored closely every day before the work started to avoid removing areas of roofing system leaving the building unprotected in case of rain. If an expected storm appeared, the work area took on the appearance of a disturbed ant hill. Under a sky choked with clouds yearning to drop sheets of rain, the workers quickly installed tarps, securing them to shelter the exposed building spaces.

However, this project was already late by several months for reasons one could attribute solely to the CM. Consequently, the negotiation turned rapidly into a confrontation between myself and the CM representatives. It involved several trips to the company headquarters in New York City. It is true I am frugal with words. It has been interpreted in different ways, sometimes to my advantage, sometimes not. But those who thought it meant I was compliant and could be steamrollered were in for a surprise. I have always been loyal to the companies I have worked for.

In the end, we settled for less than fifty cents for every dollar. The CM was fuming; he thought it was not enough; his ire was understandable, he had to cross out about one-third of a million dollars from his balance sheet. I was not entirely happy, thinking we gave too much. But it has been said that if both parties in a negotiation leave unhappy, the settlement is a good one.

This rancorous negotiation was successful enough to warrant a mention in my 1996 yearly appraisal where my supervisor noted:

"Mr. Belard monitors and manages the Construction Management firms' performances very closely and aggressively addresses deficiencies. Time and money is very effectively monitored, i. e., a request for a scope change for $342,052 was denied on the roof replacement project at Garden City."

When the roof replacement was finally and successfully completed, it was *un jour à marquer d'une pierre blanche*, a day to be marked with a white stone, that is a milestone or historic date.[2]

The CM did not get too much additional work on Long Island after this ordeal.

---

2   Under the French Empire, participation in military service was sometime left to the luck of the draw. The potential draftee plunged his hand in a bag full of white and black stones. If he drew a black stone he was drafted, unless he could pay some poor soul to take his place. If he pulled a white stone, he was exempted of military service. He could therefore think of this day as the one that may have saved him from death on the battle field, that is a day worth remembering

CHAPTER 14

Interlude

You will remember that when my work week took a dramatic plunge from sometimes as high as seventy hours a week to a steady thirty-five, I started to paint. I would not call myself an artist, but my watercolors were attractive enough since quite a few were regularly sold by a framing store in Northport.

One day, I decided to paint a pictorial map of Long Island. It took several years to complete. My wife took pictures of landmarks and during my business travels, I had the chance to visit less well-known areas of the island. I saw the fifteen million dollar mansions along the shore of East Hampton, the same ones the refined owners modestly called their cottages. Partially hidden behind immaculately trimmed hedge rows as tall as two-story buildings, these "homes" overlooking the ocean, unpretentious in their genteel and refined stylishness were reminders of how the wealthy like to live.

One of my favorite stops was the monument which acknowledges the service and sacrifice of all Vietnam Veterans. Located on Bald Hill, in Farmingville near the town of Brookhaven, it is one of the highest points of the island. At its summit stands a four-sided obelisk, thin as a needle and ascending high enough to pierce the sky. The top is gallantly painted in the colors of our nation's flag, stars on a blue background falling from the very top into sloping white and red stripes, sharply contrasting the white Cherokee marble at about two thirds from the base. It is a peaceful place, with beautiful views of the island and its surrounding waters.

The monthly company bulletin, NYNEX NEWS, occasionally featured an article about an employee, his or her hobby, a community cause, or a sporting event. When the map was completed, I contacted the staff about featuring this map. They were interested. One night, a reporter and a photographer came to my home for an interview. I showed them some of my father's and sisters' paintings, adding that my grandfather was also a painter. "You come from extremely artistic forebears, don't you" to which I replied: "Well, you need to carefully choose the right family to be born into." The featured article appears in Appendix II.

Every year, employees had to take a number of courses or attend different seminars to continually improve their skills. The subjects were closely related to respective jobs. Seminars on "Steam Systems" given by Con-Edison, "Ice Storage Systems" sponsored by Trane, a manufacturer of cooling equipment, and the like were offered.

One year I managed to get the authorization to take a two-day course in "Creativity in Art". How it came to happen I do not recall, but it was noted in my accomplishments in the 1998 yearly appraisal.

Early in 1997, a show of my watercolors was set in a gallery in Garden City. Thirty or so paintings were displayed. The opening took place on a Saturday afternoon. It was well attended by friends and family, along with a few designers and contractors I worked with at Verizon. I had mentioned the show to a friend who dealt with them. He had been a very efficient public relations person although I had been of two minds about his efforts to invite people professionally connected. In any case, a good time was had by all, possibly having to do more with scrumptious *amuse-bouches* and superb Merlots and Chardonnays than the art itself.

If a watercolor had been purchased, a red dot was placed against the protective glass and the name of the buyer put on a list. When the day ended twenty-five had been sold. I was ecstatic. What a success!

However, when I checked the buyers' list, I noticed that about half of the pieces had been purchased by acquaintances whose common thread with me was Verizon. That is what I had been afraid of. My euphoric state dropped down a couple of notches. I did not think about it too much during the rest of the weekend, but on Monday morning in the office, it dawned on me that I could be in trouble.

I called my boss in Albany and explained the situation.

"First congratulations, you seem to have some talent for people willing to put on a show for you. Now, as far as your concern, my advice would be to contact HR and ask them how you should handle the matter. You might be in conflict with the Code of Conduct."

So I got in touch with HR. It did not take them more than a New York "second" to give me their opinion: without any doubt, there was an obvious conflict of interest at the very least. At worst, some of the purchases were a disguised bribe, with the expectation that something would be eventually expected in return. So I asked them, just to be sure:

"Am I in trouble?"
"Yes you are!"
"What should I do?"
"Is the show over?'
"No, it's scheduled to last a month."
"When the show is over, you should take all the money raised and give it to a charity of some kind, the Red Cross or United Way. Your choice."
"But I said, some paintings were brought by friends or legitimate persons interested in them. Also," I pleaded, "I spent a lot of money having these watercolors framed."

The reply was chilling:

"Do you want to get into a dispute with the auditors that would be sent to make sure that all the valid purchases were accounted for, as well as the dubious ones? As far as the framing costs, did you keep invoices so that you can justify all expenses? When they sink their teeth into something, these auditors are very thorough. You may be in the hot seat for a while until they are satisfied that everything is on the up and up."

Well, this brought me down. The reality of the jam I was in finally set in. First, the last thing I wished was to get into a squabble with the number crunchers. I was wise enough to know that the only argument you ever win is the one you do not have. Second, I had to give all the money to a charity to put this sad affair behind me. So that was what I did. As soon as the show was over, and by the way, all the pieces were sold, I picked up the check and appeared at a church near the gallery with a donation amounting to a few thousand dollars. This unexpected windfall made their day. I asked for a receipt that I quickly faxed to HR. I never returned to see if they had named a pew after me.

A few days later, HR informed me that the case was closed.

CHAPTER 15

Help Wanted

When I was transferred to Long Island, my construction budget in 1996 was $6,200,000. The following year, it climbed to $9,200,000. In 1998, it remained at $8,700,000. In 1999 however, it jumped to a whopping $20,200,000, including $5,000,000 in collocation projects. Mostly because of the advent of the collocation projects, my work load became too much to handle efficiently on my own. Paradoxically it was not because the projects had become too large. In fact most of these minor projects were small in size and cost, but so numerous that each took an inordinate amount of time to manage. Driving fifty miles just to attend a method of procedure (MOP) meeting and losing half a day in the process was no longer a viable approach. This situation was further complicated when a crucial signer did not show up for the meeting and it had to be rescheduled. Clearly, it is easier to handle, let's say, a $2,000,000 project in one building in Manhattan, than a program equivalent in value spread among thirty locations scattered to every corner of Long Island. You can see the challenge I was facing.

After a few weeks of working alone, an elegant African-American woman walked into the office in Hempstead. Her name was Glendoria Moore. At first she was distant and not very cooperative. I understood later that she had been made promises which had not been kept. She was extremely bitter about it. But she had been sent to assist me, so, little by little I gained her trust and eventually, we became good friends. She had mentioned me to her mother. Each morning, this kind lady made sure that Glendoria brought me a copy of the *Daily News* so that I could do the crossword puzzles at lunch time. What service!

I initially gave Glen small jobs because her technical background was non-existent. What I should not have given her though was my beeper number. I got so many calls from her, most of them followed by the dreaded 911, which signified an emergency. Evidently, we did not have the same definition of what constituted a crisis. After a series of these calls which turned out to be of a trivial nature, I ignored most of them. We eventually became very comfortable with each other and soon, she turned into a valuable assistant.

I still fondly recall those long trips back and forth to Albany, the speakers of the rental car blasting Elvis Presley Gospel songs. Glen was a welcome companion at those dreaded staff meetings where nothing was learned that could not have been put in an e-mail. At the time, the staff meetings began with every participant having to relate something nice that happened to them in the past weeks. It seemed more like an Alcoholics Anonymous gathering than a meeting of professional individuals. It was without a doubt one of those so-called leadership skills acquired during an executive retreat in the hope it would boost management style and employee morale. During those staff meetings, hours were wasted, but minutes had to be recorded about what was said.

However, the multiplication of the collocation projects became the proverbial straw that would break the camel's back. I desperately needed help. So I asked my boss if I could bring in somebody. He agreed and I contacted Zeno Capitan who had been a member of the design and construction group before taking the six and six offer. Originally from Romania, he had emigrated in the early sixties and been lucky to land a job with the phone company. When we were in the Brooklyn office, we played bridge at lunch time. He was often a partner, the kind you do not want because he had a tendency to second guess your moves and get too frenzied about it. Anyway, what I had in mind for him did not involve playing cards, so we got along fine. Basically, I now had my own aide de camp. He would be my eyes and ears on some projects, take care of MOPs, coordinate shutdowns. He turned out to be a great help.

One of the problems was how to pay him. First, he became an employee of an architect and was paid by him through regular invoices. It worked for a while but soon, the amount this architect added to his time became so high that this arrangement was terminated.

We finally decided to have his services paid by the contractors. On every project, there is what we call an allowance. It is a sum of money included in the contract to cover unforeseen conditions, a contingency if you will. Unanticipated situations very often occur simply because, to put it crudely, "shit happens". An example will explain. Take the poor plumbing contractor who had to drill a drain into the floor of the cafeteria in the Zeckendorf building. In the absence of a drawing, he had rightly assumed that the concrete slab was of standard thickness, which is eight to twelve inches maximum. When he reached two feet with no end in sight, he started to panic because at this depth, he had already spent the budget he had allocated for this work. Of course, we all had forgotten that Zeckendorf had originally been an armament factory and that some floor areas had been designed to withstand the weight of tanks. Finally, the plumber reached the dirt after three feet of digging. He presented a justified change order that I approved without qualm. It is for these kinds of unexpected situations that allowances are warranted.

So an allowance for project supervision was added in the design documents. Zeno's time was confirmed by time sheets, the contractors did not pad his invoices and the system worked well.

As an aside, at times, the presence of the allowances was questioned by some pencil pushers. The design and construction documents, in the minds of those who never had to implement them, needed to be thorough enough to cover all aspects of the project. The importance of the unexpected was not a factor they were inclined to consider. That is why they asked why allowances were needed. Well, as illustrated by the example previously cited, more often than not, plans were not derived from a crystal ball. Unpredictable site conditions could inevitably throw a wrench into the most carefully made plans. The overall cost of the project would be affected and nothing was worse than going back to the upper echelons with one's tail between one's legs to ask for additional funds.

As a general said, the first thing to go awry at the beginning of a battle is the battle plan. Trying to explain this to a bureaucrat sipping coffee with his feet resting on the edge of his desk, as removed from the realities of a construction site as a Saudi oil billionaire prince was from a Long Island gas station, was akin to trying to grab a handful of smoke.

CHAPTER 16

The Design Professional Agreement

Around 1995 a new entity called the Sourcing Department was created as an extension of the Purchasing Department. While the latter handled all aspects of purchasing goods in the company, from toilet paper to telephone switches, from toolboxes to new buildings, Sourcing, as it soon became known, would also be involved in purchasing services. Hiring an architect is of course not at all akin to purchasing light bulbs. Although, in the minds of the Sourcing staff, it may have seemed that it should not be that different. Another new wrinkle was that the bidding process would now go through Sourcing. Before, the bids were sent by the consultant who produced the design documents, i.e., the drawings and specifications. They were then returned to the appropriate Verizon Design and Construction office where they were opened in the presence of the group supervisor and two witnesses. The date and time were written on each bid and signed by the three individuals present. The bids were analyzed and the lowest bidder was selected, after some negotiations with all bidders, if necessary. This system saved time and had worked perfectly well for decades.

Now, the bids ended up on Sourcing desks. A process that took a week to ten days had been extended to a month in the best cases.

During 1999, a novel approach was introduced by the Real Estate leadership in cooperation with the Sourcing Department regarding the selection of the design professionals to handle projects. The new agreement was based on the concept of "one-stop-shopping". A single architect would be selected for a given region for a period of five years. All design work in a given area would go to the chosen one. No more architects competing against each other through a bidding process, as it had been the rule for years. In a way, it was the Walmart model applied to Consulting Engineering. However, even Walmart has competitors to keep its prices in check by allowing the customers to compare them with, let's say, Costco or Target.

Before the new agreement was put in place, the fee for a consultant was a percentage of the Cost of Construction (COC). It could range from 4.5 percent to 5.5 percent of the COC, in the New York footprint, depending on the size of the project. These fees were lower than the ones that other large organizations, such as the School Construction Authority of New York, the Port Authority, the

Army, the Navy and the Air Force to cite a few, charged for their projects. They typically ranged from 6 percent to 10 percent of the COC. Having worked with all of them in the past, I can attest to that.

For projects involving mostly office space preparation, the architect's fee was set at $3.00 per square foot of space to be renovated. In addition, there was a pool of architects or mechanical, electrical, and structural designers to choose from for projects that matched their area of expertise. It allowed for spreading the work load, as well as the wealth.

What were the reasons that led to the implementation of a new contract? The first was that several consultants had complained that fixed percentage billing was detrimental to their bottom line. In view of the percentages noted previously, they had a point. Why the company did not give them the answer routinely offered to its own employees: "If you are not pleased here, the exit door is always open", nobody knew.

So, it was agreed that the fees would be increased. In defense of this decision, the arguments advanced by the consultants were: higher fees would mean greater expertise, expertise which would translate into jobs of higher quality, eventually, leading to lower design costs, and everybody would be happy. So there you have the second reason, higher fees would result in lower costs of the design phase of a project. This fallacy was accepted without question by the Verizon Design Department heads, as well as Sourcing.

Of course, putting such a novel contract together involved lengthy negotiations to define all the lawyerly contents that were supposed to make the contract foolproof. One major aspect of this contract was a move from fees tied to cost of construction and square footage to hourly rates. As outlined by Sourcing, "the design professional fee for each project shall be calculated and billed on an hourly basis in accordance with the Compensation Matrix set forth below". In order not to let the design costs drift to unacceptable levels, it also stated that COC greater than $100,000 shall be subject to a not-to-exceed percentage of COC, subject to equitable adjustment for supplemental services. The not-to-exceed percentage shall be 9.5 percent." It added that "hourly rates will be adjusted annually beginning on January 1, 2001 in accordance with Section 7.2.1."

In addition, the architect was made the "single point of contact" for all projects. Even if a project was mostly mechanical in nature, it had to go through the selected architect, who would then choose his or her mechanical sub-consultants, mostly mechanical, electrical, structural and all others as the case may be, whose expertise was needed to bring the project to a successful conclusion. Secondly, any question relating to the project, be it mechanical, plumbing, electrical or other, would go through the architect, who would gather the answers to the questions and relay them back. Not exactly the best way to get quick, or even precise replies, as you can imagine. Yet this was the new way of doing things.

When the contract became the law of Real Estate in

January 2000, it was impossible for us project managers to get a copy. We were going through a lot of changes during this period; we were confused and worried. Employees need leadership in normal times, and even more so in times of uncertainty. Such leadership necessitates treating employees with respect and fairness as responsible adults, not as errant children who can be brought in line with ornery threats such as "you should be happy you have a job". Still, our requests for a copy of the contract remained unanswered. In our supervisors' defense, they were often kept in the dark by upper management as well, and so did not receive a copy of the contract.

We were all kept out of the loop. As it often does, however, the loop opened, became a hyperbola and bits of information slid along its curve where they were easy to catch when they reached the x axis. Thus, only a few months after it had been implemented, we managed to obtain a copy of the contract.

To add insult to injury, Sourcing did not even have the decency to introduce the new agreement themselves. The first presentation of this new contract was made by the architect who was the beneficiary of the gift of the decade. So, the person that we were to supervise, whose work we were to check, whose invoices we were to approve was telling us what he was going to do for us. A lot of us were upset by this cavalier treatment. Once again, we were being considered second-class employees. Some of us thought we were being treated mostly with disdain. I felt like what a fire hydrant is to a dog.

Once we had the opportunity to review the contract,

its flaws were evident for whoever wanted to see them. We kept silent since we were not consulted during its preparation. As good soldiers, we adapted to the new order. First, let's be honest, any criticism of the regime during those difficult periods was seen as counterproductive. It did not matter if the remarks were technically or economically sound; you were quickly portrayed as a non-team player, the ultimate put-down. In the army, it would have been akin to being a traitor. Secondly, the projects had not stopped coming, waiting for the new contract to be in force. Work had to be done; schedules needed to be met; so we kept on.

It took a while, but eventually, the devil reared its horned head. Everything was not going according to plan. Ralph Carey, our latest manager who came from Bell Atlantic, was an engineer, the last of an endangered species in the Real Estate department. Actually, it seemed that the engineers at Bell Atlantic were much better appreciated than at NYNEX, which was a welcome turn of events. Ralph's favorite admonition was: "The devil is in the details." Lord, was he going to be proven unequivocally right with this contract! It took some time, but once again, it was demonstrated that it is in the details that plans put together without too much thought flounder every time.

When the first bubbles of the lack of reduction in savings on design fees percolated to the surface, the advice from some people was not to make any waves. During a meeting, when this problem was pointed out by one of us to a Sourcing manager who had been heavily involved in preparing this contract, his answer was: "Why do you care, just pay the bills!" Well, we cared. As part of our responsibilities, the most important was to protect the interests of Verizon and it is one we took extremely seriously.

To make matters worse, meeting the work load that a single architect now had to handle caused the number of its employees to grow by leaps and bounds. In 1996, when I arrived on Long Island, the selected firm in my area had about six or seven employees. During the early months of 2000, it grew to more than ten times that number. It became like a retirement home for former Verizon employees who had taken the Six & Six offer. There were not enough of them, however, to fill the ever expanding ranks. So new hires were added. The immediate impact was that most of these newbies did not have any Verizon experience. The number of change orders due to design errors and omissions increased dramatically. No need to tell you that the Verizon internal customers footing the costs of the projects were not at all happy.

I never possessed an inflated respect for the chain of command. I was always prepared, not to ignore my superiors per se, but to act as I saw fit to carry on with my given duties and safeguard the interests of the company who handed me a check at the end of every month. I had the knowledge to do it efficiently. My approach was: "Just give me the project folder, tell me what you expect from me, provide the funding and a schedule and leave me alone. If I have a problem which requires a decision that is above my pay grade, I'll contact you. If you do not hear from me, you can safely assume everything is all right and it will be substantiated by timely status reports." It may sound arrogant, but for me, it was only the definition of a good engineer.

When the abuses became too flagrant to ignore any longer in my area, I brought my boss up to date on the extent of the problems. Nobody enjoys being a whistle blower, but the interests of Verizon were at stake and took precedence over those of the consultants. In February 2002, I wrote a report titled "Engineering Cost Study of Completed Projects on Long Island." Its conclusions were devastating:

> While every business unit in Verizon is operating under significant budget challenges and with fiscal discipline in mind, the engineering costs of the Long Island projects reveal an opposite trend. An analysis of several projects executed in the past year shows that they cost at least twice, sometimes more, than similar projects performed earlier.

Unbeknownst to me, one project manager in Manhattan was also concerned and was preparing a report on the same subject. When we found we had the same concerns, we joined forces. Since, in addition to being an engineer, he was also an attorney, he became a very strong ally. His concerns carried more weight and they could not be dismissed in the same cavalier fashion as mine might have been. As it turned out, the same monkey business was taking place in Manhattan. Our conclusions had also been the same. They included:

- Most design fees had at least doubled or tripled as compared to those established under the previous contracts.
- Most fees exceeded the not-to-exceed clause of the new contract.

It had not been unexpected that the terms of the new contract would lead to an occasional engineering cost increase. What was not anticipated were the extent and the regularity of this surge. How did it come to this? How did the Sourcing desk-jockeys, as some like to call them in the long tradition of inter-office rivalry, come to be hoodwinked by the consultants? It is easy if you do not do your due diligence. It is hard to believe to what extent a segment of the company deceived itself about the nature of the loyalties of the vendors. Call us cynics, but isn't the first loyalty of a vendor to do whatever will translate into higher profits for his own pocket book? So it turned out that it was not possible to satisfy these two masters, the consultants who claimed they were not making enough and the company that was crying for more savings, by enforcing a contract, the terms of which led to an unquestionable mess.

At first, neither our direct supervisors, nor Sourcing, really wanted to hear our findings. They would likely have preferred to sweep them under the rug. It is only when we went over their heads and informed our director of this unfortunate turn of events that things started to move. A meeting was set up in Verizon's headquarters in Manhattan to discuss the situation.

CHAPTER 17

The Golden Goose

When our director was made aware of the situation, he did not ignore it. He wrote an e-mail to everyone involved: "Our intent in changing the method of billing was to reduce billing, not to increase it. Find what is happening."

After a bit of investigating that required neither the sagacity of Sam Spade, nor the tenacity of Sherlock Holmes, a common strategy of some of the architects became clear. First, Sourcing had established a compensation matrix detailing the hourly rate in relationship to job title. There was nothing wrong with this, it was a logical step. Unfortunately, and with consequences that should have been foreseen, Sourcing failed to ask for a list of the architectural firm personnel and their associated titles far enough in advance of contract negotiations.

So, what is a shrewd firm principal to do when handed a golden opportunity to increase his company profits? First, since the hourly rate was tied to the job title, one easy way to inflate the profits from the get-go, without much effort was evident: promote everybody within the company. That is what was done in many instances. Even a few high paying positions, which were not on Sourcing's list, were created, such as director and engineering manager, at respectively $160 per hour and $140 per hour.

It is important that you keep in mind that on Long Island I had already been dealing with this outfit for four years. I knew everybody who worked there, their names, their titles, their hourly rates. This information appeared on the invoices which had crossed my desk for approval during those past years. It was the information that Sourcing failed to request and eventually led to most of the excesses.

So, when I saw on a new invoice that an individual who used to charge $90 an hour in 1999 was promoted to director in 2000 at $160 an hour, I thought, uh-huh. On the same invoice a project manager whose hourly rate was $75 per hour in 1999 now had his hours billed at $140 a pop. Double uh-huh! Was it an indication that small cracks were appearing in the contract concocted to result in lower design costs? It was still too soon to understand the ramifications of these hourly increases. Perhaps, as the architects had proclaimed, higher fees would lead to faster design times, *ergo* lower fees.

It did not take long for these cracks to widen and reveal their true meaning. The misconception that higher fees would lead to lower design costs was soon dispelled. There was an irrefutable increase since all the invoices of the previous years where hourly rates had been used on projects were in the project history binders for anyone who wanted to see them. These were hefty raises, close to 50 percent. They surely were unheard of at Verizon, where yearly raises hovered between 2.5 percent and 3 percent for the luckiest employees.

Some of these individuals had become friends. In fact, quite a few used to work for Verizon before they took the Six & Six offer. I congratulated them on their good fortune. Then, out of curiosity, I asked if they had received a raise commensurate with their new hourly rate since their firm received the new contract. Most had not seen the contract. Some confirmed that they did not get a raise, others said they got a slight one, others again told me it was none of my business. Fair enough, but it was clear that somebody else in the firm was getting much richer.

For the sake of argument, let's do some quick calculations, starting at the low end. Let's assume that $10.00 was made on every employee. It has been noted before that the ranks had swelled to close to seventy-five or eighty people. To exclude the support staff, let's make this number sixty. $10.00 an hour per employee, forty hours a week, and fifty weeks a year during five years comes to 6 million dollars. Keeping in mind that some hourly rates had been raised by up to $50 and not passed along to the employees, somebody was getting quite rich. Now a few million dollars here and there are probably a rounding error in a corporation that was generating about $22 billion annually[1], but why should they go to somebody whose main claim to professional fame was to have hired a couple of devoted ex-New York Telephone employees who put him on the map and later on, to have been at the right place at the right time? These millions would be better allocated to boost dismal Verizon employee raises rather than fattening consultant nest eggs.

Another way to increase the revenues dramatically was to have senior level personnel performing subordinate work functions at their premium rates. A similar approach was to overstaff project teams. A typical example follows.

The project goal was to build a collocation cage which, at the time, were sprouting like dandelions in a lawn after a spring shower. It involved the construction of a wire mesh cage not larger than ten feet by ten feet to house the equipment and the installation of a fifteen-ton air conditioning unit. In normal times, the project team would have consisted of a director to define the objectives (a couple of hours of his time at most), a project manager to run the job, possibly a designer, and a Computer Aid

---

1   Source: http://www.referenceforbusiness.com/biography/S-Z/Seidenberg-Ivan-G-1946.html

Design (CAD) operator. The design would have taken three weeks at most.

This is an excerpt from invoice #1 dated 7/6/2001:

Director:	48 hours at $160 per hour
Director:	52.5 hours at $160 per hour
Engineering Manager:	62.5 hours at $140 per hour
Engineering Manager:	176.5 hours at $140 per hour
Project Manager:	9.5 hours at $140 per hour
Project Manager:	10.5 hours at $140 per hour
Asst. Project Manager:	10.5 hours at $115 per hour
Construction Inspector:	2 hours at $90 per hour
Designer:	259.5 hours at $75 per hour
Designer:	33.5 hours at $75 per hour
Senior Technician:	1 hour at $55 per hour

Eleven people were involved in this project: two directors, two engineering managers, two project manager, a construction inspector (why, since construction had not even started?) The design team who built Hoover Dam must have been proportionately less bloated! This was a perfect example of an inverted pyramid, where senior management charged more time than junior personnel. What was even more preposterous were the 259.5 hours charged by a designer. At eight hours a day, this individual worked on this project for a little more than thirty-two working days full time, almost a month and a half.
In addition, there were fifty hours of supplemental services labeled: site observation, i.e. another $3,500. What was involved in these observations to make them last

more than a week? Nobody was able to provide a legitimate explanation.

The Cost of Construction for this project was estimated to be $280,000. Therefore the not-to-exceed amount was exceeded on the first invoice!
Previously, the design of this cage would have come to two-thirds of this amount; similar projects were on file to prove it.

Here is another example of the consultant's creativity. A small room to receive a new switch was needed in a central office. Nothing fancy: four walls, some duct work changes, minor electrical work. In short, a simple design that a senior designer or junior engineer could have handled. The design fee came in excess of 14 percent of the COC. Sixty-six percent of this fee was charged by two directors. Of course the fee was reduced to 9.5 percent. Still, on a subsequent invoice for the same project, supplemental services for "extensive administration efforts" by a director appeared. One has to admire the gall. These services were of course denied.

Another incident, one of my favorites, if it can be characterized this way, showed the lengths to which the designers were going during these crazy years. A problem arose in the Long Island Technical Center located on Sunrise Highway. A few users had complained about the lack of heat in their offices. After reviewing their concerns, it was decided to install six electric radiators below the windows of their office. Not a big project. It involved sizing the radiators, a simple enough calculation; finding a source of power supply, not complicated either. When all was said and done, the installation of these radiators cost $9,500. However, trouble started when the invoice from our single-point-of-contact architect came. It amounted to $3,679. Remember that in the previous fee structure, the architect's fee would have been, for such a small job, around 10% of the cost of construction (COC), that is $950. Now, it was 38% of the COC. The invoice showed that:

- The mechanical consultant selected by the architect charged one hour by a partner at a rate of $160 per hour, 8 hours by an associate at a similar hourly rate, 7 hours by a senior engineer at $95 per hour, 3 hours by an engineer at $90.00 an hour.
- The architect invoice showed 8 hours at $140 were charged by a project manager, 2 hours at $75 an hour by a designer.

My comments on this invoice were as follows:

- The spaces the complaints originated from were a lobby and five offices located on an outside wall. That there was no provision for heating in the first place was a design error. The mechanical designer had been involved in the retrofitting of this building.
- Sizing electric radiators is a task that should not take more than a few hours by a junior engineer. Charging Verizon for a partner, an associate, a senior engineer and an engineer on such a trivial task goes against all

professional standards.

- The installation costs of these radiators, labor and material, came to $9,500. Charging Verizon 38% of the construction costs is stretching the terms of the contract between Verizon and name withheld beyond credibility.

- Consequently, this invoice is rejected. In addition, name withheld personnel spent some time on this project. Since their involvement was a direct result of the mechanical designer's design omissions, this time should be reimbursed by him to the architect.

Luckily, this is not an invoice I had to fight. One must assume the amount of hours claimed was so outrageous and unjustified that none of its initiators deemed this fabrication worth defending.

There was another clause in the contract that allowed the hiring of specialty consultants when it became necessary to evaluate design aspects of the projects that were out of the ordinary. It was intended for highly unusual tasks that came rarely on a project, such as the need for soil borings for example, or for the analysis of a potentially dangerous crack that appeared in a bearing wall, or again for the installation of grounding rods to protect a building from lightning strikes. Would you believe that, if a small air conditioning unit mounted on the roof needed a couple of beams to support it, the structural engineer designing it became a specialist, his fee reimbursable. Some simple plumbing work was even billed as a specialty. The ends to which the design professionals were willing to go to squeeze the last dollar off that lemon of a contract knew no bounds. We had entered the twilight zone.

For some architects, even this was not enough. The creative ones fattened their fees a little more by asking their consultants to pay an "entry toll" in order to be selected to work on their projects. Had a lawyer been asked to look into this double-dipping practice, his conclusions would have labeled this practice "pay to play" or more to the point "extortion." Now, mechanical and electrical engineers had to submit to this penalty, lest they be refused work.

Another way to get more money was to have a higher "Not to Exceed" fee. So, it was calculated based on the total costs of construction. Of course, this number should have excluded the general conditions, overhead and profits. Why should the architect make a profit on the profits of the general contractor or the construction manager?

All in all, the costs of the post-2000 projects increased 20 percent when compared to pre-2000 ones. In my area, quite a few compressor/dehydrator (C/D) projects were designed for Outside Plant. They spanned several years, starting in 1997. Therefore the Outside Plant project manager had all the records necessary to keep track of the cost of his projects. He became very upset, with good reason, when their costs, under the new contract, skyrocketed. What made it worse is that these projects were mostly repetitive. With the advent of Computer Aid Design and Microsoft Word's "cut and paste" feature, some installations required just a change of address on the drawings and the specifications, possibly accompanied by minor changes to fit the new building configuration. Therefore, there was almost no design involved and, still, the cost of the projects increased. In other words, the fee became almost entirely profit on some projects.

A colleague in Manhattan had another perfect example of the monetary impact of this new way of doing things. In 2002, an important re-stacking project was in the works at the 1095 Avenue of the Americas company headquarters building. It would affect office space of an approximate area of 106,000 square feet. Based on the pre-2000 contract, with architectural costs at $3 per square foot, the fee would have been: $318,000. Using the terms of the 2000 contract, the architect's fee jumped to $997,500.

Other shenanigans included sending two or three representatives to meetings when one would have sufficed. These meetings also lasted much too long, stretching beyond the point where conversation remained useful. Pleasantries were exchanged at the beginning and the end: "How about those Jets?" "Did you see *Desperate House Wives* last night?" "How are the kids doing?" It was a waste of time, but every minute was billed to Verizon, so why be concerned about the hobnobbing?
Charging travel time to the project site was also initiated. Greed knew no boundaries.

As mentioned, my New York City colleague and I finally managed to get a meeting in Verizon's headquarters in

Manhattan to discuss this matter. It included our managers and representatives from Sourcing. It was plain to see that we were not exactly welcomed with open arms, nor were our conclusions. But in order to avoid that our reports be shelved right after the meeting, they had already been sent to the next management level. Consequently, there was not much that could be done by the recalcitrant Sourcing representatives to ignore the obvious issues. So they caved in somewhat.

Following the meeting, a letter was addressed from Sourcing to the architects. It listed, "not in any particular order of importance" (as if it mattered!) some of the various issues and areas of concern that had been raised during this meeting.

- Project man-hours expended beyond upset fee %
- Design professional member(s) attendance at meetings
- Management of man-hours that are part of the upset fee % amount
- Travel time as part of billed project time.

You will notice that the elephant in the room - the internal promotion of personnel to increase hourly rates was not mentioned. Since it was an oversight by Sourcing, we may presume they "took the fifth" on this most important aspect of the problem.

Sourcing asked the architect to prepare a Total Project Summary for 2001 that would address the problems listed in its letter.

At this point, my colleague and I were kept out of the loop. Since it is difficult to keep anything secret for long anyway in a company, we learned that the architect had indeed submitted a report addressing the questions. We never saw a copy of it. Presumably, there was enough information to prove that everything was hunky-dory. Since a lot of people in high places had their imprint on this contract, it was a good bet that nobody wanted to pursue the matter in depth. So it just died. The only positive outcome was that the abuses, while they did not cease entirely, became less overt and frequent.

This agreement was great for killing time though. I never spent so many hours fighting and rejecting invoices. The architect's accountant, and I had some lengthy but nonetheless pleasant negotiations. It was not an easy task to be sent to defend the indefensible, but she did it in a professional way, courteous and charming at all times. Yet, some of these inflated invoices kept coming back, so much so, that at one point, I sent a note to the architect stating:

> Regarding the disputed invoices, I have previously (in some cases several times) discussed the reasons for non-payment of these invoices. The reasons have not changed. I would suggest that you talk to your administration and, if you feel you have been unjustly singled out, issue a formal complaint to Verizon's Auditing Department who will review it and make a final ruling.

Not surprisingly, it appeared that they did not deem it

necessary to take advantage of Verizon Auditors' expertise to further their case.

Internal pressure from above was also exerted to settle the questionable invoices, thus far not paid in full, as the following note dated 10/25/2002 suggests, regarding a meeting that I had scheduled with the consultants:

> Please leave your meeting on Wednesday with an agreement and arrangement to "put this to bed" as soon as possible. I appreciate your concerns in regard to fees but this needs to be resolved now. I don't want this to become an issue with anyone above us.

I did not dare to inquire about the meaning of the last sentence since the bloated invoices were now an open secret. Just before the meeting, my boss asked:

> "We're on the same page, right? We're clear about that?"
> "Absolutely," I replied.

What I really thought was that we were indeed on the same page, but not necessarily on the same line. The negotiations were going to be tough and I had no intention of short-changing the company.

On 11/4/2002, I replied:

> As you know, it was noted a few months ago that the "Not-to-Exceed" clause of the Design Professional

Agreement was exceeded at an alarming rate, particularly for the C/D jobs. Following lengthy meeting with - *name withheld* - I am happy to report that the negotiations resulted in a credit of $69,963 for Verizon for the C/D projects initiated in 2000/2001. While it is rewarding, it is somewhat a hollow victory since these projects have cost twice to three times more than in 1998/1999. In addition, negotiations on several other projects are bringing the total credit to $110,709.

Not a bad outcome for a two-hour meeting.

Architects throughout the company got a sweetheart deal on that contract, but what was the point of being more Catholic than the Pope? As one of our colleagues said: "It is as if Ed McMahon had knocked on the door of the architect lucky enough to have landed this huge contract and handed him a signed check with the amount left blank. You won the mega jackpot, get the most out of it".

Why Verizon let this happen in the first place is still one of the mysteries of the way corporations work. Did they really believe that the interests of the consultants would be perfectly aligned with Verizon's? Did the negotiators really think that all the loopholes of the contract, and there were many, would not be exploited to the maximum by the architects? What became clear in its first year of implementation was that it did not work out the way it was intended. A lot of money was made by some individuals during this golden age. One positive point though: complaints about the design fees being too low all but disappeared from the radar screens during this period. Still, despite the fact that this attempt had turned into a fiasco of major proportions and that it was costing the company large amounts of money, one of the proponents of this debacle showed true chutzpah. In 2003, a Sourcing employee nominated one of the perpetrators for a Verizon Supplier Excellence Award, prompting this note to my boss:

> I found it baffling that Sourcing is still entertaining the notion of nominating - *name withheld* - for an Excellence Award. While the intent of the new contract was to reduce costs, it resulted in increased billing. When this was brought to Sourcing's attention in 2002, they were forced to perform an audit of the nominee. To my knowledge, the results of this audit were never published.

On second thought, an Excellence Award was deserved after all. Didn't it require a superior intelligence to anticipate the monetary impact of promoting all its employees in order to take advantage of higher hourly rates? Isn't a well-above average acumen necessary to devise highly creative ways to exploit all the grey areas of a contract? Wasn't it the work of a superior intellect to deceive the Sourcing department in such a spectacular fashion? Masterful. Yes, an "Excellence Something" was warranted, but not by Verizon who had been taken to the cleaners. One had to wonder why an investigation was not brought about.

In 2004, this unorthodox "one-stop shopping", imperfectly inspired way of doing things was dropped without fanfare. At the beginning of 2005, things reverted to pre-"one-stop-shopping" days.

Following this debacle, many of the individuals involved in its conception were affected. Sourcing saw its payroll significantly reduced. Other employees were reassigned to positions where their ability to do irreparable harm to the company's interests were drastically curtailed. They were put on *une voie de garage*, shunted like an old railroad car on the rusted rails of an abandoned spur.

One had to wonder how many absurdly hilarious cartoons *Dilbert*[2] would have produced out of this ludicrous episode.

---

2   *Dilbert* is an American comic strip written and illustrated by Scott Adams. He worked at Pacific Bell between 1986 and 1995. He therefore knows how a phone company operates. The personalities he encountered there became the inspiration for many of his *Dilbert* characters.

CHAPTER 18

Strike Assignment

Refrigeration units in the city must be operated by licensed engineers. Consequently, I had been required to obtain a license to run these units. Expenses related to this license were paid by the company, so that in case of a strike, it would have someone to replace any unionized operating engineer. Once this license was secured, my strike assignment was as a building engineer at 140 West Street, less than a stone's throw from the two World Trade Center towers and adjacent to Seven World Trade Center. It is bounded by Barclay, Washington, and Vesey Streets. Had it not been so far from home, I would really have enjoyed this assignment.

One hundred Forty West Street is indeed a magnificent structure. It may have been dwarfed by the austere power of the towers of the World Trade Center, but their stern lines only accentuated the grandeur and grace of the first art deco building in New York City.

Designed by Ralph Thomas Walker, an architect of the firm McKenzie, Voorhees and Gmelin, it was completed in 1926. It was among the first skyscrapers designed under the 1916 Zoning Resolution[1], using the step back principle which became a key element of art deco design. The interior area of the building is 1,200,000 square feet. The lobby features marble walls and other ornate decor, including ceiling murals that depict how human communication has progressed, from Aztec runners to the telephone. Walker was inspired by Mayan architecture in designing the facade. Exterior ornamentation includes exotic foliage, along with babies and animal heads as part of the design, and a bell, symbol of the telephone company, above the door. The building was known at that time as the Barclay-Vesey Building. When it was first put into service, the building served as the headquarters for the New York Telephone Company.

My duties involved insuring the proper operation of the air conditioning system. There were four refrigeration units in the third basement (that would be completely flooded after the September 11 attack), several air handling units throughout the building, and cooling towers on the roof.

---

1   The New York City 1916 Zoning Resolution was a measure adopted primarily to stop straight and massive buildings from preventing light and air from reaching the streets below. It established limits in building massing at certain heights, usually interpreted as a series of setbacks and, while not imposing height limits, restricted towers to a percentage of the lot size.

The view from the roof was magnificent; downtown Manhattan, the harbor, the Brooklyn and Manhattan bridges and the majestic twin towers one could almost touch. Their height dwarfed even our thirty-two story building (not including five stories below grade).

Thankfully, the first strike I was involved in, in 1996, did not last long, only a couple of weeks. My assignment was at night, 7:00 p.m. to 7:00 a.m. I was alone. Wandering in this huge building was not a comforting feeling, especially in corridors leading to exits on the streets whose doors had been known to be forced open to shelter homeless people and occasional addicts.

Frequently I went on the roof by myself. I let my eyes wander over the buildings cloaked in the dark blue haze of the night. They fused with each other until the city became one single building. Its walls were punctured by a myriad of halos of brightness that made it appear as if it was built of light rather than brick, steel, glass and concrete. It stretched away in all directions, until it was engulfed by a mist that fell on it like cotton candy. What were the millions of lives being lived in these structures? Families having dinner, people at a wake, parents celebrating the baptism of their first child, the sick waiting for the respite that sleep might bring. The city lived, breathed and held fast its mysteries.

The only sounds at this height were the fans in the cooling towers, the streams of water dripping through the tower fill in the softest of pulses, and the low rumble of the motors driving the pumps pushing the water through the pipes down to the basement and up again.

The two towers of the World Trade Center loomed above. They brought back memories. I had worked on the top floor of one of them for a few months in the early 1980s. I could still recall entering one of the huge elevators. When it started its climb it was like being aboard a missile taking off. When the 95th floor was reached, I had to press both my ears to bring them back to operating order.

Living near Huntington, Long Island, did not leave much time to recover from the night schedule. Typically, subway and train delivered me home around 10:00 a.m. I had to depart again at 4:00 p.m. to be at the building on time for the night shift.

The next work stoppage occurred in 2000. It was longer and tougher. At that time, probably because of my complaints regarding the insecurity of being alone and the liability of the company should something happen to me, a colleague was assigned to do the rounds with me. Mandatory overtime and work-related stress issues led the unions to go on strike. It lasted three very long weeks. Afterwards, we managers could have had our own strike on the same issues!

Strike assignment is twelve hours a day, seven days a week with a day off after a month if you can be spared. While the hours above a regular week are paid at time-and-a-half, it quickly feels like blood money. It is stressful, particularly going through picket lines twice a day. It is grueling for those who live far away. One of my colleagues who I shared a portion of the train ride with, lived in Shoreham. This added six to seven hours of travel to the twelve hour night. It did not leave much time to relax, just enough to catch a cat nap if some idiot did not beep you during the day to pass along some useless information. The only beep that could have been tolerated was the one announcing the end of the strike.

My partner during the strike was a funny guy, full of resources. He was from the Sourcing Department, with no technical background at all. He had sleep apnea, a problem in which one's upper airway collapses, causing breathing to cease repeatedly, rendering restful slumber impossible and somewhat dangerous. So the next evening, he brought his CPAP machine, a breathing apparatus that helps combat breathing difficulties during sleep disorder. Along with it, he carried an air mattress which he dutifully inflated every night at midnight. He slept like a baby until six in the morning.

One evening, we found cans of paint in the office with a note to call a number. Some zealots had thought that, since people with free time on their hands were available, they might as well have the buildings painted at no cost. Needless to say I did not intend to do it, arguing that as a licensed building engineer, handling a brush did not fall under my duties. My colleague thought it might be fun and a neat way to pass a few hours while he was not sleeping. He went to paint a room somewhere in the building. Later on, a manager called me: "I got a phone call from your colleague. He is asking if he should paint around the water". "I do not know what he is talking about" I replied. "Then, find out." I looked for the painter-apprentice. He was in an equipment room, dabbing at the floor, carefully avoiding puddles of water created by leaking valves. The floor looked like the skin of a giant zebra given the op-art treatment.

"Why don't you tighten the packing on the valves?" I asked him.
"What's a packing?" came the reply.
"This is this part here that prevents the valve from leaking," I told him, pointing to the top of the valve.
"Now, go and get a wrench."
"What's a wrench?"

At this point, I told him to abstain from smearing the floor and go and take a nap. It was almost his bedtime anyway!

But for the long hours and the obnoxious pickets, the strike would have been a pleasant break from our regular duties. One night, around 11 o'clock, while I was in the basement recording temperatures and pressures in the machine room daily logs, the building intercom spewed my name: "Paul Bélard, please report to the Deputy Fire Director immediately." "What's going on now?" was my first thought, "a fire somewhere?" Per the New York City code, each building above a certain height and containing equipment must be manned by a Fire Director twenty-four hours a day, seven days a week.

The elevator was slow in coming, so I climbed three flights of stairs and reached the Deputy Fire Director's office out of breath, expecting the worst.

"What's going on?" I asked the deputy, panting like a dog that had tried to catch a passing car.
"Well, I got the DVD we talked about. Do you want to watch it now?"
"Sure, why not! Next time, though, why don't you wait until I come back up in order to avoid me having a heart attack?"

So we sat in his office for two hours, sipping on a diet coke and munching fries, watching a movie on the TV he had brought in to pass the time. It was called *Le diner de cons*, an uproarious French movie whose American remake was titled *Dinner for Schmucks*. After that, I retired to a room that I locked, because being the guards on the walls, we were not supposed to sleep on the job. Also another strike enthusiast was making the rounds to try to catch anybody enjoying nice dreams in Morpheus' arms. With the lack of sleep, mostly due to the long travel time to and from home, I decided that a nap was a necessity for my survival. So I went to sleep for five hours. This became a routine after eleven o'clock during the duration of the work stoppage: a movie and a nap. All that was lacking was a nice dinner and a glass of wine.

Following the attack of September 11, 2001, there was no strike in 2004. For the potential 2008, I had done my homework. I had filled a ream of paper explaining why twelve hours of work coupled with six hours of travel were not conducive to my safely performing my duties, which included operating heavy machinery. Against all odds, my request was approved and the company allowed me to rent a room in a nearby hotel. Think about it, I would leave the telephone building at 7:00 a.m. and I would be sleeping by 7:15. It was for naught though as the strike never materialized.

The company was in the midst of rolling out FiOS, its fiber-optic internet and video service in New York City. The telecommunications landscape had been drastically altered by new technologies in the past few years. The 1989 strike had been inconvenient for customers. The company saw profits reduced for a while, but the customer had been basically stuck, with no other choice than to grin and bear it. This was no longer the case. The customer could walk away from Verizon any time, knock on Cablevision, Time Warner or Dish Network doors, among others and be greeted with open arms. The unions understood this as well as upper management. Both came quickly to an agreement that a strike would be bad for everybody.

CHAPTER 19

Fast Track Projects

Technology was moving fast at the end of the 1990s. So fast in fact that projects were scheduled with completion dates without all the pertinent information required to carry them to a satisfactory end. They were known as fast-track projects.

In July 1998, we were informed that a new Tandem Switch[1] was planned for the second floor of the Deer Park central office. Although it had not yet been decided which manufacturer would supply the switching equipment, at the time Lucent and Nortel were in the running. An end date had already been established. Without the dimensions and configuration of the equipment to be installed, no detailed floor plans and engineering drawings could be developed.

---

1   Tandem Switch: It is an intermediate switch or connection between an originating telephone call or location and the final destination of the call. Source: https://www22.verizon.com/wholesale/glossary/Glossary-of-Telecom-Terms

The last week of July, Lucent was chosen as the equipment supplier and Network decided that most of the building work had to be ready by October 16th in order to receive the equipment. Two weeks later, a Digital Cross-connect Switch[2] for the first floor was added to the project. The date to receive the equipment was set for October 1st.

With such a tight schedule, taking the usual bidding route, which meant running through the obstacle course that the Sourcing department had scattered throughout the bidding process, was not going to cut it. However, despite the initial failure of the first foray into outsourcing, the drastic reduction in Verizon personnel did not leave much choice to ensure the crucial dates would be met. Outside help needed to be brought in. So another adventure in hiring construction managers was launched. It was not the approach that was faulty. Fewer employees, same amount of work, how does one reconcile the two? Bringing in outside help was the obvious solution.

The problem was the way the contracts outlining the duties of the Construction Managers were written. They seemed to be developed by people who did not know much about construction and maintenance, but thought they knew enough to dispense with the advice of those who had firsthand experience.

---

2   Digital Cross-connect Switch: It provides an electronic cross connection for individual constituent digital signals within a high-speed digital line. Source: https://www22.verizon.com/wholesale/glossary/Glossary-of-Telecom-Terms

Therein lay the rub. Regularly, the company held seminars for every employee to attend. One of them was about "Lessons Learned", the content of which might easily be shortened to "Don't make the same mistakes again, you jerk." Sourcing seemed impervious to the faults of the past. Earlier mistakes did not have a big impact on the individuals concocting these contracts, because these new adventures in outsourcing inevitably turned out, monetarily speaking, to be against Verizon's interests.

Consequently, their contracts were as leaky as an old roof. There were always enough holes in them to ensure that the profits of the selected company would be healthy. To the CM's credit, they always seemed smarter at exploiting the existence of loopholes than those who wrote the contracts were at spotting them in the first place.

Once again, Verizon was sold a bill of goods by people who promised they would do *anything* for less, who claimed to have teams of experts capable of handling any situation. One of their main arguments was that they could do bulk purchases of equipment and therefore command lower prices. Of course, if one can buy twenty air conditioning units at once instead of one, the discount incurred would not be insignificant. However, how is this an advantage when at the beginning of the year, nobody knows what equipment will be needed? Would they sample the equipment bought in years past, then buy new equipment based on this extrapolated data? If this turned out to be the case, where would this equipment be stored until it was required? Who would pay the storage fees? If the equipment sat idle for more than a year, what would happen to the warranties? As you can see, bulk purchases were not feasible.

Of course, doing things for less did not include what was not specifically called for in the contract. It happened in 1996 with the first attempt at outsourcing, and again in 2000 with the architect gold plated contract and, as sure as the sun rises in the east, it would happen yet again. Isn't one definition of foolishness trying the same things again and again and expecting different results?

Anyway, it did happen. More Construction Managers were brought in. For some unknown reason, at least to us project managers, the construction managers did not have to abide by Sourcing rules. Not having to go through the bidding process to select designers and contractors was a huge plus on these fast-track projects. It would in fact be the key in completing some urgent projects on time. Selecting the architect and contractors without having to go to Sourcing would save at least two badly needed months. It was perplexing to us why the construction managers did not have to have their bid process reviewed by Sourcing. Was it a way to circumvent them or us? Ah, to have been a fly on the wall when these contracts were negotiated!

So, as soon as those projects were handed to me, I contacted a construction manager. I had a bad experience with the CM designated to handle Long Island, so I requested permission to use another outfit. This one was based near Boston. A meeting was arranged with one of its officers as soon as I received the OK from my superiors. Quickly I persuaded him that the designer should be Gary Shumway; the general contractor Smith McCord; Pinto and Teger the electrical contractor; and Botto the mechanical contractor for whom George Josberger, who had welcomed me on Long Island in 1995, was now working. It was the best team that could be put together. He did not interfere with these choices, smart enough to grasp the value of using outfits familiar with Verizon methods of procedure and having an unblemished track record. It would of course be to his advantage.

At this juncture, the main task of the CM was to develop a CPM. The critical path method (CPM) is a step-by-step project management chart for planning all phases of a project. Basically the project schedule is divided into sequenced tasks, critical and non-critical ones, with their starting date and duration. It identifies the crucial dates not to be missed, the impact of long delivery items to prevent either bottlenecks or periods of forced inactivity. Once developed, it was thumb-tacked to one of the walls in the project meeting room and updated as the work progressed.

As mentioned, the team assembled was composed of seasoned veterans and the work proceeded smoothly. The CM was only present during project meetings, most of which he attended. Not really aware of what was going on a daily basis, his role was mostly reduced to writing the meeting minutes and updating the CPM chart.

When the projects were completed, on time and within budget, I made some calculations. Comparing the number of hours that the Construction Manager charged to the projects with the fee he collected, it turned out that he was paid $900 per hour. Brand me a suspicious individual, maybe a sarcastic one to boot, but I think outsourcing was a very lucrative career change for some. Sometimes, I wondered if it would be better for me to outsource myself!

This is indeed a high price to pay to shave a few weeks off the project schedule by eliminating the bidding process. Why did someone in a position of power not instruct the Sourcing Department to relax its rules for fast-track projects?

CHAPTER 20

September 11, 2001

Why do some people invent planes and others hurl them at skyscrapers full of their fellow human beings? How can an entire city area be amputated of several buildings, covered with smoke and ash and strewn with the bodies of those who chose to jump rather than be incinerated all in one fiery eclipse of civilization that happens so often throughout our troubled world? One cannot explain the actions of fanatics, but the following account will show the reactions of good men to these barbaric acts.

On the morning of September 11, 2001, George Famulare, the Property Manager of Southern Manhattan telephone buildings, was in his office at 140 West Street, a stone's throw from the World Trade Center complex. This interview took place in April 2011. I deliberately chose not to make any comments on the way he revisited these harrowing hours. The painful silences, the poignant sighs, the halting, at times faltering voice reveal the deep emotions that George still feels almost a decade and a half after these events took place. They are a testament to the toll this fateful day took on him and so many. So, *listen* to George:

"In the morning, a cleaning lady came to my office and told me there had been an explosion at one of the towers at the World Trade Center. I left my office, went outside and looked up and I said, um, you know, that's a funny explosion because, really, there was not of lot of debris coming out of the hole and then, somebody told me: Oh, no, no, it was a plane that hit the building. So I said, Oh… I made a comment, maybe a small private plane, a commuter plane, a Cessna. The person said: no, no, it was a jet liner."

"Could you see anything from where you were?"

"All I could see was the huge gaping hole in the north tower and a fire starting to go out. I run back into West Street because pandemonium was happening, people coming out asking questions, panicked. I went to the Command Center and I told the Fire Safety director: Listen, use the PA and calm everybody down. It's not here; it's in the building next door, calm everybody down. Tell everybody to remain in the building. Employees were coming out of the building, gathering into West Street and Battery Park City; there were hundreds of people starting to get together. I gathered Fire Safety Directors and other persons, and told them: we have to get this under control, tell the people to get calm and get off the street. I have no idea why we did what we did, but we told people: You have to get off West Street, start heading north, go away from here, and don't come back into the building. In my wildest dreams, I did not think these buildings were going to come down the way they did. When the buildings came down, as we know now, they came down and across West Street, and into Battery Park City and into the Winter Garden. It took out the overhead pedestrian walkway. Thank God we got hundreds of people out of that street or probably it would have been…you know, how much worse could it get? It would have been even worse."

"But at this point, the second plane had not hit the south tower!"

"No, the second plane had not hit the building yet."

"And the first one was falling down already?"

"No, no, no, no! We had…I do not know if it was a sixth sense or something, or just a thought. It never dawned on me it would happen the way it did, but we said to these people, you have to get off the street. The buildings had not come down yet, they had not come down, but everybody was walking up, watching and I can still see it… and I see it every day, Paul, it never goes away. What I thought being debris coming out of windows were people, with their arms and legs flailing. From ninety, a hundred stories up, you could not tell they were people until they came clear into view as they got closer to the ground, and uh…"

"One couldn't even imagine what you felt."

"The sound that you heard when these people hit, well…again, Paul, I have flashbacks regularly, and I see it regularly… uh… And then, I could not stay out there to watch and gawk, I hate to use that word, watch what was going on, so I went back into West Street to try to get control of my building. I told the people inside, you have to calm down, you have to calm down."

"Employees were still in the building at this point?"

"We were starting a controlled evacuation, OK, to get people out of the building safely, onto West Street, or Barclay Street, not on Vesey Street. We told them, go north. Go home north, get away from the World Trade Center. Um, there was a handicapped, a severely handicapped woman in the building, she uh… we had her down in the lobby. We put her in my office until we could get an ambulance there to take her away. I stayed with her; I was on and off phone with calls from uptown, 1095, telling people what was going on. I would say: Listen, a jet liner hit the World Trade Center. We are evacuating the building, we're telling people to go north. We have it under control. I have my searchers going, my fire wardens going, going up the building, thru the whole building, to make sure everybody was going out in a systematic, as orderly fashion as possible, because, again, we did not know what was going on. At the time, I did not know it was a terrorist attack. And then, I was on a conference call and I heard: Oh my God, people gasping, there is another plane coming. I did not see it and the second plane, I know that today, slapped into the second tower. At that time, you know, it was, in my mind, controlled chaos. To this day, I have no recollection of screaming of people, I have no recollection of a lot of sounds. I have conversations in my head with people, trying to focus on whatever it was that was on my brain, but we managed to get, to the best of my knowledge, everybody out of West Street safely and we started the arduous task of searching the building with my guys, from the top floor down, to make sure everybody was out, to systematically shut down, non-essential power because we did not know what was going to happen, to make sure the emergency generators were ready to be operational. We had a Power technician there, his name escapes me now, I had two elevators guys with me and two Watch Engineers, a Fire Safety Director and we walked down securing the building and making sure everything was OK. I went back into my office to make a phone call because my cell phone was going and my Nextel radio was going too, and everybody wanted to know what was going on and all I remember is hearing people on the other end, screaming, pretty much, and, I used a four letter word and my office collapsed upon me. When the south tower fell down, one of those columns, as we know today, hit the Vesey Street side of our building, It was a domino effect. My wall came down on top of me, my ceiling came down too and, all I remember you know, all went blank for a little while. If it was not for a chair that we had moved in my office to take care of the handicapped lady, it would have been a lot worse for me because that chair held up the wall and held up the ceiling and I was able to be under it…"

"So you were lying down at this point?"

"I was down on the floor, on my hands and knees. I got hit in the head by some of that debris. My guys knew I was in there. They managed to get me out to make sure I was OK. I do not know how long it was. To me, it seemed like a life time, but it was probably moments you know…minutes. They got me out. It was me, Norris, Donny Rock, Joe, the elevator guy and… oh man, it's been so long, I can't remember all the names, the other elevator guy, oh yeah, Jeff Bries. And we said, oh man, we didn't…I didn't know what happened. We were in the building and we did not know the south tower completely collapsed."

"That was the first one?"

"Yeah, that was the first. We were having a conversation. We were all covered with debris and that dust, and the sheetrock dust, and all that stuff and we looked like uncle Fester from the Addams family. We were covered like white powdered doughnuts. The only visible spots on us, black spots, were on our mucus membranes, around our eye balls, nostrils, mouths and ears. The rest of us was completely covered in all that ash, sheet rock dust and everything like that. I remember saying, you know, we have to make sure the emergency generators are on. We started to look through the building. A couple of us went this way, another couple that way. The elevators had all been recalled down to the basement…down to the first floor, excuse me. Once we realized we were in good shape, as best we could be, we started to leave. Where are we going, someone said? We're going to mobilize at Varick Street I said. Well, I have to tell you, it was probably one of the best decisions because NYPD, FDNY, The Office of Emergency Management, a bunch of people were all mobilizing around the same place. On the way, I remember having a conversation with Joe Oreo and one of the guys… and one of the guys, I don't remember if it was Lenny or Norris asked me: Who you talking to? I said: I'm talking to Joe. Joe was not next to me, he went a different way, he was not with me but I was talking to him. Um… I guess I had stuff going on in my head. Then I said, we have to go back and, and find Joe, you know. We paused on the street and I made the decision to go back to the building."

"But the street must have been crowded with people

at the time?"

"Oh yeah, but we proceeded to go back to West Street against the flow of people. We were only a couple of blocks away. We looked around for a little while and I said: Look, we have to get out of here. The Fire Department was in West Street, digging it up to get to the fire hydrants buried under the debris, hooking their hoses and started spraying water to Seven World Trade which was now engulfed in flames. We got back to Varick Street. They cleaned us off. We were all cleaned up."

"By whom?"

"Other people were at the building, the Network people. Maureen Cox at that time arrived. She was off that day, in Brooklyn, but she wanted to come in. Dave Rozensweig's guys were there, from Network. We cleaned up, took showers, washed as best we could. And then, I was with Mark Becker, Peter Miletta from Tishman, Maureen and others. A Fire Chief showed up and asked: Who is responsible for 140 West Street? I said I am. And I remember something to this effect. He said: We won't be able to get on top of... Oh, by this time, the north tower had come down also. The Chief continued: We won't be able to get on top of Seven World Trade and if it goes down, we don't know what will happen. So I said: Well, I have to go back to West Street and everybody looked at me like I was crazy. Still, me,

Mark, Becker, Peter Miletta, Maureen left Varick and headed back towards West Street. We were walking down Greenwich, and we were probably at… I don't know… Chambers maybe, I don't remember and we all looked at Seven World Trade and we saw all the flames coming out of the building and we watched it implode upon itself. Mark Becker and I threw Maureen against a wall to cover her and that stuff, that ash, all that debris came flying down the road again. And we were pretty much all covered once more with all that stuff."

"Seven World Trade was just across the street from 140 West?"

"Yes, on the back side. So, uh, I said this, and it sounds funny, but I said: after the dust settles. No it's not really funny! We decided we had to go and look at West Street and see what was going on. We could not get to it from the Greenwich side, and Barclay, because, Seven World Trade, when it pancaked as it came down, it came to rest on, I believe the seventh and eight floors of the back side of West Street and the eleventh floor or thirteenth on the Vesey Street side and it was steel leaning up against the side of the building. We had to go all the way round Battery Park City, by the docks to eventually get into West Street. We all get along West Street and there is water running everywhere. From fire hoses, hydrants, from pipes in our building, from the building that had collapsed. We start to go down to basement A, where the switchgears are.

We wanted to make sure they were OK. There was ankle-deep water in the switchgear room. Basement level E, basement level D, where the fuel tanks were starting to fill up with water. We had to make sure the emergency generators were on. So we ran to the floor where they were, only to find out that they were all snuffed out from all that debris. All the filters on the air intakes were all choked up from all that dust and everything. So we were only on battery power. Emergency 911 went thru West Street but we had redundancy. I wish I could explain it to you, Paul, but I'm not a Network guy. So I went back to Varick Street to report my findings and tell Rozensweig's people what was going on. We had to get cleaned up again and then we realized, we're not going anywhere, we're not going home. This is our mission. We're staying. So we started to walk the street. Maureen, Jeff Bries, me and a couple of other people, looking for stores that were open, where we could purchase clothes, shoes, boots, you know, underwear, sneakers, because what we had was completely compromised. We found a couple of stores that were opened and we spend the little money we had. We encountered a woman on the street who said: You look like you are the size of my husband; please come into my apartment and take whatever you want. I, I, I… just thought of that. I had not thought of that for a long time. Oh man… oooh man… Uh, we did not go in because we were still covered in stuff, but she came out carrying shirts and stuff, you know, T-shirts and stuff like that. Then, we went back to Varick Street and we met with the Network people to figure out how to proceed, what we were going to do next. If there was ever a thought in my mind, it is that we were not going to abandon the ship whatever we would have to do, that we were not going to shut out the door. We would work to make the phones operational again. So, we started the arduous task of planning to go back into the building after trying to get some rest."

"What time was it at this point?"

"Five in the afternoon, maybe later. We decided to stay at Varick, showered again. We did not sleep. We just sat and talked about what we were going to do. Then the morning rolled around, five o'clock, six o'clock, with the Network people and my team, we all went back to West Street to assess what needed to be done and how we would do it."

CHAPTER 21

The Day After

"When you went back to West Street, George, had you heard from Upper Management, had you heard from any of them?"

"The only management people I had, see… it was me, my team, Dave Rozensweig and his team. I was left, thankfully, to do whatever I had to do, to make the calls I needed to make. You know, it was hard to get in touch with us. Eventually, the cavalry came down to help the following day, but at this time, it was just me, Maureen, the Watch Engineers, the Network people and others I didn't know the names. I recall Outside Plant was there too. We realized that we had to get emergency power, so generators were brought in. During all this time, NYC Office of Emergency Management, they had the front-end loaders, the bucket loaders, they were moving cars, and they were looking for survivors, people who might be trapped. Father Judge, the priest, I remember seeing him taken out from underneath the debris. He was dead unfortunately. Taking out people in bags, putting them on gurneys and stretchers. This is all going on simultaneously; it was like, it's the wrong analogy, mice scurrying around, to see what the hell was going on. There were people all over the place, the City people, us. The Network guys were working on Emergency 911; I think the backup went to Brooklyn or 2nd Avenue, I don't remember. We had Mazzeo Electric, RMT and a bunch of electrical contractors to start running cables to temporary generators to try to power up the building as best we could. We checked areas that were safe and unsafe, rooms we could go into and those we could not. Every ten minutes, there was an alarm call: You cannot go into the building; we do not know if West Street is gonna fall down because of the trauma that it took. But this building was built like a fortress, that birthday cake, wedding cake type construction, concrete with reinforced rebars, tremendously thick foundation walls. It did not come down. By that time, the oil tanks in the basement had floated and turned because they were not strapped down and oil was floating on top of the water in basement level E & D."

"The chillers were in which basement, I forgot now, C?"

"The chillers were in basement D."

"So they were under water?"

"Yeah, the chillers were out of commission. There was no electric power, there was no nothing! So we continued to block off the building, protecting it. We had meetings every two hours with NYPD, the Fire Department, the Office of Emergency Management and others."

"Where were the meetings?"

"Some were around, um, by… at Stuyvesand High School. NYCFD were in the Winter Garden, in Battery Park City. We had meetings in trailers that had been brought to the site. And then the phone calls started from uptown, our bosses, asking questions. After a while I said: I cannot do this; you cannot ask me questions, you have to let me work. And they started to get annoyed with me, because they called me every five minutes to get an update and I told them: I do not have an update, I'm working! So finally, they sent Bobby Collins down to be my liaison. He grabbed me around the neck and he said: George, when I ask you a question, you have to answer to me because I am answering to them, so they leave you alone."

"That was a good move because Bobby is a smart man."

"Yeah, he's a better politician than me. I'm a truck

driver, you know what I mean. I'm a Marine, I'm a grunt. I'm this type of guy, you put me in the trenches and I do what has to be done, you know. Bobby could do the polish; he grabbed me every hour: What's the story? Tell me where we are at now? Tell me x, y & z. I need it for the next conference call. Then, I would go to my team, and Dominic Veltri from Design & Construction was in, and they would bring me up to speed on everything that was going on and I passed it on to Bobby. And basically, I just about spent the next 27 months at ground zero just about every day."

"The day before, I'm sure that your family must have been very worried. Did you get in touch with them, or them with you?"

"I could never contact my family for the whole of 24 hours. They all thought I was gone."

"Really?"

"Yeah, I…uh…as soon as everything happened, my mind went to…OK, George, this is what you do, and you should do it right. You know what I mean, it was my Real Estate training. You gotta do what you gotta do."

"Your wife, she must have tried to contact you?"

"I never called my mother, I never called my father, we never had good phone lines anyway. I never got hold of my wife or my kids, uh, until 24 hours later."

"It must have been terrible for them?"

"It must have been eight or ten days when Giuliani's people told me to go home. I went home, and after 8 hours, I went back to the building. And I never went home again for any length of time for nineteen months."

"What do you mean? You stayed there all this time?"

"Yes, we occupied a Holiday Inn in Chinatown, on Canal Street. I was there nineteen months, just about every single day. We usually worked from 6:00 in the morning to 10:00 or 11:00 at night and go back to sleep there, everyday."

"You had not seen your family for nine months?"

"Nineteen months! If I did go home, I just went to the bedroom and slept. I could not talk about it. Although they wanted to talk, I couldn't talk about it, you know. To this day, it's taken a long time for me to talk about it. I belong to an organization called *Serving Those Who Serve*. I had hooked up with them three years ago after I started… by this time, Paul, my lung capacity was down to 69 percent. Now it's 58-60 percent, not getting worse. I was on some hard medications for about two and a half, three years. That screwed me up. I've been on these herbs from

Serving Those Who Serve now, probably for five, six years and I have never felt better, although I cannot breathe some days, I've never felt better in my life. I sleep pretty well now. I did not sleep for all of three years, Paul, for more than two hours. I have flashbacks at night, I wake up in sweat, I see things, and I see people… I still do not have sound in my head, I do not hear screaming. I see chaos, I see people lying, although I don't hear sirens in my head…uh…I have conversations, I can play back conversations in some cases, in some areas…"

" Do you think you are blocking some of these sounds, the most terrible ones?"

" I saw doctors at Mount Sinai. They told me I had PTSD (Post Traumatic Stress Syndrome)."

" How many people beside you stayed almost continuously for such a long time? You were probably the only one, no?"

" Oh, a lot stayed seventeen, eighteen, twenty days and go home. Others would stay five, six days and go home. It would depend on the people's own life. In my mind, a lot of the weight was on my shoulders from a Real Estate's perspective. That's how I perceived it. I could not go home and do nothing. It was like I was on a mission. I was supposed to do what I was doing. Some days, when I was going home, I turned around after four or five hours. I thought: What am I doing?

I don't belong here, I belong downtown. I was old school Real Estate."

" Dave was also old school. I remember one year, you may have left already, we were working under him after one of those chronic reorganizations. During all that time, we never had a staff meeting."

" Yeah (laughing), that was him!"

" If he had a problem, he phoned. If he had an announcement to make, he used Lotus Notes. He wasn't like the other bosses we had who needed to have a staff meeting every month, listening to themselves talking for a day or so. He was such a down-to-earth guy, a real manager, a dying breed. By the way, what were the relations with upper management? They helped, interfered,…?"

" The big shots let us do what we had to do. I mean, Dave Rozensweig became the King. He was the point guy. We reported to him. He would tell me: What do you need George? What can I do to make your life easier? Just tell me and you'll have the support. You guys know your building. Back then, there were deep pockets, you know."

"I assume you were paid for all the overtime."

"Right, we were compensated for all the time we spent working. Not when we were off the clock, but you know, if I went back to the hotel at 11:00 p.m. and I ate and had a couple of beers to go to sleep, you know what I mean, we could charge that to the room. During the day, we would spend our money, but we could voucher some. We would eat like kings. And a lot of stuff was brought in for us, from the Red Cross, from McDonald's. I do not think I'll eat another McDonald's Big Mac, or a Quarter Pounder or Chicken McNugetts ever again in my life. You know, the Red Cross fed us for months, well over a year. Breakfast, lunch and dinner and all the coffee we could drink. Yes, we were well treated."

As George said, following those two days, he stayed twenty-seven months on the site, helping, directing, co-ordinating, and bringing the building back to life. You notice how he said he was a mere grunt. He was anything but. This statement from too modest a man could not be farther from the truth. On the contrary, he showed the marks of a true leader, even more exceptional, one who remained calm under the most trying and dramatic circumstances. He saw first hand human courage and, probably, human failing too. His actions in the fog of this calamitous morning, notably by clearing the streets of people before the buildings started to collapse, saved countless lives.

TV notables such as Dan Rather and Ed Bradley interviewed him. He appeared on an A&E Biography show and Entertainment Tonight. One of his proudest moments was when he was recognized by New York City

Mayor as one of ten heroes of 9/11.

At the end of 2003, George left Verizon when the company presented another one of those recurring offers made in order to shed employees from the payroll. He had started in 1973 in Syosset, Long Island. Not having taken any vacation since September 2001, it gave him enough time to qualify without undue penalty.

He has now founded a successful house inspection company in Orange County, New York.

CHAPTER 22

Cleaning Up

This interview with John Quatrale took place on December 15, 2017.

"So John, when did you get involved, just the day after or later?"

"We arrived on the scene a couple of days after 9/11 to find that the facility at 140 West Street had been flooded. I was an environmental manager for Verizon at the time. Our group handled things like oil spills and environmental issues, leaking tanks, hazardous wastes, dealing with the Environmental Protection Agency (EPA), and things like that. The power had gone out and since the basement of the building is ninety-seven feet deep, it's below the depth of the Hudson River. When the power was lost, the main pumps that run all the time there to keep the basement dry failed and in a short period of time, two levels of the sub-basement had filled with water."

"Where were those pumps? I knew there were five levels but I never went down beyond basement D where the chillers were located."

"Well, basement E has a sump, a concrete pit about the size of this conference room, I say twenty feet by twenty feet by fifteen feet. A series of pumps are constantly on to pump out the infiltrations from the river. The pumps are located on basement level D and extend down into the sump on level E."

"So the pumps operate all the time?"

"Yes, because of the proximity of the river and the lowest basement, as I said, below the river bed. So when these pumps failed, this basement filled up and under New York City Fire Code, the fuel tanks have to be in the lowest part of the basement which was level E. There was a 20,000 gallon and a 10,000 gallon tank, a main storage tank of diesel fuel and day tanks to supply the emergency generators on levels C and D. When the water rose, these tanks started to float as they were not strapped to the floor. First, all the pipes broke and when the tanks could not float any more, you know, they were pushed by water pressure and floated up against the ceiling, the hydraulic pressure crushed them and oil and fuel were squeezed out of the tanks. This mix ended up floating on the water and contaminated everything it got in touch with including tons of material that had been stored in the basements over the years including files, carpet, and furniture, lumber, other building materials, paint, etc. At this point, the water was up to the middle of level D where the refrigeration equipment was. When Con-Ed power failed, the back-up engines on level C and D kicked on for a while, but soon they stopped working too because the fresh air intakes had been clogged up with dust and debris created when the towers fell. With no air to cool them, they overheated and shut down. After they cooled a bit, they started again for a while. It went on like that for a few hours until they broke down for good. It was hectic, a real mess and again it all goes back to the power failure and the pumps not operating any longer. So we started the job to pump, to skim and retrieve as much of the oil as we could and then remove all the debris. The basement had been used to store furniture and files and packing crates and cardboard cartons, and who knows what over years and years. Everything had been contaminated with oil and had to be disposed of properly. We brought several environmental hazmat response contractors who worked for about four months to bring the place to its original conditions. They had their own generators on the street to power their equipment. We spent about five million dollars to clean the place up. We finally got to the point where commercial power had been restored and the main pumps were able to do their job again. When the water receded, we had to start the clean-up of the spaces that had been inundated. That was done primarily by power washing with a citrus based product. At the same time that the water came up from basement E, the firemen were using city water and from our building, they were shooting that water to try to contain the dust and smoke that was floating above the piled debris of the two collapsed towers. There was a lot of water coming down throughout the building, maybe also from some broken water mains in the street, and it caused a lot of damage. Eventually it went down to level B and flooded it also. That was the old medical center where a hundred years' worth of employee's medical files were stored. They were completely saturated with water, totally destroyed. We did not even know about it at first. If you can believe it, we only found out a few weeks later because all the efforts had been focused on the floors below. When we finally entered that floor, everything was soaked, paper floated on the water everywhere and there were stalactites of mold hanging from the ceiling. It looked like a science fiction movie, three foot long masses of mold dropping everywhere from the hung ceiling. It was like those vines that hang from trees in the South, you know, yeah, kudzu, that's it. But it wasn't green, it was a sick grey. It was a real hazardous type of situation. If you breathe even a few particles of that mold, you'd be very sick quickly. So that was part of the work that we did. We had an asbestos abatement company working on site and they demolished the entire space using all proper protections. They disposed of everything."

"Did it smell bad?"

"I do not know. We had respirators on."

"What happened to the tanks?"

"After level E and D were pumped down and the oil removed, every surface was power-washed with a citrus based solvent. After this was all done, I believe some tanks were repaired, others removed. I know that temporary tanks were put in the streets to fuel the emergency generators for a while. It took about a year before the tank room was in operation again. The tanks were strapped down so they could not float and they were constructed something like a submarine so that they could withstand the pressure of being under water, should it happen again."

"What happened to the water that was polluted?"

"Well, we pumped the water from the bottom so that we did not pick up the oil. We did that for weeks and it was just dumped into the City sewers. It was all clean water at the bottom. And it wasn't until near the end when we got to a mixture of oil and water that we pumped it in temporary tanks we had on the streets. We let the oil separate; we used booms, you know these floating barriers to contain oil in spills, and oil absorbent materials to skim off the oil and then the water was drained into the sewers. The oil was taken to facilities to treat it and recover what was possible."

"Of course, you were not alone."

"We had an entire team of specialists: Mike was there, Claudia, some of the guys from New Jersey came in, Jerome and there was the safety group, Ken, Evan, John, Fred. They were the occupational safety people at the time. They quickly set up a respiratory program for people. Everyone who was going to work downtown had to go to the Verizon facility on thirty-eighth street first to take a class, then be fitted with a respirator. We couldn't go in the building without respiratory protection. Hillman Environmental, another contractor, was set up in the lobby of 140 West. They were providing suits and respiratory equipment to everybody right there. Hillman was also screening the building every day with meters to see what the volatile levels were, such as petroleum fumes. Also, on the upper floors, there was a lot of asbestos abatement done. So they were also doing samplings in the air to check if asbestos particles were where they should not be. I was not involved with the management of the asbestos work. It was Ellen Davis and Steve Lane and their people. The upper floors of the building were pierced when the World Trade Center came down and a large steel beam broke the wall. Some of the asbestos that had been used in the World Trade was reported to be in the air and came into the building. So there was some extensive work done to get rid of it."

"How long were you there?"

"I worked there for four and a half months, from September well into January of 2002. I do not have any lasting health effects, although my wife insists that I have more sinus conditions, congestion and things like that, but it might just be age, *laughing*. I went through the physicals that the company did, blood work, respiratory tests and I was fine. I signed up for the registry and I do not have any lasting health problems that I know of."

"Which registry?"

"The 9/11 registry.[1]"

"Did you stay in a hotel or somewhere else?"

"No, I never stayed in the City. I lived in Nassau County at the time but I went home every day or night. I

---

1   The World Trade Center Health Registry is now the largest registry in U.S. history to track the health effects of a disaster. Enrollment in the Registry was voluntary for people who lived, worked or went to school in the area of the WTC disaster, or were involved in rescue and recovery efforts. To enroll, people completed a confidential survey in 2003 or 2004. Each enrollee answered a series of questions about where they were on 9/11, their experiences and their health. This initial data allowed health professionals to compare the health of those directly exposed to the WTC disaster to the health of the general population.

worked sometimes eighteen hours straight. We worked every day for many weeks, with no weekend, no holidays. Uh, *pause.* It was a tough time. It was a big effort on everybody's part. I refer to it as the high and low points of my career. I was exposed to so much, I learned so much and it was undoubtedly the biggest project I was involved in, and hopefully the only one. And the sadness of seeing what happened made it the worst also."

"You were also looking at the work going on at the site of the Trade Center."

"Sure, the ambulances, the stretchers that were carrying bodies in the first two weeks, or pieces of people who died. It was tough to be around you know. But I mean, we were there on behalf of a big company and we had to help put the networks back on line. Nobody could work in the building because of the petroleum fumes so we had to clean it ASAP. The network guys had the stock exchange back in service very quickly. They had temporary cables laid out on the streets if you remember. It was amazing to see what the employees could do so quickly in those kinds of conditions. Everything was done to get telephone service restored, you name it, everything. Dave Rozensweig was in charge. He was a network guy and everything went through him. We were our own group reporting to Steve Schmidt and Steve Henry, in Virginia, but we had progress meetings everyday with all involved. As far as the clean-up we knew what to do. But of course it was not the case about what to do for the rest of the building. We were in uncharted territory. At the beginning, there was no shortage of opinions. They were debated at length. After the first chaotic days, a final strategy was put in place and all efforts were directed to attain this goal."

"We met with Dominic Veltri and his Design and Construction team, Justin Goldberg, George Hinkle, others I do not recall all the names. It was intense you know. The pressure was on to get that place running again. And they spent several years and I do not know how many millions of dollars to get the building in shape only to sell most of it a few years back as condominiums."

"Well, it had to be done anyway. But yes, I read about the sale. If you have a few million dollars, you can buy a condo with a view of the harbor."

"Yeah, right! Other environmental work we did had to do with all the manholes around the area. There were a lot of concerns that some may have been contaminated by asbestos, or oil, or human remains. So we facilitated the clean-out of most of them. Another million dollars was spent scrubbing hundreds of them in lower Manhattan. Con Edison did the same with theirs."

"The oil that was contaminated, what happened to it?"

"Everything that was removed was put into a vacuum truck by hazmat contractors. It was taken away for proper disposal as hazardous materials or wastes. Some stuff like the oil went for treatment and recycling. There was a kind of giant vacuum cleaner on these trucks and it was used to suck everything, oil, dirt, debris. They're called guzzlers or vac-trucks with a ten inch hose. They can suck the boots off your feet if you're not careful. The oil and water went into tankers called frac-trucks because the oil would separate from the water after six or seven hours. Then you can dump the clean water and put the oil in another truck and take it to a site to be recycled."

"During these long hours, where were you eating?"

"First we ate at the Red Cross. They set up a chow line in St. Joseph College, which was not far. They really knew how to do it. We had three meals there."

"Then, they used cruise boats in the marina behind Battery Park City. They pulled the boats there and set up cafeterias on these boats. The boats were already set up for catering and there was no need to go through Lower Manhattan with everything that was going on. The whole area was locked down for a few weeks, from Canal Street at the beginning, then Chambers Street. There the police would check you, your badge; they went through your bags and things like that. Anyway, now supplies could be brought in through the harbor and it was easier. Some days, we ate on these boats. It was pretty good, hot meals and so on. Finally, the company brought meals to the building and we always had plenty to eat. So it started with the Red Cross, followed by the ships, and then the company. Yeah, that's how we ate. Everything was a huge undertaking, from chaotic triage of the first days to a more organized response as time went by. It was the worst of times and the best of times as I said. There was a camaraderie that developed and endures up to now. We had a luncheon this week you know, Mike, Claudia and I. We were all there. We worked together for hours, days, weeks, months. It created a bond."

"Like soldiers on the front line."

"Right, I had never been part of the military, I was in the environmental group and worked mostly by myself, so it was a tremendous opportunity to be part of a huge endeavor the like I'll never see again, to forge these strong bonds. It's like I became a member of an exclusive brotherhood, you know."

"Did you go through any moment that scared you, where you felt you were in danger?"

"In the early days, we were kind of on edge, we felt uncomfortable. I remember being near the building, outside when some contractor was rigging building materials, bricks or cinder blocks with a crane up the Barclay Street side. There was a moment when something went wrong, some load became unsecured maybe. A big bang was heard, things fell. There was an instant stampede of people, from Barclay Street through an alleyway maybe ten or twelve feet wide. Instant panic set in and all of a sudden I was in a group dressed with rubber boots, and galoshes and white suits, running away. There was such an overwhelming fear that we all wanted to get away from the building. Somehow somebody thought that it was coming down. It wasn't, but something caused that irrational fear and I can tell you, it spread so quickly that you were not thinking anymore, except to get away. My heart was racing in my chest; it was a feeling of panic I had never experienced before in my life. I can get anxious every once in a while, but this was the first time that I felt such a fright; your heart rate goes haywire, adrenaline courses throughout your body, you can't think clearly anymore. Yes, it was scary. This happened the first week if I remember right."

"Do you have any nightmares?"

"No, thankfully, I sleep all right. Maybe I had some bad nights the first weeks, but it did not linger. I do remember that day as being one of the most terrifying of my life though."

"Did you tell your wife about your days?"

"Yes, sure I told her most everything. I was exhausted but it helped to talk. I had a baby, she was born October 27, 2001. So my wife was home with the newborn and my son was two years old at the time. I'm glad you brought that up, because I did not realize until recently that it made it very hard for my wife not being around much for four months. My mother would come as often as she could to lend a hand. I missed being with them, being a family like you'd want to be when you have a baby and a two-year old. She would stay at home, and be alone. It's hard you know. I probably put that away for a while. But everybody bears the cost of such a tragedy. You do not realize it a first, but your family, the people around you, they worry about you when you're gone for hours. They may think another plane or something will cause more heartaches."

"Where were you when the planes hit?"

"I was in Hempstead, the same office you were in sometimes. Mike, Dan and I, we heard it on the radio and we went to the roof. You remember, it was a beautiful crisp fall day, crystal clear. We could actually see in the distance. It was about twenty some miles as a crow flies from Hempstead. We could see that dust plume that was hovering over lower Manhattan and trailing towards New Jersey. We knew it was something bad. It took a little bit to learn how West Street was impacted. The first persons we saw when we got there were Rick Winner and Dominic Veltri kind of scratching their heads, probably thinking: OK, what do we do now?"

"Well, nothing like that had happened before, so it is quite understandable that the first actions to be tackled were not that obvious."

"As the government said, it was a failure of imagination. Nobody thought that terrorists would get hold of jetliners and use them as missiles. Yeah, it was an experience. I would have gladly gone on with my life without it, but it was an experience you could never get anywhere. Still watching the stretchers carrying bodies or remains of bodies going by every day, it is something that stays with you. We did not sign on to be emergency responders, we did not sign on to see people jumping off from floors as high as 1,500 feet but some did, including George Famulare. The scale of the damage to our building, to the surrounding ones, the total disappearance in a couple of hours of these two giant towers, it was hard to take in. It looked like the area had been bombed.
You asked me before when I was called to go. It's funny, but I cannot remember anyone directing us to go. We just went because we knew our expertise would be needed and we could help. Early on, I was on the site already, I did get a phone call from my boss, he was a lawyer. He basically told us: you know you're going there on your own volition. That was of course the lawyer talking, stressing that people were not being forced to work there. I found that to be kind of off-putting, especially at the time. I remember it well, I was in my kitchen and I got that call and he read me something that had been prepared by the Legal

Department. It basically said that the work we were doing there was risky and if we chose to remain there on our own, the company could not be held liable. I said, whatever, good bye, that kind of thing. What else could I say? I don't recall being asked to sign anything, I just had a verbal disclaimer."

"But really, I can't remember anybody explicitly telling me to go there. But it was my job at the time. If I heard of an emergency somewhere, I coordinated a response and sometimes went without waiting for my boss to tell me to go. That was my job, that's as simple as that. I knew there were environmental hazards to be cleaned up and I went. Of course, what I did not know was the extent of it. Never in my wildest dreams could I have imagined that it would become my life for the next few months."

CHAPTER 23

Restoration

The day before the planes crashed into the World Trade Center towers and brought them down, Dominic Veltri was in charge of the Design and Construction team for New York City. His role in the reconstruction of 140 West Street was recorded in May 2018. His recollection starts here.

"On Monday September 10, I was at West Street. We had a façade project in progress. I had met Fred Corrado from Tishman to discuss it, and somehow, we found ourselves on the top of the building. I looked below at the roofs of Four and Five WTC buildings right across the street and I recalled commenting on how clean they looked from where we stood. They were so nice and pristine."

Who could have predicted that the very next day, we would be living in a world that had changed forever?

How could Dominic have foretold that these unblemished roofs would be buried by a blizzard of debris hailing from the falling towers?

"A staff meeting had been scheduled in New Jersey for the next two days. I could not attend the first day because my wife was pregnant with our son; she had a nine o'clock appointment with her doctor to have an amnio done and we went together. I drove down to Bronxville. As we were parking the car, the radio said that a plane had hit a World Trade Center tower. My first thought was that it was a small plane, probably an accident. As we walked into the doctor's office, a TV was on, reporting that a second plane had smashed into the second tower. I turned to my wife and told her that this was no accident. The doctor asked us to come in and we were there about one hour, maybe one hour and a half. When we left, we put the radio on in the car to listen to what was going on. As I drove back north toward Westchester to get back home, we saw all kinds of fire trucks, emergency vehicles speeding south on the Sprain Brook Parkway, all sirens blaring, red and blue lights flashing. On the radio, reporters were trying to unravel what happened, stating that one of the buildings may have collapsed. When we got home, I put the TV on and we watched everything in real time. Later, I called my boss. The towers were in my area, next to our building at West Street. I asked him: "What do you need me to do?" "Can you go down there and assess the situation?" he said. I replied that it was not possible; at this time, the city was closed off. No cars, no trains were allowed in. Nothing was running. So he told me to see if I could contact some people down there, try to get the extent of the damages, and, if any, put together a budgetary plan to do a restoration. I remember calling Bobby Collins and together, we put together a kind of abstract budget because, although we had spoken to some people on the site, the information we got was so fragmented it was impossible to get a true picture of what needed to be done. So our numbers were high because of all these uncertainties."

"Not having seen the building yourself, it had to be mostly guess work."

"Well, we knew the electrical systems were heavily damaged, so were the emergency generators. But as you said, I could not evaluate the damages with my own eyes, so this budget was, as a consequence, built out of sketchy info, but it already ran into millions of dollars. I called my boss back, a few times actually. He had cancelled the staff meeting and sent everybody home. I remember telling him late at night that I would go down there the next day. I did not know how, but I would go. I got up early the next morning, around four o'clock. I managed to get a train to Grand Central. I can't remember how I made it to the building; I may have walked for all I know. I had to show my Verizon badge to get through the cordon that had been set up by the police across the downtown area.

Finally, I was standing at the corner of West Street and Vesey Street and looking up and around. I cannot explain what I saw. I simply stood there, frozen; it could have been an hour, it could have been five minutes. Time stopped, my mind went totally blank. Somebody came to me and said: "Hey Dom, what are you doing?" I think it was George Famulare who saw me and came over. We started talking, then he walked me through the building, at least where we were able to go, just a quick tour. He told me what was flooded, what did not work. You know, seeing Seven World Trade Center leaning against our building, and the steel beams that had pierced the façade, and the debris, the dust, it was overwhelming. I was probably there most of the morning. I remember trying to get a call to my boss a couple of times. Cell phone service was not good; it was very hard to communicate from down there. I told George: "OK I'm leaving." He said: "You're leaving? You just got here!" I said, "I cannot help you standing here in the mud right now, but I'll be back. I can't do anything from here right now. I got to go to mid-town, to my office in 1095. We'll be back." He looked at me; he could not believe I just got there and I was leaving. So I went back to my office. It was about one o'clock."

"Did you take any pictures?"

"No, the cell phones at the time were not that smart yet. In the office, a bunch of people had pulled the building plans and were putting together what information we had about the building. We started to mobilize at that point. There was a man named Bob McNally (spelling?), a project manager for Tishman. He was an older gentleman and very knowledgeable about the construction business. We had a meeting and started to come up with some ideas about what we needed to assemble to try to fix this heavily damaged building. I called my boss and told him to throw away the estimate I had sent him the day before because it was completely off the mark. We needed a better budget for what it would cost to put the building back in operation. First and foremost, we had to provide power to reinstate some phone service immediately. We ordered generators to be placed in the streets adjacent to the building; looked at how we could bring them in. The logistics were not easy. Once the generators were in place, power needed to be brought into the building. Maybe we could back feed some of the existing boards to help Network. We worked a long time, I think I didn't get home until eleven or midnight. The next morning, I packed a bag and went downtown. By then, we had called electricians and other contractors. We realized we needed all kinds of plywood to safe off some dangerous areas. The contractors were ordered to find these materials and bring them to the site. There was no big plan at first, just small steps. Lighting was needed to see what was going on. The first few days were devoted to stabilizing the building, running up temporary power lines, cleaning work areas and assessing more clearly what had to be done."

"You were allowed to get into the building?"

"The second day we were. There was a lot of concern about buildings falling down around us, alarms going off all the time. So we were told to be very cautious entering the building. Not too many people were allowed in, but there were a few structural engineers to take a look at the damages and provide recommendations. Eventually, we segregated areas that were safe to work in and those which weren't were cordoned off. We started coordinating with the Network folks in order to bring back communication ASAP. The stock exchange was nearby and it was the priority. So the marching orders were to provide power to the Network people. The plans kind of evolved as we went along."

"When did you start working with all the government or city agencies and other groups that were involved?"

"I think it was the first day. There were meetings once or twice a day within walking distance and I recall going to quite a few of them. Verizon was always represented. We stated our progress, requested help or whatever."

"How was the financing set up? Did you have a certain amount of money to pay the contractors?"

"Not in the first days. We issued contracts and kept

track of all expenditures. Obviously, we were standing in the mud; there was debris and water everywhere. We had no desks. We were finding people, tapping them on the shoulder and telling them what we needed. Eventually, we reconciled all of it and people started being paid within a few days. You know, Paul, there were about seven hundred contractors on site every day during the first few weeks, carpenters, steam fitters, electricians, laborers and what not, and the expenses climbed accordingly."

"You said before that you packed a bag. Did you stay downtown for a while?"

"Yes, I stayed straight through five days before I went back home. We were working most of the time. The first night, I remember catching a couple of hours of sleep on the floor in the Varick Street central office. Eventually, we stayed in a hotel nearby in Chinatown. We were on site at five in the morning until eleven at night. We got something to eat, took a shower, went to sleep a bit and started the next day. The first couple of weeks were very chaotic. Later we started to get into more of a rhythm, planned the maintenance of all the generators that were running all the time, worked on contingencies in case one of them stopped working. Between George and me, one of us was always on site for seven months. When he was going home, I stayed and vice-versa."

"I understand that Network was the priority but when

did you start replacing what was flooded in the basements: the tanks, the chillers, the generators?"

"The new stuff came months later. Until then, everything was temporary. Basically, for the first seven months, we were in emergency mode. We started with restoring power, then moved to rubble removal. When the phone equipment started working again, it produced heat and we had to ventilate and eventually bring air conditioners, truck-mounted chillers. We restored some of the fan units in the building, connected them to the portable chillers and used them to cool the switch rooms. We got more generators in and soon, space became an issue."

I remember seeing pictures of a multitude of power cables snaking through various openings like black IV drip tubes keeping the building on life support. They make Dominic's recollection even more vivid.

"We had to put fuel tanks on top of scaffolds, so they needed to be reinforced to withstand the additional weight. We put chillers on top of a sidewalk bridge. All the temporary infrastructure was on the street and we had to stack things vertically because space was at a premium."

"Dominic, did you get any help from the city inspectors at this point?"

"We had extensive cooperation from the New York

City Building Department. We told them what we wanted to do and they replied OK. As for permits, we could start without them and they would eventually be formalized. Eventually, we had to catch up with a lot of paperwork: action was first, red tape came later. We got along well."

"You all did very well because there wasn't any precedent for this type of disaster."

"No, absolutely not. There was no playbook for this. After a few weeks, while the emergency work was still being done, we started to make plans for fixing the building and its infrastructure. We knew it was all lost: the switch gears, the chillers, the generators, the fire pumps, the oil tanks were all flooded, so we had designers looking at options and developing master plans and specs. We worked with Con Ed to get new transformers and rework the building power feed. Obviously, a lot of the flooded equipment had to be relocated to safer areas. Only the fuel tanks stayed in the basement, but they were properly secured this time.

"At the time, you were a second level manager."

"Yes, I was in charge of Manhattan; New York City actually. However, I was on special assignment exclusively to focus on West Street for close to two years. Rick Winner took over the rest of the city and, as you know, Joan DiBono became your boss for a while on

Long Island and upstate."

"Do you remember some harrowing moments?"

"Yes, there were some. Sometimes piles of debris were removed and cars and fire trucks were found underneath. It was upsetting. And there were the smells and the sounds. It was hard to talk to people who weren't there. They would say: "I saw pictures of this, I saw pictures of that and I can imagine what you went through." And I told them: "You have no idea what it's like." I remember it as if it was yesterday. Seven World Trade Center was finally removed and it was Halloween. We realized that two major columns of our building had been hidden all that time and were damaged. We were afraid that the façade might come down so we had to come up with a stabilization plan right away."

"You mentioned the smells and sounds. Can you elaborate?"

"It's hard to describe. In the building, the smell of petroleum and the chemical stuff they use to clean it was overpowering, even with a respirator on. Outside, with the respirator off, it was dry, musty, dusty air that prickled the throat. My mouth was always very dry."

"You had a respirator on inside?"
"For the most part, yes. There were asbestos sensors

and other devices everywhere to monitor the air quality and we had been trained on how to use the respirators inside at all times."

"Going back to the first time you saw the extent of the damages, you must have scratched your head and thought, what am I going to do?"

"Like I said, when I first got down there, I stood on the corner for I don't know how long, in a kind of a daze. It was like watching a movie in slow motion, with no sound. All the peripheral noises were blanked out. In a way, what my eyes saw; collapsed buildings, twisted steel, dust, shattered bricks, water everywhere, my brain could not process. I talked to other people about it and most had the same reaction; that first glimpse at the extent of the devastation, it was just too much to absorb."

"When you talked to your boss, did he grasp the magnitude of what had to be done?"

"I related to him what I saw, the damages, what could be fixed and what could not, the flooding. Yes, I think he understood. He was an experienced engineer, but nobody in these first days could really grasp what it would take to regain control of the building. It was badly wounded but the gravity of the wound was yet unknown. He came down a week or so later, and he was like "Wow, I can't believe it." It was that kind of a reaction. The other thing that was interesting, Paul, is that we had a lot of meetings, conference calls and whatever we needed to do, and some people who had not been there said something like I can really appreciate what you're going through. To me, it was like: no, you really can't, you had to be here to fully understand. I was frustrated with them but I realized that they just didn't know and they would not unless they came here."

"Well, that's true for a lot of situations in life. How was your relationship with Dave Rozensweig? He was the Network executive supervising the work wasn't he?"

"Yes, he was. What was interesting about him was… well, he was the field general on the ground, but he allowed us to do what we did best without much interference. We did not have carte blanche of course. When we presented our plans for each day, he sometimes challenged this or that, questioned us, but was not wishy washy. He did not obsess over things of no consequence at the expense of the big picture. He understood the responsibility of command; he was there with us all the time, not far away and e-mailing his orders. If he felt the plan was sound, he said go ahead and provided the means to carry it out. He valued our opinion, understood the ramifications of what we were doing. In the beginning when restoring the Network was the only priority, he was very demanding, expecting results and if you said a certain task would be done by five o'clock, it was not five fifteen, you know what I mean. As long as we were honest with each other, we had a great relationship, and we did. He trusted our abilities and we trusted his leadership. He was really the executive in charge down there, involved in all high level conversations with us or other agencies. If he needed us for something, he called us; if not, he left us alone."

"As far as your health, do you have any issues related to your long presence on site?"

"Not that I know of. I mean, you know, it's already been seventeen years and we're all getting older. No, I do not think I have any problem that could be attributed to being down there almost two years."

As Dominic said, if you were not there, facing this reality not easily fathomed, that a telephone building had become collateral damage the moment that the Towers were hit by passenger jet planes turned into missiles, you could not visualize or, for that matter, conceive of the challenges that would eventually have to be overcome. Even for those who were in the midst of the rubble, it must have been, at times, an impossible task to face. Who could have anticipated what had to be done in the confusion of those first days? The expression "the fog of war" comes to mind, and yet, this comparison is flawed. The Army does not go into battle without a plan, even if the best ones have a tendency to fall apart as soon as the first bullet is fired. Faced with a situation that had no precedent, absent of guidelines to describe step-by-step what had to be done, initiative, inventiveness, experience, as well as coolness and a little bit of luck became indispensable assets that would lead to success. Thinking out of the box became the rule, not the cliché it has too often become. So every morning, what needed to be done had to be identified; what could go wrong foreseen. Is there any doubt that most of those in charge must have felt the loneliness and coldness of leadership? Still, in spite of all that could have gone wrong, and maybe did at times, they kept on no matter what and prevailed.

In 2004, *New York Construction Magazine* honored Verizon for the restoration of the building. Dominic was quoted: "If ever a building deserved a second life, it is this fortress. This building was built to last. It's heavily reinforced and, as they say in the industry, has great bones. Most buildings would have collapsed from the pounding this venerable structure sustained." True enough, but the broken bones had to be properly repositioned with splints and a cast later applied for them to correctly heal. It took teams with leaders like Dominic to make it so.

There is a saying that out of bad always comes some good. Too often we are not what we think we are. We are not what we say we are. Only actions do not lie. True leaders are forged in the crucible of the unexpected, not implementing parts pulled out of a five-year plan. Confronted with a situation that required resourcefulness and creative thinking, a new generation of standard-bearers emerged from reclaiming the mutilated building at West Street.

CHAPTER 24

Freedom Kiss

Following the September 11, 2001 attacks by nineteen terrorists, fifteen of whom were from Saudi Arabia, the US Government decided logically to pounce on Iraq. France declared it would neither support nor participate in the invasion. This provoked resentment from certain quarters against everything French. Congress, in a daring act of courage even went as far as renaming French fries "Freedom" fries. Of course, the most ironic aspect of this idiocy is that French fries did not even originate in France, but were from Belgium; but how would our batch of cultured representatives know?

For a while, I was subjected by colleagues to gentle ribbing. They would arrive every morning with something quirky to say about the French. In my counterattacks, I quoted Americans about their opinions about my country of birth or other relevant facts. It became a sort of game. I tried to be prepared for their mild insults. When the war became inevitable, some comments became more pointed. Although I seemed to take them in stride, they pained me a lot.

"Hey, did you hear what they said about the French on The Simpsons - that they were cheese-eating surrendering monkeys?"

"Now you're hurting my feelings. You know, when America has fought as many wars as France, won some, lost some, you can give it lessons on surrendering. By the way, the French lost 210,000 soldiers and 390,000 civilians during World War II, which is 1.44 percent of the population at the time; The Americans lost 407,300 military personnel and no civilians, that is 0.32 percent of its population. Less than one-third of the French losses, do you think it's not enough to deserve some respect?"

"In early 2003, George Will from *The Washington Post* described retreat as 'an exercise for which France has often refined its savoir-faire since 1870.'"

"Well, George conveniently left out World War I, didn't he? Anyway, we must have taught you well because you had your share of retreats too. Didn't you retreat from Canada in 1776? Didn't one side of America surrender to the other after the Civil war? The Bataan Death March did not happen without your troops surrendering at one point, uh? And what about the retreat from the Chosin reservoir when the Chinese kicked you out of North Korea for good? And last but not least, you did not leave Viet Nam with your heads held high, did you?"

"Did you hear about this Congress woman who wants to bring back all the American soldiers interred in France?"

"Well, this is a stupid idea. Why doesn't she propose to ship back the Statue of Liberty to France while she's at it? "When good Americans die, they go to Paris," said Oscar Wilde. I don't know why he said that because he was Irish, but I'm sure the soldiers that are going to Iraq would rather go to France."

"Did your hear about that guy in Jersey who's pouring French white wine in the gutter?"

"Well he probably drank all of the contents of the bottle, pissed in it to fill it again and called the TV station before pretending he was emptying a bottle of Chardonnay in the street to show he supported the invasion of Iraq. It would have been easier to do like Congress. Call it Freedom wine and be done with it."

Not everybody disagreed with France's stance. In an episode of *Saturday Night Live*, it was reported on the satirical segment Weekend Update: "In a related story, in France, American cheese is now referred to as idiot cheese."

Sometimes, the discussions took a more serious turn. I was once approached by a more belligerent coworker who called me an ungrateful SOB in regard to France's position. I told him he had the wrong person because the French ambassador at the United Nations felt no obligation to call me to explain every speech he gave at the United Nations. It did not deter him from pursuing his argument.

"Well, if we had not come in 1945…
"June 44," I interrupted him.
"What 44?" he asked, startled by my interruption.
"It was in 1944, June 6 to be exact. Please, go on."
"If we had not come in France, you all would speak German."
"Actually, that's not true. The balalaika would have replaced the accordion as our national instrument, we would be eating borscht, and the Reds would be drinking our wine."
"What are you talking about?" he said, confused.
"We would be not be speaking German, but Russian."

So, being a history buff, I explained to him that, during Operation Bagration, the largest campaign of the entire Second World War, the Soviet Union recovered all its lost territories from the Germans and ended the operation in the suburbs of Warsaw, Poland.
The entire campaign had lasted a little less than two months, from June to August 1944 and its largest advance was of about 600 miles. It had taken about eight weeks also, for the Allies to extricate themselves from the Normandy *bocage[1]*, advancing only thirty miles or so.

---

1   The bocage is a region where the fields and meadows are enclosed by earth banks carrying hedges or rows of trees. During the Battle of Normandy, it made progress against the Germans extremely difficult. American personnel usually referred to bocage

It put the Allies roughly 600 miles from Berlin, while the Russians were only 325 miles from it. So I concluded, "If the landing had not happened or had been repulsed, the Russians would have eventually steamrollered the Nazis by themselves and taken all of Western Europe. Hence we would speak Russian in France, not German."

He chose not to argue with these facts. It is a well-known and sad reality that history is not the subject that improves the average American student's GPA. Indeed one of my colleagues came over one day and told me: "Yesterday, I saw *The Patriot*[2]. Man, I did not know that the French helped us during the War of Independence." Well, yes! "Breaking news: French troops and navy aid rebels; involvement decisive contribution to American victory." Thanks to Hollywood, at least some history is coming to light.

Still, he kept bugging me.

> "I noticed that you do not have an *I support the troops* sticker on the back of your car. Why not?"
> "So you paid $3.00 for this sticker manufactured by a who-knows-who hawker who's peddling it off

---

as hedgerows. The German army used these numerous sunken lanes to implement strong points and defenses to stop the advance of the American troops.

2   The Patriot is a 2000 American epic historical fiction war film which takes place in South Carolina during the American Revolutionary War. The movie ends when English General Cornwallis is besieged at Yorktown, Virginia, where he surrenders to the surrounding Continental Army and the French naval force.

of the war and the suffering it leads to, and you think your patriotic duty has been done? When they come back diminished in body and mind, our soldiers, where's your support?"

"Well, they are heroes," he answered somewhat meekly.

"Some are and some are not. In any case, for me, a miner who dies in some dark underground tunnel is as much a hero as the unlucky soldier who gets killed on the front line. Every worker who toils day-in, day-out to make America hum along and keep the military supplied with all its needs, deserves to be told every once in a while *Thank you for your service.*"

Apart from a few instances, it was all done in good fun. I do not know why Congress fixated just on the fries, there are so many other expressions that they could have used to express their wrath. For a while, I used to leave the office in the evening telling them:

"Now, if you'll pardon my Freedom, I'm gonna get the hell outta here and take a Freedom leave. I'm going home. When I get there, I'll enter the house through our Freedom doors and I'll pet my Freedom poodle. Then I'll give a long and patriotic Freedom kiss to my wife and for a while sit down at the table to enjoy a nice meal prepared by our Freedom maid: some perfectly salted and crisp Freedom fries, *uf corse*, followed by a salad covered with Freedom dressing. Later, if I'm still hungry, I may fancy a scoop of Freedom vanilla ice cream. Tomorrow morning, before coming to the office, I'll have a couple of Freedom toasts, maybe a slice of buttered Freedom baguette, accompanied by a nice cup of piping hot coffee brewed in our Freedom press. In the evening I'll take my wife to a Freedom restaurant. And if we are in the mood, I'll make sure I have a Freedom letter[3] nearby."

---

3 A French letter is the name that the English gave to a condom. One explanation for this idiom may be attributed to the fact that during WWI, condoms were packed in small paper envelopes and issued to English troops. Since most of these troops were in-France, the name French Letters may have been coined at that time when they were distributed like regular mail.

CHAPTER 25

Montauk Central Office Roof

Another winter had arrived. My boss and I had been called to the central office in Montauk. Across the fork of the island that jutted into the Atlantic ocean, a frigid wind straight from Canada hissed through the bare tree branches. It hit my face like a fist made of ice. There was a rawness in it that chilled the bones. Curled leaves scurried through the parking lot like suicidal lemmings. It was a cold and grey day. Sky and ocean merged in the distance, erasing the horizon.

We were puffing little plumes of condensed air and tapping our feet while waiting for the property supervisor who had asked us to come, forthwith. We knew the building roofing system had problems, which for a roof are always leak related. In fact, the roof was scheduled to be replaced by the next spring and the funding had already been secured. We wondered what the reason was for this summons.

Blowing on his bare hands, my boss asked "what is so urgent that we have to meet like this?" Looking at the building, the supervisor explained that leaks had developed during the night, dangerously close to the switching equipment. The reason for our presence was that he wanted the roof to be replaced immediately. My boss and I looked at each other, stunned by this request. Replace a roof in the middle of the winter, what a stupid idea, akin to trying to change a tire on a car that was still moving. He pointed to the sky the color of pewter. "It may not be that threatening today" he said, "but it is a reminder that bad weather is on its way." It did not persuade our friend.

The cold did not encourage lingering outside. Inside the building, the supervisor showed an area where tarpaulins had been hung under the roof, repeating that we should go ahead with the replacement of the roof at once. We tried to dissuade him again, arguing that a few months of bad weather were here, and that it meant snow and ice. If the existing roofing system was removed and a snow storm arrived, stopping the work, it would be a disaster, particularly when the snow would begin to melt, putting all the switches inside at risk. These tarpaulins would protect the equipment from any infiltration. It was done all the time in central offices to protect the switching equipment until leaks were repaired. Obstinate, he did not want to hear about it, claiming it was not what he wanted.

What was not the best idea was replacing a roof when the possibilities of snow storms were real. As a matter of fact, on the scale of not so good ideas, it ranked pretty high, somewhere between saying no to a request from your supervisor and being stuck in the middle of Russia as an invader during the winter. Since he was not our boss, we demurred. He was adamant though and went up the line to further his case. Somehow he succeeded. We were ordered to start the replacement work. So we met the contractor and gave him his orders. Flabbergasted, he looked at us with the astonished face of an oyster that had swallowed its own pearl. His first reaction was "a what the f..." face. Then he asked me "Have you gone out of your mind?" With a very Gaelic shoulder shrug, I raised my hands palms up in mock surrender, and replied "My friend, what can I do, it's beyond my pay grade!"

But sometimes, good fortune favors the unprepared as well as innocents. The weather remained clement and everything turned out all right. The problem is when these lucky people equate magnanimous providence or a fluke winter with an exceptional intelligence. "See I told you so, there was no need to be afraid!", they would tell you, proud as a peacock for what was purely a stroke of luck.
What a difference a year makes. If the roof had been replaced at the same time the following year, a snow storm would have buried the remaining steel layer on which the roofing materials rest just as the existing roofing had been removed. It would have stayed snow and ice bound for two months. Then when the thaw came, there would have been a shower throughout the central office. The customers at the tip of the island would have lost their phone lines probably for months.

CHAPTER 26

Ask Not What The Company Can Do For You

Why our department was only working thirty-five hours a week while others worked forty, I do not know.
In 1994, however, that changed and not for the better for us. NYNEX decided that, in the interest of making the hours of work within different entities of the company consistent, the work week would be forty hours for all employees. There was nothing inherently wrong with this decision. After all, who still worked thirty-five hours a week? Well, there were the French, of course! Following the return of a socialist-leaning government in the eighties, the working hours were reduced from forty to thirty-five a week. But the French model does not fit cozily with the Puritan work ethic. In all honesty, how could the United State economy survive under such a system? Thirty-five hour weeks, five week vacations after the first year of full employment, and retirement at sixty

years of age with a substantial salary including full medical benefits. It would simply collapse, wouldn't it. This is not what the capitalist system is all about. Think of it! It would mean spreading the country's wealth more equitably, increasing taxes on the one-percenters, and reducing the profits of the HMO's who reap obscene benefits from the illness of others. It is socialism at best, communism at worst. The fact that Jesus Christ preached something similar in the gospels is always conveniently forgotten.

So it was that our department worked five more hours a week. It was an extra load that most could easily accommodate, without breaking an additional bead of sweat. Where it hurt however, was that HR failed to remember to adjust the salaries to reflect the increase in working hours. Consequently, this increase of almost nine percent in working hours resulted in a corresponding percentage loss in salary. If you take into account that the medium raise for the following years did not keep pace with inflation, averaging two percent in a good year, much less, by the time I left the company at the end of 2008, it turned out I had barely made up the lost pay resulting from this additional five hours without compensation during the following fourteen years.

Was it unethical? Even Clarence Darrow would have difficulty arguing it did not blur a few ethical boundaries! We were hired without a written contract, presumably to eliminate any paper trail. *Les paroles s'envolent, les écrits restent* to cite another French proverb; "The spoken words fly away, the written words stay." Yet, we believed, naively perhaps, that there was an implied moral one, with some ethical bond between the company and ourselves when they hired us under certain verbally stated conditions, one being the thirty-five hour week. It unquestionably violated the terms of this unwritten contract.

Was it legal? Probably not! But once again, nobody complained, so it came to pass without even the smallest ripple. It is still shameful to admit it, but the truth was we had become not much more than mere robots, somehow stripped of the capability to react to unfair decisions. So the new ruling became the new law of the realm. This was an example of asymmetrical corporate warfare, where the more powerful side was playing by its own set of rules. In short, the edict from the ramparts of Upper Management was: "It is my way or the highway." In any case, status was not quo any longer. Add to this the ever increasing participation of the employees in health plan costs; it was not a total surprise that the attitude of many towards the company changed dramatically.

If we sometimes joked about it, it was in a bitter way. One evening, I left the headquarters building at 1095 Sixth Avenue around four-thirty instead of five o'clock to catch an early train. In the elevator lobby, my boss Bob came out of one as I waited.

"So Paul, half a day today?"

I pretended to look at a watch on my wrist - I do not wear one any longer because there are clocks everywhere, on the PCs, on the cell phone, in the office, in the car – and

I said:

"Well, I guess my watch is still in the thirty-five hour a week time zone."

At least, he was kind enough to chuckle.

Quite a few employees adhered to what they would call an "undertime" concept. Basically it was like overtime in reverse. Since they had to be present more hours for the same amount of pay, they worked less during these hours. The real pros were the ones who managed not to do any productive work during these five no-pay hours. One of my colleagues put it better by paraphrasing an old Russian proverb: " They pretend to pay me and I pretend to work."

Another unilateral decision that stuck in our throats occurred during the lead up to a potential strike in August 2008. As was not uncommon, negotiations about the renewing of the union contract had stalled. Consequently, there was the ever present risk that the union personnel might go on strike upon expiration of the contract. As usual in that case, management was called to the rescue. During the days preceding the potential strike deadline, emergency plans were put in place, and each management employee was given his duties. On the night of the possible strike, all were dispatched to the location of their strike assignment. This time, 140 West Street was not my assigned location. The company did not want to pay for licenses, be it for professional engineers or refrigeration machine operators. So I had let mine lapse. Instead, my assigned location was a central office in an unsavory area in Brooklyn. We were also instructed to arrive at our strike location one hour before midnight. This would be the time at which we would know if a strike had been scheduled or not. It meant that I left my house at 10:00 p.m. Another colleague was with me in the central office; we chatted, read the paper, solved crosswords and sudokus, waiting for the phone to ring with the news. The hour of midnight passed without a call. Half an hour after midnight, still no ring. Finally, shortly after 1:00 a.m., the news came that talks were still in progress, but that a strike had not been yet voted. We waited for a while when a call came telling us to go home. We learned later that a supervisor, one who presumably did not have any family life, wanted us to stay in our assignment until a decision regarding the strike was made. As it turned out, we would have been stuck for a very long time since it took another week or so to finalize the contract and eliminate the specter of a strike. That night, our director's good sense prevailed and we were sent home. I reached my house around 3:00 a.m., having spent five hours on company overtime.

When the time came to be paid, a special code had to be included on the time sheet for these hours. We were told that they would not be paid. To add insult to injury, we were not even thanked for our dedication to the well-being of the company. Granted, we did not have a choice; still, it would have been nice to be recognized; even better, to be given compensation time. This is another example of actions by the company that were not legal. Isn't it one of the pillars of the capitalistic system that work must be compensated?

At least, thanks to the understanding of my boss, the mileage to and from that central office was reimbursed.

The following story tells of an incident that happened during another work stoppage, the now legendary 1989 strike. You will see how an action that started with good intentions mushroomed into an unbelievably long series of trials and tribulations for a colleague who will be called James. His strike assignment was at the Patchogue garage. One day, he received a call from the dispatch center that tracked any incident happening in buildings: there was a leak in the Southampton central office. Being the lucky one to have picked up the telephone, he was to go there immediately to investigate and correct the situation. Modern telephone switching equipment and water do not mix well. Less than half a glass of water dropped on switching electronics can put the telephones of 60,000 people out of service in seconds. Being a conscientious employee, James went to the truck pool, grabbed some keys from the board, and went to the truck whose number was on the key identification tag. The keys did not fit. He repeated the operation with another set; still no luck. Had the strikers mixed the keys to cause confusion? In any case, pressed for time, James decided to take his own car. As he reached the Southampton central office, strikers were on the sidewalks along the driveway leading to the parking lot in the back of the building.

Company instructions on how to deal with the pickets

were very clear: "Do not confront them, even if you are being harassed. In all cases, they must let you pass to enter the building. This is the law." As James turned into the driveway, the strikers closed ranks in front of him. He drove slowly, so as not to hurt anybody. The picket captain rushed to the car and kicked the front fender. At this point, James decided sensibly to back up and park in front of the building. The strikers were suddenly more subdued, because they had become aware of the dent caused by the captain's fit of temper on the fender. James noticed too and when he entered the building, he told the guard to call the Police. The leak fixed, James made the officers aware of his intention to sue the union members because he did not intend to pay for the repair out of his own pocket, to which one policeman answered:

"You know, if you sue the strikers, you cannot claim this as an accident. You must file a civil complaint and in that case, your auto insurance is out of the picture and will not help you. Also, be warned, if you do sue the strikers, they will all claim that you ran into them. This is what they told me. If you are still of a mind to press charges, you must come to the Police station so that I can file my report by the end of the day."

Having not yet decided how to handle the problem, James followed the Police to the station house. There, he was surprised to see that two of the strikers, both females, as well as the male picket captain were also present. The policeman, and the two women encouraged

James to side with the workers, arguing that the Company was no good, that the strike was right and so on. Figuring that the company would most probably reimburse him for the minor damage to his car, and with assurances that the company would deal with union member's activities after the strike, James chose not to press charges. In exchange, the union members agreed not to pursue their fabricated view of the incident. Back in Patchogue, James called his District Manager to report the incident. He was told to have the car fixed and the Company eventually reimbursed the $460.00 cost of the repair.

Case closed, you would think? No, and far from it! A few days later, James received a summons from one the female union members informing him that he was being sued for $10,000,000 for physical damages caused by the incident. It appeared that one of the two women who had been at the police station (coincidence or advanced work, you be the judge!) was chronically sick. The suit argued that the incident aggravated her already precarious situation, and she had three thick binders packed with medical bills to prove it. Dumbfounded, James called the legal department. He was told that, since the alleged accident happened with his own car, even though on company business, the company could not get involved per New York State Law and that he should put the claim through his personal auto insurance policy. In other words, James was on his own. As luck would have it, this latest fender bender placed him in a risk pool and he was thrown out by the Insurance Company. Believe it or not, James was assigned through the New York Insurance Fund to the same company that had dropped him. But now, since James was considered a high risk, his premiums almost doubled. The strike incident was starting to hurt him financially.

Lo and behold, while this suit proceeded at justice's snail's pace, a second suit was filed by the second woman. This one came one year later for an additional $1,000,000. She claimed that she was injured during the incident, while pushing a baby carriage on the picket line, and she had medical bills to prove it. This brought the total being sought in damages to $11,000,000.

The trial lasted four days during which James was derided by the plaintiffs, being called "a mad dog" driver. At the time of his first deposition two years back, James had given his estimate of the width of the strip of grass between the building and the drive way. In his deposition at the trial, it differed by a couple of feet, which caused the plaintiff's attorney to label him a liar who could not be trusted at all. If he lied about the width of the grass strip, the attorneys questioned how much more was he lying about? James was likened to the proverbial fisherman whose fish gets bigger each time he tells his story of the catch.

The second plaintiff came into the court hobbling on a cane. The same morning, this woman had been seen briskly walking with the cane daintily resting on her shoulder in the parking lot.

The jury went into deliberations. It came back soon after with questions:

- The first concerned the definition of pedestrians' contact with a car. Does it mean a car hitting a person or does it mean a person initiating contact with the vehicle? This was important because if the pickets initiated the contact, James was not liable. The reply from the judge was that it should not matter who hit who, contact was contact.

- The second question concerned the right of way in a driveway. The prosecution argued that a person has the right of way on a sidewalk, even when he/she crosses a driveway, and contended that the car should yield to a pedestrian. The defending attorney argued that a car has the right of way when on a driveway crossing a sidewalk. The fact that strikers were no ordinary pedestrians did not sway the judge. He chose to instruct the jury in favor of the prosecuting attorney.

At this point, it was clear James was going to lose the case and so he did! Then came the question of monetary awards. If the worst happened, would the insurance pony up only to the limits of the personal auto policy? At this stage, New York Telephone agreed to cover any judgments in excess of the personal policy limits. All these things took their toll on him and family as well.

A decision was finally reached regarding damages with-one woman receiving $60,000, and the other $30,000. Later on, they left the company and one can only hope they lived happily ever after. Because the awarded amounts fell within the limits of James' policy, the entire matter cost New York Telephone only the $460.00 they had reimbursed him for the fender repair. No offer was made to compensate him for part of the increased insurance premiums or for the mental anguish suffered by him and his family.

Of course, the entire trial was a travesty, a pretense of justice rendered. The prosecuting attorney assumed that the judge was extremely upset because his time had been wasted on a matter that should not have come to court. In his opinion, it should have been settled between the Union and New York Telephone. It is difficult to deny that the judge was right in this assessment. The New York Telephone attorneys who attended the trial expressed an opinion that an appeal should be filed due to the judge's biased guidance during the trial. Of course, New York Telephone would not file, nor pay for the appeal and the matter was dropped.

To use an expression the company is fond of, what were the lessons learned? These were easy to draw:

- Do not use your own car for company business, even if there is an emergency.
- Because you do the right thing for the company, do not assume the company will do the right thing by you in return.
- While you do not press charges for a wrong done to you, do not expect that others will do the same.

Why did the company not step up to the plate? James was an honest and loyal employee. He fixed the problem in a timely manner.

What he financially lost was a fraction of a drop in the bucket of what the company would have lost if the leak had reached the switch. Hundreds of telephone lines would have been shut down for a very long period.

Still, all he got in return for being responsible was indifference.

CHAPTER 27

Pension Plan

On December 6, 2005, an e-mail with the following subject heading, date and time reached all Verizon managerial employees.

Subject: Management Retiree Benefits Restructured
Date: 12/05/2005 09:02 PM
Sent by: Verizon Message Center

It had been purposefully sent at a late hour when almost no one would be at their desks.

It started innocently enough with: Verizon will restructure its management retirement benefits effective June 30, 2006. These changes will affect management employees in Corporate, Domestic Telecom, Verizon Information Services and Verizon International.

So far, nothing out of the ordinary! There had been countless attempts at restructuring before and the fact that it applied only to management employees was nothing new either. With no unions to defend us, we were fresh meat to be slaughtered at will. I often wondered whether managers would win a job discrimination lawsuit, as they were always taking the brunt of the measures to make the company more profitable: incessant layoffs, increases in health care costs, paltry raises. It looked like the managers and the union employees worked for two different companies. Was Verizon still a true "Equal Opportunity Employer?"

The e-mail continued: We are making a number of changes that will bring our plans more in line with current trends, including an enhancement to our savings plan to encourage employees to save and manage their own financial future, and a restructuring of our pension and retiree healthcare plans which will lower Verizon's ongoing costs.

When changes are made to be more in line with current industry trends, this means only one thing: bad news! The current trends that are selected are never the best ones in the business. It is similar to "benchmarking", theprocess that compares a company's way of doing things with other firms in the same line of business. You can be assured that the one with the lowest salaries and the worst benefits, will become the "gold standard". Can't a company be sure of itself without having to look outside for the best or worst ways to operate?

What followed were changes being made to:

Management Savings Plan

Management Pension Plan
Management Retiree Healthcare

The changes in the Management Pension Plan were drastic:

Verizon management employees will not earn pension benefits after June 30, 2006.

Beginning Jan.1, 2006, new management employees will not earn pension benefits.

Well, roll over in your resting place, Samuel Gompers[1]. Just like that, in the dead of night, Verizon announced that the pension plan was done away with. Nothing has ever been given freely by corporations. It has always involved a fight. Some courageous people thought the working more-often-than-not poor had a legitimate cause for better conditions that should not be squashed by the corporations that employed them and that could not have existed without the fruits of their labor.

---

1   Samuel Gompers was the first and longest-serving president of the American Federation of Labor (AFL) Under his leadership, the AFL became the largest and most influential labor federation in the world. It grew from a marginal association of 50,000 in 1886 to an established organization of nearly 3 million in 1924 that had won a permanent place in American society. In a society renowned for its individualism and the power of its employer class, he forged a self-confident workers' organization dedicated to the principles of solidarity and mutual aid. It was a singular achievement. Source: https://aflcio.org/about/history/labor-history-people/samuel-gompers

Many of these courageous individuals lost their jobs as well as perfectly working limbs, and sometimes their very lives at the hands of company-hired goons, local police, and State Army reserves. It took years of dedicated commitment to compel companies to provide their work force with better conditions and protection during its working and retirement years.

What the company had offered for decades was called a defined benefit plan, commonly known as a pension. As did Social Security, which is another type of defined benefit plan, it guaranteed a monthly payment once the employee left the company to enjoy his retirement. The amount of the payout took into account salary and years of service. Last but not least, these pensions were insured by the Pension Benefit Guaranty Corporation (PBGC). PBGC is a federal agency that ensures the payment of pension benefits when private company pension plans are unable to pay all promised benefits.
A single e-mail wiped out these gains in a matter of seconds.

In the early 1970s some high earning individuals from Kodak lobbied Congress to allow a part of their salary to be invested in the stock market and thus be exempt from income taxes. This resulted in section 401(k) being inserted in the tax code, allowing companies to offer additional retirement benefits to high ranking executives, above and beyond their defined pensions.
In a perfect example of unintended consequences, over time, some smart accountant somewhere found out it

was more lucrative for the company to shift from the traditional pension to 401(k)'s for all employees. They became known as defined contribution plans. In doing so, the company saved its annual contribution to the pensions, which it is believed was around 6% of each employee's salary and its PBGC premiums. As an added bonus, most employees place their 401(k) in Verizon stock, which is a way to prop up its value.

Yes, some companies are still matching a percentage of what the employee is putting into the 401(k), but these contributions have more often than not been scaled back. In effect, these plans which were initially designed to supplement Social Security benefits and employer pensions have become substitutes, not supplements, for employer pensions. The 401(k)'s have some advantages. The plans are portable. Therefore if the employee decides to switch companies, they can be rolled over. However, as noted in an article published in the *Los Angeles Times*, in October 2017, titled "Your 401(k) Won't Give You A Decent Retirement", pensions are vanishing and 401(k)'s will not save a large majority of people. The most important and least mentioned weakness of a 401(k) is that it is not insured by the Pension Benefit Guaranty Corporation. In other words, any losses incurred due to the vagaries of the stock market would not be covered by any insurance.

What followed in the e-mail was an explanation of how the pension would be replaced by other financial tools, notably this 401(k) plan. This was a poor substitute. Even during the best of times, this plan would never be as at-

tractive and, certainly not as secure as a pension plan since it was dependent on the returns of the investments that are selected for them. In other words, they are at the mercy of Wall Street. The crash of 2008 has proven how Wall Street views the interest of the common man. He is just a sheep that can be sheared at will.
To its credit, Verizon did not eschew the fact that this move was self-motivated and based on monetary matters. It indicated in the e-mail that "the restructuring was expected to provide pre-tax net savings to the company of approximately 3 billion over the next 10 years."

Although it was initially received like a devious kick in one's privates, what struck me most was the lack of reaction from the employees. Yes, they were angry; yes, they were disheartened. Still, beyond a few choice words, there was a complete lack of long-term reaction.
I had been educated in France; during my first job at Michelin Tire Corporation, I was an engineer and member of a union. Without a shadow of doubt, if this measure had been introduced in a French company, all workers, and I mean all of them, would have been demonstrating in the streets within a Paris minute. These workers are not afraid to show their discontent. Here, what did we get? Not a peep! Just another resigned shrug that seemed to confirm that lower management was inherently "screwed" and that this nail added to the coffin was not unexpected.

Is there something in the character of the average modern American that resists challenging corporate authority? Even Abraham Lincoln recognized the importance of labor when he said: "Labor is prior to, and independent of, capital. Capital is only the fruit of labor, and could never have existed if labor had not first existed. Labor is the superior of capital, and deserves much the higher consideration".

Some may argue with the last sentence. I contend that the person who invented the telephone deserves higher consideration than those who came after to implement it. However, it should not lead to poor treatment of the workers. But it did; leading labor to fight back. A century ago, workers did organize against the excesses of the corporate world. Examples abound of lives lost in gaining rights, although they do not appear in too many school books for some peculiar reason:

> The Homestead Strike against Andrew Carnegie's steel empire in Pennsylvania. Also known as the Homestead massacre, resulting from a battle between strikers and private security agents on July 6, 1892.

> The Herrin Massacre is one of history's most notorious scab labor tragedies. On June 22, 1922, in the town of Herrin, Ill., striking coal miners surrounded a mine full of nonunion scabs. Armed with rifles and farm implements, the strikers promised that if the scabs surrendered, they would be escorted safely out of town. Instead, the scabs were marched through Herrin and into the woods, where twenty of them were murdered and others seriously injured.

The Pullman Strike was a nationwide railroad strike which began in Pullman, Chicago, on May 11 when nearly 4,000 factory employees of the Pullman Company began a wildcat strike in response to recent reductions in wages. The American Railways Union called a massive boycott against all trains that carried a Pullman car. It affected most rail lines west of Detroit and at its peak involved some 250,000 workers in twenty-seven states. During the strike, thirty strikers were killed.

The Ludlow slaughter, where the deaths of nineteen people occurred during an attack by the Colorado National Guard on a tent colony of 1,200 striking coal miners and their families at Ludlow, Colorado, on April 20, 1914. Among the dead were two women and eleven children who were asphyxiated and burned to death.

The Battle of Blair Mountain, the largest labor uprising. For five days from late August to early September 1921, in Logan County, West Virginia, some 10,000 armed coal miners confronted 3,000 lawmen and strikebreakers, who were backed by coal mine operators during an attempt by the miners to unionize the southwestern West Virginia coalfields. At the beginning of the strike, a gunfight erupted and became known as the Matewan Massacre. Later, gas and explosive bombs left over from World War I were dropped on the strikers in several locations The United States Army's involvement led to the end of the strike. It is estimated that up to 100 miners were killed and thirty lawmen.

The Columbine Mine massacre occurred in 1927, in the misnamed town of Serene, Colorado. A fight broke out between Colorado State Police and a group of striking coal miners, during which the unarmed miners were attacked with machine guns.

The massacre in Thibodaux, Louisiana in November 1887 which followed a three-week strike during the harvest season by an estimated 10,000 workers against sugar cane plantation owners. On the 23rd, local white paramilitary forces attacked workers and their families. Although the total number of casualties is unknown, it is believed that 300 overall were killed, wounded or missing. Victims included elders, women and children. I placed this event last because it is unknown to most, probably due to the fact that all those killed were African-American.[2]

These are only a few examples of the struggles that pitted workers against owners for rights that are now considered a given, such as the forty-hour week and the elimination of child labor to name only two.

---

[2] John C. Rodrigue, "Thibodaux Massacre", in Eric Arnesen, editor, Encyclopedia of U.S. Labor and Working-class History, and Rebecca Jarvis Scott, Degrees of Freedom: Louisiana and Cuba after Slavery

Have we gone soft? Or is it a result of having too much to lose, maybe? There is a theory that contends that if you drop a frog in boiling water, it will hop right out. On the other hand, put the same amphibian in cold water, slowly heat it up and it will not move until the water starts boiling while the poor amphibian is cooked alive. Throughout the years, had we become these frogs? Had we been so brainwashed with the rugged individuality of the cowboy that survives on his own volition in the Wild West? What we seem to forget is that this cowboy is free because he has nothing much to leave behind. His possessions fit in the saddlebags hanging on the side of his horse. In the words of Kris Kristofferson: "Freedom's just another word for nothing left to lose." Forget the cowboy mystique. What we have acquired is the herd mentality. We like to think we still are wild horses but forgetting the blinders that cover our eyes, we let a few smart cowboys lead us wherever they want us to go.

Upon reading this e-mail, one of my colleagues considered a move to AT&T. He called a friend of his who worked there. To his surprise, he was told that AT&T had frozen their pension plan about a year before but had kept it quiet, so it did not appear in the press. Should hiding such a drastic change from the public be qualified as an enhancement of the savings plan, as noted in the e-mail. Checking the dictionary, "enhancement" has several synonyms such as improvement, augmentation, enrichment; devaluation, reduction, depreciation are not. As difficult as it is to accept, the pension plans are going the way of the horse-drawn carriage.

One day, maybe our grandchildren will ask us: "Grandpa/Grandma, tell us about the good old days when there were pensions"!

You recall that this message was received on December 6. It would have been more appropriate had it been held one more day and given on December 7, the day in 1941 when the Japanese deviously attacked Pearl Harbor. Taking delivery of this sneaky message on the anniversary of a major national disaster would have been more appropriate. However, December 7, 1941 is a date which will live in infamy; December 5, 2005 will just live in obscurity.

On October, 2012, a letter signed by Marc C. Reed Chief Administrative Officer was sent to all Verizon retirees. It began as follows:

Dear Mr. xxx:

I am writing to inform you about a change we are making regarding the funding and payment of your monthly pension benefit from the Verizon Management Pension Plan. This change will not affect the amount of your monthly pension benefit or the amount of any benefits that may be available to your beneficiaries. Beginning with the transfer of about $8 billion in cash and pension assets to The Prudential Insurance Company of America ("Prudential") in December, 2012, Prudential will assume the responsibility for your pension benefit.[3]

---

3 The entire letter is shown in Appendix IV.

The letter stated that *"this change will not affect the amount of your monthly pension benefit..."* Was the Verizon CAO simply disingenuous, claiming willful ignorance in not telling the whole impact of such a move or could it be he had not done his homework? Be that as it may, retirees did not agree with his assessment. A month or so later, they filed a lawsuit to halt Verizon's plan to sell off 41,000 employee protected pensions to Prudential.[4]

The main concern of the retirees was that the conversion of the pension to an annuity would remove the federally insured safety net provided by the Pension Benefit Guaranty Corporation (PBGC) which protected their pension up to the limit of $55,800 per year, per retiree for an unlimited number of years.[5]

Retirees also noted that Prudential could also sell or transfer all or part of its ownership of the annuity asset to another company.

---

4   See Appendix V.

5   The current system of pension protection has its roots in the 1963 bankruptcy of Studebaker. The carmaker fired 4,000 workers at its manufacturing plant in South Bend, Indiana, and terminated its pension plan. With no national safety net or pension law in place, workers found they had no pension and little recourse. Concerned about this new threat to pensions, NY senator Jacob Javits championed legislation in 1967 to safeguard retirement benefits and establish a federal insurance program for workers who fell victim to their employers' troubles. Source:https://www.institutionalinvestor.com

The argument was that, while Prudential looked like a dependable insurance company, the American business landscape was scattered with the bones of many once too-big-to-fail financial giants such as AIG, Lehman Brothers, and Bear Stearns to name but a few. Should the insurer experience a default or asset shortfall, the protections would be replaced by varying coverage, generally determined by state of residence. They cited eight states that limited coverage for annuity holders in case of a default or shortfall to a lifetime maximum of $100,000.

These were valid reasons to be concerned. Retiree association President C. William Jones said: "Retirees and their spouses, especially in states with the lowest protection levels, will be seriously harmed and left with as little as two years pension replacement in case of insurer default. Verizon's pension spin-off and conversion to a non-PBGC insurance annuity offers zero protection or upside for tens of thousands of Ma Bell's orphans."

In effect, like the employees pensions which had been converted to 401k, the retiree pensions would be tied to the whims of the stock market should the suit be dismissed.

Then started a long judicial slog. Filed in 2012, a District Court dismissed the suit in 2014. The Supreme Court was petitioned in 2015. The following year, it vacated the lower court decision. Where the suit presently stands is unknown.

CHAPTER 28

Excellence Awards

To honor the employees who had contributed to the well-being of the company above and beyond the call of duty, as they say in military circles, the Verizon Excellence Awards were established early in 2000. They were like what the Oscars are for the film industry, or what the blue ribbon is for the homemaker who bakes the best apple pie. The awards were given in recognition of "teams, individuals and business units for exceptional and sustained results on behalf of our customers, our communities and the company."

The award ceremony took place once a year with great fanfare. Participation involved the following:

- Towards the end of the year, the achievements deemed to have been beneficial for the company were submitted in writing. A specific format was required and a word limit was set. This was a good move. Otherwise a few submissions slightly shorter than the King James Bible would surely have been proposed.

- The submission was then to be sent to a panel of judges who would in secret decide which individuals, teams or units were worthy of being nominated for this highest acclaim.

- Early the next year, the chosen were informed by e-mail of the good news. Along with the announcement as a finalist nominee, an invitation was extended to a reception during which, the final winners would be announced.

As a member of a team, I was nominated not once, which would have been quite an achievement in itself, but twice. On two occasions, our team was granted the honor of being selected for outstanding contributions to the good health and reputation of Verizon. I was particularly proud of this because I had initiated the process that led to the nominations.

Towards the end of the nineties, a big push was put in place by Outside Plant, the section of the company that covered the transmission lines outside the Central Offices to the end-users to improve the reliability of the network of telephone wiring. There are multiple reasons that cause wiring to fail. Above ground, the storms that bring about havoc are the main offenders. Another cause is the rats and the squirrels that have developed a liking for the wire insulation. Underground, the most important reason for failure is water. It seeps into the cables and causes short-circuits. To prevent this water penetration, air is constantly pumped into the inside of the cable envelope, so as to keep the water at bay. Over the years, the means of pumping air had deteriorated and failures were on a drastic increase, putting at risk the users and the company revenues. It was thus decided to revamp the whole pressurization system.

A pressurization system is made of several machines called compressor-dehydrators. The compressor injects air into the telephone cable jacket, at a pressure sufficient to prevent water infiltration. The dehydrator insures that this air does not contain water, which if it did, would of course defeat the whole purpose of the process. The compressor, composed of moving parts, generates heat that must be dissipated to avoid breakdowns. The most common means to do this is to use city water in New York City and cooling tower water in other areas. This was the way compressor-dehydrators were cooled until very recently. The water came in at about 60 degrees Fahrenheit year in and year out and left with an increase of roughly 15 degrees. However, the price of water, especially in New York City, had increased dramatically, as had the costs of dumping this water into the sewer system, since the cooling involved a once-thru system. In addition, the municipalities frowned more and more upon using potable water for process cooling purposes and were starting to clamp down on these applications. Hefty fines were put in place to discourage the perpetrators. Consequently, other means of cooling the compressors had to be devised.

The obvious one was to generate our own chilled water. This was done with a small packaged cooling machine that delivered water between 45 and 50 degrees Fahrenheit to the compressor cooling jackets in a continuous closed loop piping system. The main advantage was that city water was no longer wasted. The disadvantages included the energy costs to run the chiller and condenser and added upkeep expenses since these units needed preventive maintenance and were bound to break down every once in a while. It became the system used in New York City and Nassau County.

I had been interested in alternative energy systems for a while. One of them was the use of ground water, or well water, as a cooling agent. It involves using the ground as a heat sink to dissipate the heat generated by the equipment. At one time, I had visited a bank in the Melville, Long Island corridor that used ground water for cooling its chillers. It was a fascinating installation. In addition to the lack of a cooling tower which drastically reduced the energy and maintenance costs, there was an added factor. The ground water was at an average temperature of 60 to 65 degrees Fahrenheit. Compare this to the water temperature coming out of cooling towers during the summer which was about 100 degrees. Since most chillers are rated for a condenser temperature of 100 degrees, supplying cooler water to the chillers greatly increased their efficiency. In fact, the bank chillers were rated 300 tons, but the use of ground water allowed them to deliver beyond 400 tons. Great stuff that left me properly impressed. However, the bank had installed its well water system before the environmental codes had been drastically tightened. Nowadays, ground water use is severely controlled on Long Island. Environmental impact studies, permits, and hearings are required to put up roadblocks to the practice.

Still, the water was coming from the ground, and the ground was cooling it. If the water could not be used, maybe the ground could. I investigated the principle. Basically, two systems emerged. The first involved a series of loops of piping buried below the frost line, long enough to allow the ground to cool the water. The second involved the drilling of wells in which a water pipe was installed. Both systems needed ample space. Space was at a premium in the City and Nassau County, but was more plentiful the farther east one went.

When the compressor-dehydrator replacement program reached eastern Suffolk, it was the time to be bold and try something new. I talked to the team leader in charge of this program in Outside Plant, John Schmidt, to get his consent. After all, he was in charge of the project and the funding. He thought it was worth trying. He, however, insisted that a chilled water back-up system be installed in case the ground water cooling system did not perform as expected or failed. The use of City water was still allowed during short-term emergencies, so a system having belts and suspenders satisfied him.

Not being an expert in the design of ground water cooling installation, I hired one, and the design was on its way. Soon, enough information was available to choose an adequate site. On the list of sites was Yaphank. It was a small Central Office with enough land to install the cooling system. The latter involved several wells, close to 500 feet deep. They contained copper tubes that brought the hot water from the compressor/dehydrator plant. This water was cooled by the ground surrounding the well and then, returned to the plant.

The equipment for digging 500 foot holes is not something seen every day. It elicited quite a bit of interest from the neighbors. One asked us if we were drilling for oil, thinking that maybe his backyard, which was abutting Verizon's property, would make him a rich man.

The installation proved quite successful and led to our first "Excellence awards" nomination under the name "Geo-thermal chiller team." The letter we received stated: "Reaching the finalist stage of the program symbolizes that you made an important contribution to our success and to helping us to deliver on the Verizon Promise. I am very proud to be associated with folks like you who have achieved this high honor." We were proud too, and excited. Being finalists was no small achievement. Nearly 1,000 nominations were submitted within the Network Service Group. After judges reviewed the submissions, 175 teams and individuals were selected as finalists. A subsequent judging phase determined which winners were chosen and whose names would be pronounced after the "pass-the-envelope-please" moment.

As you already know, we were nominated, but not crowned. Still, we were quite happy because being part of the chosen few was not a small feat and quite an accomplishment in itself. It was a rare sign of respect and we accepted it with pride.

Yet, we remained tenacious. The next year, we did a similar installation at the Shoreham Central Office. This building was comparable to Yaphank's, so comparable in fact that the installation was closely boilerplate. Taking full advantage of the Computer Aided Design, we reused the Yaphank drawings for the Shoreham compressor/dehydrator installation. Basically, it involved merely changing the address on the drawings and specifications, plus a few minor modifications here and there to accommodate the slightly different configuration of the building and the site.

At the end of the year, we submitted this project

again to the Excellence Awards' committee. Needless to say, we were a little nervous during the selection process. The possibility that the committee might recall having seen a similar project in the not too distant past was real. Should it come to this, our submission would have been rejected off hand, with possibly a slap on the wrist or more. Lo and behold, it turned out that, either the reviewing committee did not have an elephantine memory or it was appraised by an entirely different set of eyes.

Be that as it may, against all odds, a letter starting with: "Congratulations on being selected as a Network Services Group Verizon Award finalist" reached my desk. Hallelujah, we were nominated again. This time, we went all the way, reaching the finish line as champions. We returned from the ceremony in New York City, lugging our trophy made of marble and glass which weighted a little less than a small pick-up truck back to our respective offices. I placed mine next to the one that was given to the finalists of the previous year. I must say that they formed a pretty nice combo, a great tribute to team work, persistence and recognition.

I had another satisfaction in the form of a note from my director, Ralph Carey:

> "Paul, congratulations on being nominated. The nomination itself is an honor. And to be nominated by another organization, to me, is more

validation of our/your value to the business."

The allusion to being nominated by another organization was a little dig at the teams who nominated themselves for work performed in their own organizations, in the hope that friendly judges would be more sympathetic to their submission.

CHAPTER 29

Real Estate Mysterious Ways

God moves in a Mysterious Way is the title of a famous hymn by William Cowper. This cryptic sentence also describes the way the Real Estate Organization operated at times. A case in point will explain. Close to the end of every year, in order to grab as big a chunk of next year's budget as possible, projects put into the five-year plan are initiated. This plan lists locations that will soon require infrastructure improvement or replacement, including roofs. Their maintenance had too often fallen by the wayside, mostly because what you did not see soon belongs to the category "out of sight, out of mind". Some roofs were so neglected that vegetation was growing all over them, making them resemble at best a fallow field, at worst the Hanging Gardens of Babylon. Little trees were growing from the drains, grass from between slabs that covered the asphalt plies.

I had listed three of the Long Island roofs as candidates.

Replacement design and construction documents were completed in late fall and sent out for bidding to General Contractors (GCs). When the bids came back, they were analyzed, both by Sourcing and our group. The winning GCs were selected. When the budget for the next year was in the works, three estimate cases were written to obtain the funding. They were not approved. This was not unexpected as, of course, the amount of capital dedicated to construction is not infinite. What was more perplexing, however, is what came afterwards.

A few months later, these projects came back to life. Capital had been secured and they were allowed to proceed. However, somebody decided that they were to be bundled with other projects and handled by a Construction Manager (CM).
For most people, this decision would not be mystifying. Yet, for us, as project managers, it was baffling. As noted above, bids had been received; the lowest bidders had been selected. Putting them under the supervision of a Construction Manager did not make sense for two reasons. Firstly, it was adding an unnecessary layer to a construction team of roofing specialists. Secondly, this added layer was not going to be working at no cost. Of course, the Construction Manager's arguments were always the same: "The large pool of contractors we have access to and the possibilities of volume purchase allow us to get competitive, very low, low prices." We had heard that so many times that it was not even worth arguing. However, would these prices be so low as compared to the ones already on hand to offset the CM fees? It always

remained the open question.

In this instance, it turned out to be a moot point. The CM chose not to go out to bid again with its large pool of contractors. Instead, he simply hired the GCs who had initially been selected for these projects. No surprise there: it saved time and money for the CM and, consequently, for Verizon. At least, this was the rationale that was fed to us. Against our arguments, the arrangement was implemented. The roofing contracts were awarded to the GCs by the CM.

So, when all was said and done, I made some tabulations for the projects in my area. It was very simple. In one column were the prices that would have been paid to the General Contractors had they done the work without CM's interference. A second column documented the complete payments that were made to the CM. It did not come as a revelation that the total cost of the second column was in the range of $300,000 more than the first. Almost a third of a million dollars and there was nothing to show for it.

We were not privy to all the reasons that led to these kinds of arrangements, but how did they make sense financially? Where they a disguised gift to the CMs? As project managers, all too often kept in the dark as to the why's and wherefore's, these shenanigans drove us crazy. They hurt the General Contractors who without a doubt were squeezed a little to lower their initial bid. More importantly, they hurt Verizon at a time when money was very tight. For this amount of money, another leaky roof could have been replaced and the reliability of the telephone equipment enhanced.

I put all this in a memo. Of course it did not come as a shock that I was asked not to distribute it.

Meanwhile, the inventory of second managers waltzing into our lives was periodically restocked. Let's see, we were in 2002. How many direct supervisors did I have in twelve years? I could count five.

Every time a new one showed up, an adjustment of style was necessary to get attuned to his personality and his way of doing things. It is not to say one had to train ourselves to mimic his manners, but one had to find what made him tick and what put him off.

Following the disaster of September 11, 2011, my current boss was temporarily detached to other duties and in came Joann DiBono. Her predecessors had all been good, supportive and reasonable bosses in their own right: Bill Drum, Charles Knuth, Bob Huber, Bob Keyser, Rick Winner. She was however the first woman under whom we would work. It was not a problem for me, but some members of the team with a penchant for machismo were a little leery of her presence at the helm of the team.

She quickly dispelled those doubts. In fact, she proved to be one of the best leaders we ever had. We quickly found out by her actions that speaking merely to hear the sound of her own voice was not part of her personality. "Wasting time" was not an expression that was in her vocabulary and was reflected in the way she handled the responsibilities of her function. On top of this, she had an unerring radar to detect bullshit at all levels, which we admired. There was not an ounce of corporate politics in her. She invariably backed us up, giving us our assignments and letting us carry them out without undue interference, unless, of course, we sought her advice. Problems that arose were seen as mere obstacles that could be eliminated one way or the other. She was respected by all of us. So much so that we all nominated her for a Verizon Excellence Award. Our arguments were that, in addition to being a dedicated mother of two and being pregnant with a third at the time, she was handling her duties as a second level manager in an exemplary manner. In short, she was a credit to Verizon. She was never selected as a finalist, but in our eyes, she was and remained a winner. We truly missed her when she was transferred to other duties.

As far as the directors were concerned, the shuffle was even worse. During my career, nine of them occupied the position, three from New York Telephone, one from NYNEX, three from Bell Atlantic, and eventually two more plucked from the old New York Telephone organization.

CHAPTER 30

Of Conference Calls, Matrixes & BlackBerries

The years 2007 and 2008 were tough. Not because the projects had become more difficult; they had not. But the department protocol, and that of the entire company one would assume, was becoming more and more paper and computer oriented. The paperwork became more time consuming than the technical challenges. Also many decisions were hard to fathom, as in the case of the example given in the previous chapter.

Simultaneously we had entered the era of matrixes and conference calls. Once again technology proved to be unstoppable. That it had some good sides was not in question. Conference calls allowed you to be present at meetings from your desk rather than driving for hours or flying to a far-away location. Microsoft Excel spreadsheet software using a grid of rows and columns to organize data and allow manipulations like mathematical, statistical, engineering and financial operations, was useful in presenting data in a compact form. In short, it became the backbone of the communications with our superiors. Where this goes wrong, however, is when it is thought that everything can be reduced to and explained by numbers. Yes, Pythagoras famously said "All Things Are Number"; Galileo, Newton or Pascal, and many others thought the same way, but these mathematicians were all geniuses, a rare occurrence among middle managers in an American corporation. Still, these spreadsheets became the tool no department could live without, mind-numbingly humdrum as they were. Since it was deemed by some that an Excel spreadsheet was too pedestrian a name, a more exciting one was given to these rectangular arrays of rows and columns, graphs, histograms and charts: They became matrixes. We entered the matrix mania era and convinced ourselves that they were the path to the truth, even if they were sometimes manipulated to make this truth more palatable.

So it was that conference calls and matrixes came to consume the largest part of our daily activities.

The first half of the day was spent in front of a computer. The primary task was to sift through the amount of e-mails which popped up every morning and separate the inconsequential from the relevant. Then, the next hours were spent putting together one of these dreaded matrix requests or with the phone on speaker listening to people in love with the sound of their own voices. I was afraid that, because of these hours of immobility, barnacles would grow on my back. In the instance that my name popped up requiring my input, I formulated my reply while asking "Can you repeat the question, please?" The afternoons were a liberation. I visited the job sites where I became a born-again project engineer. Hearing the hum of the motors, smelling the acrid odor of the welding torches, chatting with sub-contractors, this was heaven. We were now directed by a bunch of pale-faced bureaucrats for whom "being in the field" meant not much more than an outing on the golf course. Most were based in Basking Ridge in New Jersey, the new company headquarters, touted as follows on the internet:

Thousands of employees representing all different teams work in the Basking Ridge office so it's a great place to meet new people every day. When we're not working hard, we're eating great food. The cafeteria offers specials every day: sushi stations, custom salad bars, taco bars and more. All that great food gives us reason to work off the calories – that's why fitness thrives here. The rent-a-bike program, Pilates and massage therapy are employee favorites. Summer Lunch Jams give our employees an opportunity to take the stage and show off their musical talents.

Great food, massage therapy, summer lunch jams, sounds like an advertisement for Club Med. Who would not be enticed to work there?

Back to the pencil pushers working hard to burn off the calories of the sushi ingested in the cafeteria. These people had become masters of the obvious: "experts", as we say in French, "at bursting doors that were already opened." The department had turned to a passive mode. "Proactive? What are you talking about? We are here to put out fires, not to install the firebreaks that could prevent them." This was a sad state of affairs.

Until 2007, a certain amount of funding had been allocated to our department for emergencies, such as equipment breakdowns, or jobs that did not require a large amount of money but were needed immediately, such as cutting holes in partitions or walls to accommodate new telephone cables. In a sense, it was our petty cash. As long as the expense did not exceed $50,000, it did not require the writing of an estimate case to justify the expenditure. In 2008, these amounts were drastically reduced for network jobs and dropped to zero for infrastructure jobs. However emergencies still occurred.

So a new rule was instituted. For any emergency repair, a form had to be filled out, explaining the nature of the problem and the required expenditure associated with it, and then sent up the line. At first glance, nothing was wrong with this procedure. However, it seemed that Basking Ridge had become a bureaucratic black hole. Although it was in the same time zone as New York City and Long Island, it appeared to be in a different word-definition zone. Did the word emergency have a different meaning over there? It appeared so because the sense of urgency that an emergency connotes did not translate into much resolve on their part.

This phenomenon was in evidence when a large crack appeared in a sidewalk at the Smithtown central office. Several people had already tripped on it. While nobody was injured, it was only a matter of time before a more serious accident occurred. The property manager, conscious of the likely implications, got a couple of quotes to fix the broken side walk, sent them to me to fill out the appropriate forms and pass the emergency request along. Naively, I thought that in view of the small amount of money required (a few thousand dollars), associated with the potentially dangerous situation, the repair would be approved in a couple of days.

How wrong I was! These guys were into foreplay big time. They teased you with calls to get more detail; they baited you with more forms to explain the problems; they pestered you with "what would happen if the money was not allocated?" "I tell you what will happen while you are making up your mind: somebody will twist an ankle or worse, break a leg. The company will be sued for a thousand times the cost of the repair. And by the way, you will lose your job."

I knew the company would be sued for a fact. I had been handed quite a few subpoenas during my career. They all had to do with accidents. They enjoined me to go and give depositions in lawsuits involving employees who had suffered mishaps on my jobs. One of them had tripped on one of the concrete car stop blocks in a parking lot that was under renovation. Another one was from a subcontractor who had fallen from his own ladder which he had placed on a desk. One had to guess that the fact it happened on the property of a company with very deep pockets entitled a person to some compensation.

As mentioned above, I had to attend many examinations before trial. An account follows concerning the employee who tripped over the concrete block in a parking lot that was in the process of being resurfaced. The plaintiff was suing the Telephone Company and the construction manager; the Telephone Company was suing the outfit that did the work on the parking lot, as did the construction manager. As you can see, it was one of those "pointing the blame at somebody else" affairs. So it was that I found myself in front of four attorneys. What follows are some excerpts of the recorded testimony. Of course this is not an exhaustive transcript of the entire testimony, just some questions and answers to give you an idea of the proceedings.

> Attorney 1 (A1): Please state your name for the record.
> Reply (R): Paul Belard
> A1: Where do you presently reside?
> R: *I gave my address.*
> A1: Good morning, M. Belard. My name is xxxxx, and I represent the plaintiff in this matter, xxxxx. I'm going to be asking you questions this morning with regard to work being performed at xxxxx. Do you understand?
> R: Yes.
> A1: By whom are you employed presently?
> R: Verizon.

A1: For how long have you been employed by Verizon?
R: Under that name or --
A1: Under any name. What other names has Verizon been known by?
R: Bell Atlantic, NYNEX, New York Telephone.
A1: Back in November of 1996, you were employed by whom?
R: I believe it was NYNEX at the time.

It took a litany of questions that covered eighteen pages in the testimony report to get to this point.

A1: Mr. Belard, are you aware of an incident involving an xxxxx that took place in November of 1996?
R: Yes.
A1: How did you first come to learn of that?
R: I believe it was in September of the year 2000 when I was asked to come and testify in the city.
A1: Do you know xxxxx personally?
R: No.
A1: I have nothing further.

First, you will have noticed that four years elapsed between the incident and this testimony. Justice may move forward, but it grinds at its own pace. Second, I could not begin to sort through the meandering ways the lawyer had to take to get to the crucial point. I do not even think the fact he was paid by the hour had anything to do with it, but he had my head throbbing.

Now I was interrogated by a second attorney, mainly about work that was performed on several parking lots on the property over several years.

A2: Sir, I'm going to show you what was marked on July 13th, 2000 at the plaintiff's deposition, which are color lasers of copies of the alleged site of the accident, and I ask you to take a look at those photographs.

What followed were questions about work done on several parking lots surrounding the building and related invoices.

A2: Looking at the photographs that are in front of you, if you had gone to this particular parking lot and observed the condition as depicted there, would you have come to the conclusion that the work had been completed or some other conclusion?
A4: Note my objection.
A3: Note my objection.
A1: Note my objection.
A4: You can answer.
R: No, I would not have concluded that the work was not finished.

I did not have a clue what the objections were about. At this point I was completely at sea. A4 was the Verizon attorney, here to insure that the interests of the company were protected and to guide me. I felt at times that these lawyers made an issue out of tiny details that did not appear to have any bearing on the case. As somebody who likes to go straight to the point without beating around the bush, it was discombobulating.

Then came the third attorney. These are also some excerpts of the exchange:

> A3: Good morning, Mr. Belard. My name is xxxxxx. I'm the attotrney for xxxxx in this case. Are there currently car stops at that lot now?
> R; I think there are.
> A3: When -- I'm sorry finish you answer.
> R: I think. I'm not sure one hundred percent.
> A3: When was the last time you were at the lot?
> R: Last week.
> A3: Did you drive to the lot when you were there last week?
> R: Yes.
> A3: Did you park?
> R: Well, I parked across the street.
> A3: When you walked up, did you walk through the front door or the side door?

What the heck had these questions to do with somebody tripping? I thought.

> A3: In 1996, did NYNEX have the car stops replaced?
> R: I don't know.
> A4: Just objection. Again, there hasn't been a foundation that there were car stops.
> A3: Were there car stops in 1996?
> A4: Prior to November 1st?
> A3: Prior to November 1st.

R: I don't recall. I mean, I would assume there were. I don't know.
A4: Don't assume. Testify in terms of what you recall.

This is just a sample of all the questions that needed to be answered on a project I had barely had any involvement with since it was handled by a construction manager. Although I was a non-party witness, my testimony was thirty-six pages long. All in all, I had wasted one day during which my regular workload was piling up on my desk. You will now understand why I did not relish being given the third degree by lawyers.

That is the main reason I did not appreciate the lackadaisical attitude of this individual who could not approve a few thousand dollars to avoid a lawsuit. Because of his failure to act, I, not him, may have to endure an inventory of circuitous questions by attorneys. And yes, the settlements to these lawsuits were a hundred times larger than what it would cost to fix the crack at the Smithtown central office.

Still, these people seemed to live in La La Land where reality had a hard time penetrating. I did not want to believe that his sluggishness to reach a decision was backed by disingenuousness, but as time passed, it was difficult not to think so. I felt like telling him "just approve the damn money and go back to sharpening your pencils or unbending paper clips".

Slowly but surely, the Real Estate department was sliding into an unreal state.

It took several weeks to decide to allocate the money. This is where one-dimensional thinking leads to a lack of common sense which in the end was hurtful to the company's bottom line. Some said that the ultimate payback of these paper pushers was to waste the valuable time of those who have to work in the field. We have all been in situations where we had to face some obdurate bureaucrat: a lesson in humility in the face of inanity.

Following the introduction of the conference calls and the matrixes came the advent of the BlackBerry. There was something irresistible about this gizmo. When it rang, it had to be answered right away as if the fate of the entire company was hanging on this call. Its owner moves a few feet away and starts pecking at the small key board. It does not matter if she/he is in a meeting, or in a discussion; a call is enough to remove the "callee" from any current activities; nothing else exists.

Yes, we had beepers before, but if the call was important, it was marked urgent with an added 911. If the cell phone was ringing, you could check the number of the caller and decide whether to respond or not. But there was something about a call through the BlackBerry, the first smart phone, and later about its offsprings, that made it impossible to ignore. It was of course the integrated e-mail and instant messaging. Now the anonymity of a pager or a cell phone call no longer existed. The written words were like an order to be answered immediately upon receipt, prompted by the fear of missing something important. The pull of technology was becoming more and more addictive.

Coincidentally, one of the last seminars we were required to attend was "Be Here Now". Contrary to what was first thought, it did not mean "Be Here Now" for the company's sake. On the contrary, it introduced the notion of a better balance between our personal and professional lives. At last, a seminar that was not used solely to promote the interests of the company. Rather it encouraged us to take a deep breath regularly and to quiet our minds before exiting the office in order not to bring our professional baggage home. The more we can be fully present both at home and at work it assured us, the more fulfilling our lives will be in both places.

So it was ironic that at the same time that we were encouraged to spend more time alone or with loved ones came these devices that put us within reach of any maniac who decided to call you in the middle of the night from a different time zone or during the weekend simply because she/he could. Nine-to-five did no longer exist. Work overlapped like never before with personal and family life. The era of the electronic leash had arrived. For all intents and purposes, we had become tethered to the office.

As technology advances, the leash becomes shorter. Every little tug on it becomes more difficult to ignore. One wonders if the contents of "Be Here Now" have been altered to take these technological advancements into account.

CHAPTER 31

Promotion

On couple of occasions, I had been asked whether I would consider a promotion. It was a question I did not even have to think about. My answer was a categorical no. If I had been ten years younger, I would have given it some thought because it would have been a necessary step to other levels. Presently, moving up to second level manager would be the last advancement. For $4,000 or $5,000 more a year, sitting in on interminable conference calls that would extend late into the evenings would become the greatest part of my days. I would find myself with people under me who I would have to grade, or in the worst case, taking into account the perilous times we were living in, dismiss.

Once, one of my bosses chickened out and I had to give the exit interview to an employee who had been terminated. I too tried to weasel out of it. Why wasn't it done by an HR person? While I was not an expert at exit interviews, I knew they were usually done with employees quitting a firm on their own terms, to assess if some procedures and policies could be improved. The usual questions include reasons for leaving, what was liked or not liked, any problems with supervisors or company rules. If the person interviewed was fired, his or her answers might be biased and tainted by emotions, therefore not very useful.

That encounter was a nerve-racking experience for me; I could only imagine what it was like for my colleague. We had worked together well, shared rides to staff meetings during which we got to know each other. Frankly, I did not know what led to the dismissal, except that we had entered an era where the company was shedding personnel left and right. A mistake that a few years ago would have led only to a reprimand was now a ticket to the exit door. I did not wish to conduct an exit interview ever again.

I was not power hungry, not "because power corrupts" as the saying goes. I simply deemed a hierarchical upgrade would place me in a cage that would limit my movements, get me away from what I was trained for, was good at, and liked to do. My department leash was pretty slack in my present position. It would become tighter with a new rank. The hours would be longer and, more importantly, I would enter an area of company-politic quick sand. God only knows how many promoted souls had been sucked into it. Too many choices would have to be made based on political pragmatism and bureaucratic expediency. My education and temperament had not equipped me for these battles. I was not a political animal; too many murky lines to cross. In addition, it would mean cutting down on the time I devoted to the restoration of books and painting. Both activities demanded attention, concentration, and always released me from the stress of the day's doings. They brought me relaxing moments and financial benefits too, enough to offset the raise attached to the promotion. In short, I was happy being right where I was, as a first level manager. Why should I give up this sweet spot?

Besides, if I had said yes, where would this new position in the pecking order put me? Away from Long Island, in another group where I did not know anybody? Or in one where I knew everybody? Becoming a boss is not easy. It is even trickier when you become the leader of a group you have previously worked with as a peer. How do you reach the equilibrium between being in charge, giving strict orders, or being everybody's friend in the hope that it will smooth the relationships with former colleagues? Where is the middle ground? How to strike the right tone; not letting the ego and influence go to one's head; avoiding leading by fear and intimidation which alienates subordinates and usually results in poor performances, and being friendly without falling into the classic pitfall of "too much familiarity breeds contempt?"

During some of the projects I handled, I may have had fifty or more persons working for me. I was grateful however not to have had any Verizon direct reports working under me. When I had to sanction some of my contractors for poor performances, I did not have a union representative on my back to fight the decision to take them off the bidder's list for a while, kick them off a job site or to deny payment of some dubious invoices.

This was not the case of my property manager friends. They managed a crew of watch engineers, all members of a union. These craft people all knew how to file a grievance about a real or imagined wrong they felt had been perpetrated against them.

To be clear, there is nothing wrong with filing a grievance. It is guaranteed in the First Amendment; if it is important enough to be in the Bill of Rights, it certainly must apply to the workplace also. As stated in Sean C. Doyle's work titled *The Grievance Procedure: The Heart of the Collective Agreement*, a grievance is a procedure put in place to challenge questionable decisions that are made by others in the workplace[1]. God knows there were too many. In the case of Verizon, the grievance process was outlined in the CWA[2] Stewards' Hand Book. It specified that: One of your jobs as a steward is to keep management from intimidating employees. It then went on, stating that there are two types of grievances: Discipline grievances where the employee may be sanctioned and other types of grievances.

Typically, the sequence of a grievance followed a well-

1	Source:
2	CWA: Communication Workers of America, a union founded in 1938 in New Orleans.

defined path:

-       The employee brought the grievance and the stewards met with first level managers.
-       If no solution was arrived at, the grievance moved to second level managers.
-       If no solution was reached again, the grievance went to a company Labor representative, and eventually to arbitration where the problem would get settled by a neutral third party.

A large percentage of the grievances were legitimate. Others were border line and a few could be classified as ridiculous. Dave, a property manager friend related one instance.

"One day, I was called into the Long Beach Central Office. A watch engineer had filed a complaint and I went to support the property manager in this area. You see, during the first meeting, the employee filing the grievance brings in two union stewards. So, two managers must also be present. Once we were seated, the watch engineer stated his protest. A new second level manager had come into the area and put the kibosh on all unnecessary overtime. The problem was that he was cursing the manager's edict like a fishmonger. We had to tell him to watch his language. Still, he kept on berating this individual, arguing that it was the first time in quite a few years that he didn't make $100,000 a year. When he said this, there was a stunned silence. I looked at my colleague, then at the stewards. We all had the same look on our faces. This watch engineer had been earning $100,000 or more for several years? You know, there was nobody in this room who was making that kind of money, far from it. This admission brought the meeting to a quick end. The stewards both agreed that the grievance was unfounded and rejected it. You know, Paul, why was this grievance brought in in the first place, I've no idea? The Steward's hand book states: Must the Union grieve every employee complaint? No. A grievance does not have to be filed if the Union believes it is unfounded, or without any basis in the contract. In addition, overtime is not a right, but is only approved for special occasions."

This anecdote brought to mind a discussion I had with a watch engineer at the 140 West Street building on August 2000. At midnight, the union contract came to expiration. In the event of a strike, all managers that would fulfill some of the craft duties had been dispatched to their strike posting. Since I would be in charge of the chillers supplying air conditioning to the building, I went down to the watch engineer's office to meet him. He was a nice guy. He showed me the office which was very pleasant. There was a radio, a TV, a VCR with bootleg tapes of the new movies which one could buy on almost every street of Manhattan. He even disclosed the cache of the X-rated ones. After the entertainment aspect, he showed me the microwave, the fridge which contained miscellaneous foods, drinks and even a couple of beers, which was a no-no. The company Code of Conduct is very clear on this: alcohol is strictly prohibited on the work premises. There was also a cot for catching a little sleep during the night watches.

Waiting for the stroke of midnight, we chatted a little bit. At one point, he mentioned that he was making in excess of $100,000 per year. I was flabbergasted; I was barely making that kind of salary at the end of my career. Later, thinking about it, the watch engineers working in the city were required by law to be present at all times to monitor the centrifugal refrigeration machines. It meant they were working days, nights, weekends, and holidays. With this amount of overtime, sometimes doubled or tripled depending on the time of their shift, it was not surprising that their paycheck increased accordingly. Their job was probably one of the best you could have in the company. Chillers and their ancillaries were reliable machines that did not give much trouble; no wonder they had an extensive collection of movies to pass the time. They were licensed professionals, respected as such, and who was going to bother them in the middle of the night or on Sunday afternoons?

CHAPTER 32

Mergers

The successive mergers brought us in contact with new approaches to work. For example, on a lighter note, the alliance with Bell Atlantic first got rid of men's ties, which we had worn for years. Bell Atlantic employees were more relaxed, maybe because the weather was significantly hotter below the Mason-Dixon line. They arrived with their shirt collars open. Since this alliance was more of a takeover, they were aped. So the casually knotted ties disappeared into Salvation Army bins and were rarely seen again.

Another good change for us brought on by the Bell Atlantic merger is that our director was now an engineer. He was liked and respected by all. A no-nonsense individual, he favored the use of expressions such as "the devil is in the details" or "we did not get to the Rubicon to go swimming". A trend which was prevailing in American management practice in the 1980s was that managers were not expected to technically understand the things they managed. The CEO of Boeing could become the CEO of Ford. The phone company followed the trend.

We had been through these depressing times with several directors lacking in technical savvy, but the arrival of this director was a breath of fresh air. For a while, our department was run as it should be, by a professional who understood the problems we had to deal with and who trusted his crew. It did not go on for long, because this director soon retired, but it was nice while it lasted. Coming from areas where the local laws, when they existed, were less stringent than in the New York area, these newcomers sometimes proposed things that made us roll our eyes.

In the Central Islip office, the parking lot size had to be increased and of course, a permit was required by the town building department. Everybody complains about Washington edicts, but these departments are much worse. They rule the towns like they are their personal fiefdoms, making you jump through hoops to get the proper certificates before you can build or add something to an existing structure. In addition, they have a well-earned reputation for their lack of speed in making things happen, not to mention a penchant for coercing demands that sometimes border on corruption. These officials, being who they are, never give anything for nothing when they deal with a company with deep pockets. They suggested that an area next to the parking extension be transformed into a little park with benches, flowers, and bushes. A large placard, bearing their names outlined in gold, would also be installed for all the residents to see how their elected representatives were at work for them. Their "offer" was accepted.

There was a hamburger shack in the proposed area. The company paid an unheard of amount of money for this joint, so much so that the owner thought he had gotten the power ball winning ticket. The next step was to demolish the little structure. One Bell Atlantic employee suggested burning it down for the purpose of giving the local Fire Department some training. Obviously, he equated the suburbs of New York City with some rural hamlet in West Virginia. I could just see myself going to the Central Islip Town Hall and to the Fire Department, asking them for authorization to set fire to a structure less than twenty feet away from a central office serving tens thousands of customers and abutting a major thoroughfare. It was not difficult to imagine them rolling on the floor, in spasms of laughter.

When General Telephone & Electronics Corporation (GTE) joined our ranks, we had to deal with an influx of Texans, one of whom was in charge of a project in which I became involved. We were expecting a tall fellah, maybe with a ten-gallon hat and decorated leather boots stitched with white and red threads, a kind of John Wayne, if you like, wearing a T-shirt warning "Don't mess with Texas, my God and my guns." Would he say "Ya'll" and "This ain't my first rodeo"? After all, the Texans have a reputation to uphold.

So, who *did* show up? Well, basically myself! The Texan was short of stature, a touch stocky. However, I was more photogenic and where my handshake has often been qualified as hearty and robust, in some instances as nearly bone-crushing, shaking his limp hand was like squeezing a bunch of beached flounders left on the shore by the ebbing tide.

Still, this man did something that nobody else had been able to do during all my years in the company. He made me throw a little bit of an outburst. The last wave of layoffs had been announced, the very one I was sure I would be a casualty of. We were under a great deal of stress; maybe he was too. In any case, my temper was on a short fuse. The building we were upgrading was a supply center. Trucks would come and go and a fuel tank was required to fill their tanks. Maybe, in Texas, it would have been a simple affair. It was not the case here where the Building Departments must issue permits before anything can be done.

So here I was, every weekly meeting, having to bring him up-to-date on the state of the fuel tank, when he knew darn well that it would take a couple of months before a decision was made by the Town. Week after week, there he was, asking the same question with the stubbornness of a querulous spoiled brat. I should have answered him: "Hey partner, we're not in Texas anymore. Things are done differently up here in these parts by us yankees." But no, I was on the defensive. I had held my growing frustration in check for too long with this petulant fellow and one day, I exploded and let him have it with both barrels. I remember trembling as a wave of anger swelled inside me. Heat climbed to my face and my burning cheeks must have turned the color of fire hydrants. I realized how long it had been bubbling close to the surface, but this time, the safety valve did not work.

Unfortunately, the staunch control that had served me well in my professional career had failed me miserably. I had allowed my emotions to get the best of me and in doing so, perpetrated my second cardinal sin.

The first one was committed a few years ago: The train had just arrived in Huntington when I got a beep with the dreaded 911 following the number of the caller. An emergency! This was before cell phones were allocated; I needed to get home before I could call back. The phone number of the caller was not unknown, it belonged to a contractor presently involved in a chiller replacement project in the telephone building located on Third Avenue. He informed me that, while drilling a hole in a terra cotta clad wall, a telephone cable had been damaged and several thousand customers were without service. The ultimate sin, the loss of customers, had been committed on one of my projects. He continued, confirming that Network had been informed. A crew of splicers was already on site working on the repair. But how long would it take? A couple of hours, or days? How much revenue would the company lose? I considered going back to the city, but to what end? It was now in the hands of the splicers. I called my boss. In a rather cowed voice, I explained what happened. Apparently, it was not the first time he heard of this kind of incident. He took it in stride, asked me to call him first thing in the morning and wished me a good night.

That was not the case. I tossed and turned, already imagining myself standing on line at the local unemployment office. I had been in this situation a couple of times before. I did not relish being part of this second class humanity who had to rely on aid to make ends meet. Waiting in line to get to the window was like being in a soup kitchen. One felt marginalized, no longer part of the productive class, somehow having lost the status of full human being. Some of my unfortunate fellow citizens were individuals for whom bad luck was not an abstraction any more but a relentless reality in their lives. This stigma was etched in their faces as it was in the photographs of disenfranchised people during the depression. It was more than losing a job, it was losing health insurance, it was losing the ability to pay all the bills, but more debasing, it was losing one's dignity.

I had instructed the contractor to call me at regular intervals to keep me abreast of any development. I had planned to go to the site to face the music, but according to him, no company big shots were present, only the splicing crew. Oddly, he even added the splicers were whistling while doing what they were supposed to do. Really! I took some solace from that comment; maybe it was not so bad after all. But who was I kidding? If the splicers had already been there twelve hours, how good could it be? Their happy mood was probably due to the fact that they had earned twelve hours of overtime.

So I headed for the office as if I were going to my beheading. When would the dreaded phone call summoning me forthwith to some Network honcho come? Each time the phone rang, my heart playing xylophone on my ribs intensified. I could feel the swish of the axe blade aiming for my neck. Will I be fired; will some money be taken from my paycheck? As you can see, this waiting was interfering with my ability to think straight. But, as Marie-Antoinette said: "In times of crisis, it is of utmost importance not to lose one's head." So I struggled to remain calm.

In the meantime, I managed to find out that these cables imbedded in the wall should have been identified by a marker on this wall. It was a Network crucial rule and it had been ignored.
At least, I had some kind of defense should I be brought in in front of accusers. By the middle of the morning, the service had been reestablished, but not my peace of mind. My fears turned out to be moot because nobody questioned me about this incident. Why? Colleagues who had experienced similar incidents had been called on the carpet and read the riot act. Honestly, I did not know why the same fate failed to befall me. Needless to say, I did not make the tiniest effort to discover why.

Back to the present, with the Texan I had forgotten that after all, he was representing the customer. Even inside the phone company, the customer was king. My role was, within reason, to meet his demands. Lambasting him, definitely not a good move on my part! The last thing I wanted was to be fired with nothing to show for it because I was unable to hold my tongue. At least, were I to be laid off, it would come with severance pay.

When I had calmed down, I took a deep breath and phoned my boss to inform him of my outburst. I started meekly to explain what had happened. He cut me off: "Paul", he said, "he already called me." My heart started throbbing again. He continued: "He asked me to remove you from the job." He paused, and I waited for the ax to fall. "I told him you were one of my best engineers and that you will remain on this project. And by the way, I've been told by others that he can be a jerk sometimes." Lord, I would have hugged him if we had been in the same room.

CHAPTER 33

Another Foray Into Energy Conservation

When I took over Long Island, I reported to a director based in Albany. He was enamored of seminars and he gave us the opportunity to attend plenty of them. He was not technologically inclined, nor did he wish to become so. Therefore the subject of these workshops was never technical.
I had attended plenty of seminars before reporting to him, among them: "Diversity and Sensivity Training", "Empowerment," "Sexual Harassment," and "Lead by Example."

"Empowerment" was a seminar intended to give us more responsibilities in the way we handled our work. Its mission statement was, "To instill in employees the will to realize their full potential through a variety of techniques designed to facilitate self-empowerment." Unfortunately, the thought of giving us more power did not last beyond the length of the seminar. As soon as it was over, we again found ourselves under the thumbs of our superiors.

To the seminars sponsored by the company, the director added "Coaching the Coaches", "Winning Ways", and the unforgettable "Don't Be a Victim." He also had a weakness for role-playing situations. We had to act in too many of them. Once, he had us put a red ball on our noses. It was a foam sphere with a slit in it. We all looked like a bunch of circus clowns in need of a birthday gig. I am not sure what the intended message was but it will really come handy some day!

Still, a few such seminars such as as "Coaching the Coaches" had made our relationship with contractors and customers smoother. Nonetheless, these workshops had no impact whatsoever on the quality of the projects. If a member of the group had no technical background before going through these seminars, she/he was still as ignorant at the end. She/he could not tell if a ductwork had been properly installed, nor could she/he make sure that the specifications had been adhered to. The Real Estate technical expertise had been slowly diluted. As seasoned employees left, an influx of marginally qualified individuals had been brought in at diverse levels. The generic manager was now reigning supreme and damn the quality of the work put out by the designers, the contractors and the construction managers.

I liked this director a lot. We had an excellent relationship and shared a common taste for foie gras accompanied by a slightly chilled bottle of Sauternes. We had dinner once at my home during one of his visits to Long Island and it was a marvelous evening.

He was now the head of a group whose goal was to implement energy conservation measures. This was not a new initiative. A thorough and highly professional manual on the subject had been released in the early 1980s, following the drastic increases in energy costs that resulted from the production cuts and an oil embargo against the United States by the oil cartel Organization of the Petroleum Exporting Countries, known as OPEC[1], in the mid-seventies. This comprehensive manual had been put together by experts who knew what they were writing about. Its recommendations were still relevant twenty years after it was written. I had been involved as a Subject Matter Expert in energy conservation in the early 1990s. I was a strong believer in its irrefutable positive impact on the good health of the environment. I had been a part of the green light program in the company, and had written an article published and distributed nationally in the trade magazine *Energy Users News*[2] .

---

1 In October 1973, the Organization of Arab Petroleum Exporting Countries (OAPEC, consisting of the Arab majority of OPEC plus Egypt and Syria) declared an oil embargo against the United States and other nations that supported Israel in the Yom Kippur War. The impact was a surge in oil prices and an emergency period of severe energy rationing in industrialized nations.
2 This article appears in Appendix 1.

In other words, in the area of energy conservation, all the low hanging fruits had already been reaped. Some a little higher were also picked, such as the use of the ground as a cooling agent.

So for a while this new energy team ambled over a well-trodden path. One of their first modest initiatives was to install posters urging the occupants to turn off the lights when they left a room. Cartoon characters emphasized the message from five-foot-high posters, one of them named Sparky. Really! For years, there had been little stickers next to the switch instructing the last person leaving the room to turn the lights off. It was somewhat successful, but relied on the last person to be responsible. To take the human element out of the equation, motion sensors were later installed. If no movement was detected after a preset time, let's say ten minutes, the lights turned off automatically. So, sorry Sparky, you were a little late to the party.

Another endeavor of this group was to hire outside consultants to perform energy surveys in buildings, and propose energy savings. Some consultants were good, others were borderline scam artists. There was a report about a building in my area that listed so many savings opportunities that when you added them all, these savings amounted to more than the building's actual energy bill. The best way to check the accuracy of these reports, for those who lacked the technical expertise to challenge their findings, was to ask the consultant: "Will you share a substantial portion of the savings rather than being paid up-front?" Even the better qualified ones declined this method of compensation. If proof was needed that these reports too often were full of empty promises, there it was.

Some recommendations were technical aberrations. One proposed to install a variable speed motor on the fan supplying air conditioned air to several rooms. This concept was known as a Variable Air Volume system (VAV). It permitted modulating the amount of air according to the needs of the occupants rather than supplying a constant air flow regardless of the time of day. In the morning, some rooms do not require as much cooling as in the afternoon, when the sun is at its peak. However, the consultant did not include any changes to be made on the duct work. To illustrate the fallacy of this incomplete concept, let's assume that you have three sprinklers watering your lawn installed on the same hose, one after the other. What happens if you turn the spigot to deliver only half of the water? Will each sprinkler spray only half its previous output? No, water follows the path of least resistance. It will flow through the first sprinkler as before, a little less through the second and the third one will be taking a rest. The same happens with a variable speed drive and the air outlets throughout the duct work. The closest ones to the fan will deliver the same amount of air as before, the subsequent ones a little less and the farthest ones will not see any air at all reaching them. What was missing in the report was that these air outlets must be modulated in sync with the fan in order for each to deliver the amount of reduced air flow. This is basic engineering. Some reports were so loaded with technical inconsistencies that they were useless.

There were still a few of us left, engineers with the knowledge required to perform these surveys, but we were all overburdened with more and more projects heaped upon our desks. The use of external help was therefore necessary. But the use of these consultants went beyond that, which left the distinct impression that some individuals in the company no longer believed in suggestions originating within the organization; they had to come from the outside and command a hefty fee to be given any credibility.

One of the problems with relying on consultants was that it is mostly an unregulated profession. A person who opens a nail salon needs a license. This is not the case for anyone or any outfit proclaiming to be management consultants. To reduce the amount of disreputable firms in it for the quick buck, or even the honest firm lacking the experience required to give sound advice, the individual signing the reports should be a State-licensed professional engineer and therefore liable for the report recommendations. At the very least, this should have been a minimum prerequisite to hiring an energy consultant.

Notwithstanding these faux pas, the group came up with a revolutionary and bold proposal. It involved the use of fuel cells to generate clean energy and supply it to the telephone buildings. Though the technology was not unknown - it had been used by NASA in its spatial experiments - it had not been exploited on a large scale. In fact, an exhaustive study had been performed by the Network group in Verizon. Its conclusions were unequivocal: Fuel cells were still too expensive to be of use in telephone installations with a decent payback time, which had been generally set at four years. So proposing such an endeavor was a daring move. The director showed unexpected audacity in his unflinching support for it.

He put Jon Chestnut, an outstanding young engineer from Pennsylvania, in charge of the project. Before we even knew of this venture, Jon did all the ground work. He dealt with fuel cell manufacturers, selected the most appropriate, and, more importantly, obtained several grants from diverse national and regional entities that would make this venture economically more palatable. It turned out to be the most difficult part, mostly because fuel cells were indeed very expensive. Without any outside monetary help, the project would not have seen the light of day. Against all odds, Jon obtained grants from several agencies, including NYSERDA; the New York State Energy Research and Development Authority; DOE; the Department of Energy, and a few others. The legwork expended in contacting these authorities, and meeting and convincing them had been Herculean in its breath.

But Jon succeeded. If anybody should get the full credit for the successful completion of this project, it is he.

CHAPTER 34

Fuel Cells

A fuel cell is an item of great complexity based, as often in technological advancements, on an idea of surprising simplicity. It is similar to a battery, like the one that allows you to start your car. Such a battery is self-contained, with all of its chemicals stored within. These chemicals react, producing electricity. When they lose their potency, the battery "goes dead". It can be recharged a few times but, eventually, it will have to be thrown away and replaced. In most fuel cells, natural gas continuously flows into the cell so it never "dies". As long as gas enters the cell, electricity goes out. The main constituent of natural gas is methane, composed of carbon and hydrogen.

A fuel cell is a thing of beauty. It does not pollute the atmosphere, emits nothing but heated water that can be recovered to drive absorption chillers or heat portions of a building. It is made of three components: a fuel processor, a fuel cell stack and a power converter.

- In the fuel processor, the hydrogen is extracted from the natural gas stream.
- In the fuel stack, the beating heart of the unit, hydrogen combines with the oxygen contained in the ambient air and the resulting chemical reaction produces a direct current.
- The power converter transforms the direct current into an alternative current.

Following the work performed by Jon Chestnut, not the least of it the acquisition of grants to make the project economically viable, the budget was approved. I wrote an estimate case for about $20,000,000. Once it was signed, the work could begin. A project manager was needed and the director, saying that he needed a solid guy to be in charge, selected me. Your confidence was an honor I am proud of, so thank you for taking a chance on me Rod Sluyter.

The next step was to put together a team. I included the property manager of, among other buildings, Zeckendorf, the building that had been chosen to receive the fuel cells. Since he would eventually be in charge of the operation and maintenance, his presence was essential. Don Nitsch, from the Power Group would take care of the electrical questions, and they proved to be many. Although I could handle a PC reasonably well, an expert was needed. Dan Malaszczyk, who was more savvy than

I regarding the capabilities of a computer, was involved in preparing presentations and reports.

The team was small, but I had no doubt that I would be a better team leader having them to rely on. Also, according to business lore "the difficulty of getting anything started increases with the square root of the number of people involved." In other words, the likelihood that a project will start rapidly and on firm footing is inversely proportional to the number of persons involved in the start-up team. This did not happen on the fuel cell project. As soon as the go-ahead was given, we were up and running.

Was it a little surprising that nobody else tried to insert himself in this small team? No, because we were taking a trip into uncharted territory, at the frontier of known technology. There was no play book to rely on. We needed to write it. A lot of stars would need to perfectly align for this endeavor to succeed. We did not fool ourselves; it was a project fraught with risk. The possibility of failure was indeed a likely outcome. Most people tend to take full credit for success. There were too many unknowns and consequently, many people stayed away from the hazy undertaking until the air became clearer. You could count on them to implant themselves in the project when the time came to take some credit if a successful outcome presented itself. So we were mostly left alone. That was fine with the team. Most of us had never been comfortable with the shackles too many supervisors can put on any enterprise. With no management nannies making us jump through hoops like circus seals, life was good. The less supervision, the better. And in the end, it worked!

The next step was to select an engineering firm for the preliminary design. As noted earlier, I had worked for a few of them. Now I was on the other side and I enjoyed it thoroughly. I chose an outfit located in midtown Manhattan, a firm which had already done some value engineering work for our department. During a few meetings, a sound approach was established. Soon, a design was reviewed and accepted. However, one aspect of the project that had not yet been explored was the associated operating and maintenance costs of the cells. I instructed the consulting firm to submit such a study. When it arrived, the project came to an abrupt halt. The costs of running the installation were prohibitive, mostly because a crucial part of the cell, the fuel stack, had to be replaced every four to five years at a cost of $300,000. Until this point, the project had been sold mostly on its savings and fast payback time. This was no longer a tenable position.

At this stage, most of us thought the project was dead, but thanks to a resilient new director, it was revived a few months later. Under an elegant change of scope, the project became a pilot plant that would be operated for only five years. Useful data about how fuel cells performed would be recorded and shared with various entities, including of course the ones which were financing part of the project. When parts of the cells would start to fail, the plant would be abandoned. The time limit would therefore avoid the cost of replacement of vital and expensive parts.

I tried to put aside some of the money allocated to dismantle the plant after its years of operation. My proposal was rejected. I could already imagine a graveyard of fuel cells rusting behind a chain link fence in a condemned area of the parking lot. What a disgraceful end it would be for such an enlightening project.

Anyway, this was in the future. Back to the present, for the construction phase, a Design and Construction firm was selected. Together, we went through the teething pains of a design on which plans and specifications could be based. Some of the most difficult problems to solve were how to wed the fuel cell electrical output with, on one side the commercial electrical grid from the Long Island Power Authority (LIPA), and on the other side the electrical system of the building itself, including the emergency generators that would kick on in the case of a commercial power blackout.

Faced at times with issues that appeared insoluble, it was difficult not to feel the coldness of the hole we would find ourselves in if things did not turn out the way they were supposed to. I must confess that some of the anxieties we faced were hard to ignore. Too often, as team leader, I wondered if this time, I had taken on more than I could manage. To have spent millions and have nothing to show for it would have been merely upsetting for some people, but for the team, it would have been the kiss of death. Particularly on the electrical side of the project, one would have needed a calculator to tally all the things that could have gone wrong. Without the know-how of Don Nitsch and his people in the Power Group, it is a probable good bet the project would not have succeeded.

Against all odds, the installation was completed successfully. Interference from above had been minimal. The only instance I can recall is that some higher-up had requested the design and construction documents to be reviewed by a team of lawyers. Why, since the administrative portion of the documents was similar to the one used on other projects? And as far as the technical section, what in God's name could they comment on? They were not engineers and probably would not know if they were looking at the drawings upside down. Unexpectedly they came back with some trivial comments on the administrative segments sprinkled with pinches of legal mumbo jumbo to give them an air of authenticity. To their credit, they had the decency to make no observation on the technical parts.

Several invoices where their time was billed at a healthy $650 an hour hit my desk. If you never really understood what lawyers did that was worth that kind of money, this little episode would have done nothing to alter your opinion. I approved these invoices with the feeling that, once again, the company had enriched some individuals with nothing concrete to show for it.

I have always been mesmerized by plants; by all their moving or static parts; by the whine of engines and pump motors pushing liquids through untold lengths of piping; by valves opening, closing or modulating flows in accordance with instructions that few individuals can understand; by the whooshing of fans forcing the air through ductwork. Engineers and technicians, we are part of a secret society that can comprehend the meaning of colored lights flashing on control panels, of needles shivering against the dials of instrumentation gauges, of the staccato of relays and switches and of arcane messages displayed on status screens. We also know that when it works as flawlessly as a Swiss watch, it is a kind of miracle, because so many things can go wrong and often do.

When the plant went into service, it purred like a satisfied cat. The elation of having created something cannot be readily explained. One just feels for a while like a wizard or a lesser god, but a deity nonetheless.

To celebrate the successful completion of the fuel cell plant, a ceremony was organized. Among those present were Ivan Seidenberg, Verizon's chairman and CEO. He was accompanied by a phalanx of subordinates. The press was also present in good numbers. All went well. It was a simple affair. No champagne bottles were hurled and broken against the hull of a fuel cell. With a few aptly chosen words, Mr. Seidenberg extolled the virtues of the project. His speech was well received. Then he again took his seat and one could tell that his mind had at that moment switched to other problems. When the director took the podium, he asked the project team to stand up. Its members were suddenly more numerous; tangential participants finally decided to come into the limelight now that the project was a success. Photographs were taken and a good time was had by all.

At this time, an introduction to the chairman and CEO is appropriate. Wikipedia tells us that he started his career in telecommunications as a cable splicer straight from high school. Inducted into the armed forces, he was wounded in Vietnam. He earned a bachelor's degree in mathematics from Lehman College, and an MBA from Pace University. He became head of NYNEX in 1994. He took a senior position at Bell Atlantic after that company merged with NYNEX. When Bell Atlantic morphed into Verizon, Mr. Seidenberg became sole CEO of the company. An interesting man indeed.

He was sometimes sighted in the cafeteria in the company's headquarters. I glimpsed him a couple of times, carrying his tray to a table to break bread with other employees whom he may or may not have known. When he appeared, one could sense a stillness taking over the area he walked into. There were whispers accompanied by quick jerky movement of the head to inform colleagues of his presence. Looks were openly curious; others artfully blasé or indifferent. Several employees were spellbound as if they were witnessing the Annunciation. One expected a few to approach him, kneel and kiss his ring. To paraphrase Churchill, he was however an enigma wrapped in a mystery. What happened to the splicer that was hired in 1966 at the entry-level salary of $76.50 a week[1] and rose to the position of Verizon's President and CEO with an annual compensation of $30.93 million in 2010[2]? This is a story that so far has not been told[3].

Now it was time to pay the piper. All the agencies that had provided funds for the project expected comprehensive and numerous reports. As we know too well, most bureaucratic organizations thrive on paper, even in this digital age. So many reports had to be written that we felt sorry for all the trees that had to be felled to fill untold numbers of pages. I am greatly indebted to Dan Malaszczyk for taking the data, photographs, charts that he was given and putting all of it together into these reports in an attractive and very professional manner. Without him, I would have been up the proverbial creek. The reports were well received, with very few requests to amend them. When they were all accepted, we could finally utter a sigh of relief and declare: Mission accomplished.

Later, the project was mentioned in several publications.

The US Department of Energy, Office of Science, published the following:

> Climate Change Fuel Cell Program
> SciTech Connect

---

1   Source: http://www.nydailynews.com
2   Source : https://www.forbes.com/lists/2010/12
3   As a matter of fact, in May 2018, Ivan Seidenberg' book "Verizon Untethered" was published.

Project Manager: Paul Belard
2006-09-21

Verizon is presently operating the largest Distributed Generation Fuel Cell project in the USA.

Situated on Long Island, NY, the power plant is composed of seven (7) fuel cells operating in parallel with the Utility grid from the Long Island Power Authority (LIPA). Each fuel cell has an output of 200 KW, for a total of 1.4 MW generated from the on-site plant. The remaining power to meet the facility demand is purchased from LIPA. The fuel cell plant is utilized as a co-generation system. A by-product of the fuel cell electric generation process is high temperature water. The heat content of this water is recovered from the fuel cells and used to drive two absorption chillers in the summer and a steam generator in the winter. Cost savings from the operations of the fuel cells are forecasted to be in excess of $250,000 per year. Annual NOx emissions reductions are equivalent to removing 1,020 motor vehicles from roadways. Further, approximately 5.45 million metric tons (5 million tons) of CO_2 per year will not be generated as a result of this clean power generation. The project was partially financed with grants from New York State Energy R&D and the Department of Energy.

In Verizon's Corporate Responsibility Report of 2005 entitled "Living Our Values", the project was listed in a lengthy article, accompanied by a flattering picture of

Jon Chestnut and myself. The write-up appears in Appendix 4.

We all waited for John Chestnut to get a promotion at the conclusion of the project. He deserved it. A few months after the project's completion, the company went to another one of its shedding periods. John was put on the "at risk" list. It meant he would be part of the next wave of lay offs. What a shocking way to reward him for the exceptional work he did on the fuel cell project. Without his dedication, his relentless stamina, his dogged resilience, the project would have been dead on arrival. Luckily, he found a position as a project engineer and deservedly got a new lease on his professional life with Verizon.

Our lives are chock-full of people we meet, with whom we travel on the same path a few hours or days or months. Then we never see them again. Jon was one of these individuals and it made me regret that I could not spend more time with him, get to know him better. People come and people go. One of the random happenstances that make life what it is. It is one of the small misfortunes of this life that this happens too often.

In 2007, almost three years after the project was completed, I got a call from one of the team members.

> "Hey Paul, I did not think you'd be that secretive.
> "What do you mean?"
> "I learned through the grapevine that the New York Chapter of the Association of Energy Engineers had

selected the fuel cell projects as one of their winners for 2007. There was a gala to celebrate the winners. What gives? Did you get this award and keep it to yourself? You were the project manager, no?"
"Oh, come on, you know me better than that! This is the first time I am hearing about it. Maybe Jon Chestnut got it. It would make sense, but he would have said so. Or his boss since rank has its privilege. Let me find out more."

I called Jon, then every team member. Not a single one had been informed of this award, nor invited to the ceremony. This was bizarre. Finally, we discovered the name of the winner. We were all stunned. Some of the most polite reactions:

> "Who is this guy? We have not heard of him or seen him during the entire project."
> "Why is he getting an award he doesn't deserve?"
> "Does this fella have any scruples or an ego the size of the Empire State Building?"
> "We did the goddamn work and the commemorative plaque is given to some dude who had not been involved at all in the project, do you get it?"
> "That's pretty slick, not doing anything, reaping the benefits and getting the glory, that's worse than plagiarizing, it's professional appropriation."

We all understood the need for some individuals to hog the limelight. Still, a simple e-mail stating that the award had been received on behalf of the Fuel Cell project team would have gone a long way to assuage the feeling of having been manipulated. It was, however, not the best time to make waves, so in the end we let it go.

As for me, yes, it was the company headquarters' chiller replacement *déjà vu* all over again; you do the work and somebody claims the sole credit. This time though, it was not because I failed to toot my own horn. Our project had been highjacked.

CHAPTER 35

Metaphor

Every once in awhile, the entire department was called to a meeting to review the health of the company, a "State of the Union" for Verizon, if you will. You need to understand that it was an era of information overload. We were constantly bombarded at any hour of the day by so many e-mails that these presentations were short on breaking news. If we were lucky, there was a PowerPoint presentation or a lecture backed up by slides. With the lights turned off, quite a few of us grabbed the opportunity for a little shuteye.

I thought of the remark Gertrude Stein[1] made early in

---

1   Gertrude Stein was an American novelist, poet, playwright, and art collector. She moved to Paris in 1903, and made France her home for the remainder of her life. She hosted a Paris salon, where the leading figures of modernism in literature and art, such as Pablo Picasso, Ernest Hemingway, F. Scott Fitzgerald, Sinclair Lewis, Henri Matisse among others would meet.

the 1900s: "Everybody gets so much information all day long that they lose their common sense." One can only imagine what she would have thought of the deluge of data we were inundated with every day? She was right about the fact that it leads to a lack of good judgment, as the following example will confirm. An idea that was floated during these reviews was as follows: Why not ask the project engineers to assume the role of the property managers for a few months and vice versa? The rationale was that if one member of one group was confronted with the difficulties of his counterpart in the other group, a better understanding of the problems they faced would be beneficial to both.

One of the first remarks raised by a participant was: "No disrespect for the property managers intended sir, but would you propose to an assembly of lawyers that they become paralegals; or to doctors that they should assume the role of registered nurses?" Another, with a more tongue in cheek approach" chimed in: "Why don't you suggest this idea to the football leagues, let the quarter back become kicker for a while and vice-versa."
In this age of generic managers, this asinine experiment may at some level have made sense. Since individuals do not have the required set of skills to execute efficiently the duties a position calls for, does it really matter where they are asked to exercise them? Thankfully, the proposal was soon forgotten.

During one of these meetings that often enough doubled as pep rallies, our director told us we were all in the same boat. He signaled to show a picture to illustrate his point. It was, yes you have it, a boat. It was a nice one too, but there, in a simple photograph, the metaphor of what we had been up against for the past few years was displayed in full view for all to see. The boat was covered with a tarpaulin. How many people can get into a boat protected by a tarp? None! Of course, a participant did not waste any time in pointing out this incongruity. As the room erupted with laughter, one member started to sing *Row, row your boat*. For the first time, our glib director was at a loss for words.

A colleague tapped me on the shoulder and asked me if I had read the book *Don't Forget to Sing in the Lifeboats*. Later on, he told me it was a book he thoroughly enjoyed because it was full of wise quotes, some very inspirational that could be applied to the situations we were finding ourselves in. The title came from a quote from the French philosopher Voltaire: "Life is a shipwreck but we must not forget to sing in the lifeboats."

At about the same time, a major crisis had developed. It seemed that funds attributed to one building had been used to correct some urgent deficiencies in another. It was an understandable move by a down-to-earth project manager with the interest of the company at heart. Monies had not been required in full on a project, so why not transfer a bit to another building in need of some?

From the reaction of our director, it seemed like a major

scandal had been perpetrated. An urgent conference call was set up and we were all taken to task. In the director's defense, moving funds from where they were initially allocated did not follow all accounting practices to the letter. However, should not preserving phone service trump them at times? Apparently not.

I was also mentioned during this epic conference call. It seems I allocated the funding required to resurface parts of a parking lot to the wrong accounts. I put them as Maintenance and Repair (M&R); the director insisted it should have been a Capital Improvement, thus subject to tax deductions. My answer was:

> "Had the entire parking lot been resurfaced, it would have been a capital improvement; however only portions of it were, so the work fell under the M&R category."

We agreed to disagree. Later, several auditors were at odds as to which account was the right one. Did I feel vindicated? Yes.

As a result of these accounting questions, audits across all departments took place. A legion of seasoned accountants descended and pored through drawings, invoices, and purchase orders. They came with the finality of a swarm of angry locusts assaulting a field of ripe grain. They had experience with numbers, company policies, accounting practices. Their manners were polite, calm and cool. One took over my own ergonomic chair, immediately establishing the pecking order. They asked many questions and answered none. They recorded their input on note pads. They leafed through project binders, asked more questions. They seemed impervious to fatigue. Meanwhile, I had to sit in a very uncomfortable chair and my rear-end was slipping slowly but surely from a butt-burn into a coma.

CHAPTER 36

Appraisals

At the end of every year, we had to go through the torment of the appraisal. During my first years, this appraisal was done by my supervisor without much direct input from me. He was in charge of a small group and was close enough to each member of his team to write knowingly about what we were doing. As workloads increased at all levels, that close contact between boss and subordinate was lost. With a supervisor located in Albany, 170 miles or so from my area, and with only intermittent interactions, what did he really know about my accomplishments? Every member of the Design and Construction group was in a similar situation. So before writing appraisals, our supervisors asked to be given an outline of our achievements, including our aspirations, and our negative points.

When I was in the Air Force as a second lieutenant, my captain had to give an evaluation about me to his superiors, probably to find out if I was a good prospect for being a permanent officer and a gentleman. We had had very few interactions, certainly not enough for him to develop a true assessment of my potential. So he asked me to tell him my skills and my shortcomings. I was twenty years old or so, what did I know of the ways of the world? So, trustingly I told him everything. When I saw my evaluation, he had written more or less verbatim what I had told him, except where he exaggerated my weaknesses. I guess he did not see me as Air Force material. He was right, I did not see myself as Air Force material either. Following orders to the letter has never been my strong suit.

Anyway, from that day on, if somebody asked me to assess my performance, stressing what my strengths and vulnerabilities were, I did not mention any weaknesses. Let them find out and tell me.

Eventually we were basically writing ninety percent of our own performance reviews. Besides the actual project results which could not be sugar coated, you can be pretty sure that everybody put themselves in the best light with tripe such as:

- Thank you for giving me the chance to develop my people skills, and work habits and to grow professionally.
- Your support allowed me to meet the challenges that arose in my projects with increased self-reliance, an unruffled attitude and "learning by doing".
- Your strong leadership made me a better and more

valuable team player, as well as an instrumental asset for your group and the company at large.

- Under your guidance, I learned to nuance my thinking and negotiate the customer's needs versus the budget available with more self-confidence.

I wonder if anybody went as far as saying: "You made me a better man." You may think I am exaggerating, so carefully read the following, which is part of an appraisal one of our peers proudly displayed for all to see.

> "I would like to take this opportunity to thank my manager *name withheld* and District Manager *name withheld* for giving (sic) the opportunity to work on challenging and interesting projects. I would also like to commend them on their support throughout this past year and for their guidance on some very difficult projects. I appreciate the confidence they placed in my ability and for allowing me to manage perhaps the most fast-track undertaking our department has been involved in the past few years. Additionally, I would like to thank them for recognizing my efforts and for documenting them accordingly in this performance evaluation. However despite a positive review, I express my concerns at this time given the impending transition within our department, I continue to be given the opportunity to develop my management skills and apply them to a challenging work load."

How's that for laying it on with a trowel! Who's to say

that the old adage "flattery will get you everywhere" may not have some truth behind it?

Just to show how one is perceived differently by various people, here are some comments on my appraisals by supervisors throughout the years:

- 1993: Paul needs to work on his oral communication skills. Paul can organizing (sic) his ideas and they are typically in logical order but he needs to slow down a bit when he is verbalizing his thoughts and ideas. If there is an area that Paul can work on it would be his decision-making capabilities.
- 1994: Due to his accent, it is difficult to understand him at times. Paul is a very good decision maker. He has the knowledge in project management and confidence in ones self (sic) to make these decisions.
- 1996: Though Paul is quiet and appears not enthused, he provides the direction to his suppliers and customers. He expresses his ideas and feelings unemotionally to groups that require motivation. Paul is low-key but is effective when working with his peers.
- 1997: Mr. Belard has very effective oral and written communication skills. I encourage Paul to be more patient and use more tact towards consultants and contractors who do not meet his expectations and towards customers with wishes that are unrealistic or well beyond what the budget would permit.
- 1998: His inter-office memos, Lotus notes, oral conversations are timely, and well presented. During my three weeks of absence, Paul acted on my behalf which he did very well.

I would be lying if some parts of this book were not self-serving. It is important to me to show that, while I do not hold a grudge against the company for my involuntary separation, it was not based on a dereliction of duty, but dictated by economic pressures.

One unforeseen consequence of these repetitive layoffs was the undeniable fact that being a good performer became a harder concept to quantify. Consider a group of employees: mathematically, only half of them can be in the top half when evaluation time comes. Since the appraisals had to fit the Bell curve, as the group became smaller, some members became underachievers not because of their performances, but simply because of statistics.

Two years before I was let go, I received an "on-the-spot" award for the work done on the fuel cell projects. It was backed by a check. The amount was enough to purchase one bag of groceries, but nonetheless, it was a nice gesture. To a thank you note addressed to my director, he replied: "You are very welcome & the spot award is my way of recognizing the effort and passion put into making this project successful. You deserve the recognition and words only go so far. Thanks again."

My last appraisal in 2007 read: "Paul has been a good contributor in delivering the capital program, especially FTTP[1] and administrative overlay on Long Island.

1   FTTP: Fiber to the Premises: It involved bringing an optical fiber via a distribution network from a central office all the way to the premises occupied by the subscriber.

He has good work ethic and is flexible on taking on assignments and prioritizing work. Paul manages his projects well and is self-motivated. I will look to Paul to take on additional responsibilities in 2008 and I expect him to be successful.

As we will see, 2008 turned out to be a little different!

CHAPTER 37

Rhode Island

The number of projects that kept coming in did not allow for a moment's respite. We were like Sisyphus pushing the boulder up the hill just to see it rolling down again when it reached the summit. No sooner was a project completed, two new ones were coming down.
As the projects multiplied, my supervision was done from a higher and higher altitude. In this rarefied atmosphere, it became more and more difficult to breathe and consequently, to operate efficiently. Thus, I relied increasingly on the designers and the contractors, entrusting them with more and more responsibilities. Isn't delegation an essential characteristic of a good executive?

What is crucial though is to surround yourself with competent people. This is why designers like Gary Shumway and Jim Nicolazzi, general contractors such as Smith McCord, Sugrue, Madad, Pinto & Teger, Mazzeo Electric and others where godsends. The fact that no deadlines were missed, that projects came within budget rests in large part on their professionalism, attention to detail, respect for a job well done, and years of experience acquired by working for the phone company. They were indispensable assets without whom I could not have accomplished my job. It was never truer than when another island was added to the one I already had.

In 2006, somebody thought I did not have enough work on Long Island, so Rhode Island was added to my territory. It was 1995 all over again. The local project manager had retired, voluntarily or not; who knew nowadays? His projects were handed to me without any passing of the baton. To put things in perspective, I was already responsible for Nassau and Suffolk Counties, each providing telephone service to a respective population of nearly 1,500,000 and 1,400,000 inhabitants. By comparison, the entire state of Rhode Island had a head count of only 1,000,000, which is 1,900,000 less than my former territory. Small in numbers, but also 300 miles away. Nevertheless, coming in cold was going to be a challenge.

I took it in stride though. No longer did I fool myself that my life was under my control. Like so many of you, I have been whipped, beaten, and bitten on several occasions. At work, we were at the mercy of the whims of a boss; in an airplane, our fate was in the hands of a pilot, in a train or subway, of an engineer. Setbacks and misfortune had been plenty. I could not say I got used to them, but they had hardened me and I had learned to cope with them without resentment. So, what is another trial by fire? Against all odds, this added assignment turned out to be very satisfying. I enjoyed the trips there. I drove early in the gloom of a new day to Orient Point in order to catch the ferry to New London. Once I adjusted to the rhythm of the engines, it was a smooth trip that was not conducive to getting any work done on the way. If the weather was good, a climb to the top level allowed a nice view of Long Island Sound, a leaden green in the wee hours of the morning turning into various shades of blue as the sun rose. It was indeed a soothing way to start the day. What a sheer pleasure it was to breathe the crisp salty air.

Later, sitting in a lounge chair, I could soak in the sun's rays, its light dancing on the crests of the waves, and watch fishing boats scurry along, leaving undulating and shriveling trails in their wake at times a blinding white. On occasion, I might see a water-skier with a rooster tail of shimmering froth behind him. From New London to Providence, the drive was equally pleasant, the straight road cutting a path across wooded rolling hills.

The Verizon crew were a nice bunch, professional and well aware of what their responsibilities entailed. They were instrumental in making this impromptu assignment an easy transition. I am grateful to have worked with such dedicated employees.
There was however a flip side to these trips. While I was away, nobody was there to pick up the slack in my absence. It had become par for the course for almost all of us. It was worse upon returning from vacation. As good as it was to go away to relieve the ever mounting pressure, the return was devastating. Desks were drowned in

a sea of paper, voice mail packed to capacity with phone calls. The e-mails numbered in the hundreds. By the time I had finished sifting through all that information, I had a splitting headache, and the stress would go back to pre-vacation levels.

Nevertheless, I arranged a few trips to Providence at the end of a few weeks. My wife came along and we spent the weekends visiting the state. Newport was, of course one, of the primary destinations. It has an interesting history, from being a major center of the slave trade in colonial America, to becoming by the turn of the century the summer playground of the robber barons*[1], those *nouveaux riches* with more money than taste. Did you know that sixty percent of slave-trading voyages launched from North America started in tiny Rhode Island? Some years it reached more than ninety percent? A great many of the ships sailed to and from Newport. The town was active in what was called at the time the "triangle trade". Sugar and molasses produced by slaves in the Caribbean were shipped to Rhode Island and distilled into rum, which was then carried to West Africa and exchanged for more slaves. We certainly did not know this when we entered this beautiful town for the first time. No mention was made of it in the sleek brochures at the tourist

---

1   The term robber baron derives from the Raubritter (robber knights), the medieval German lords who charged illegal tolls unauthorized by the Holy Roman Emperor on the roads crossing their lands and along the Rhine river — all without adding anything of value, but instead lining their pockets at the cost of the common good. Source: Wikipedia.

bureau.

They highlighted Newport's famous Jazz festival, its gentlemanly regattas and its assortment of imposing mansions.

Our little jaunts took us to the magnificent if ostentatious palaces dotting a stretch of coast line. The mansions were used only a few weeks a year, mainly for the purposes of partying and outshining their rich neighbors. It was difficult to reconcile this opulence with the hordes of workers who toiled long hours, all year round, for meager earnings, without any protection, living in squalid hovels. They were the ones who had allowed these unscrupulous magnates to amass untold fortunes. One cannot help but think of Balzac's famous words: *Behind every great fortune there is a crime*. These tycoons were not very different from the slave traders. They both made their fortunes at the expense of human misery.

Still we visited the grandest of these summer "cottages", *The Breakers*. Some smart people think Vanderbilt named it so because its construction left him almost broke, but it may assume this tycoon had a sense of humor.
America is a country with abundant resources, certainly enough to offer well-to-do lives to all its citizens. Instead, too often, these assets have been used by a minority of pillagers to accumulate riches so great that even in nine lifetimes, no deficit would be perceived.

Besides being ruthless and unprincipled, they were clever men. They knew that their reputation as greedy plunderers would not put them at the top of the Pantheon of great men. So they turned to philanthropy as a way to regain some dignity for posterity. By creating libraries, colleges, and museums, they hid their worst deeds and put a veneer of humanism on lives mostly devoid of concerns for basic human welfare.

CHAPTER 38

RIF

In the late 1970s, as a marketing manager for a French company that dealt with Eastern European Countries, I travelled to Romania several times. Ceaucescu was still in power and ruled his realm with an autocratic communist hand. He was still nine years or so away from being put against a wall with his wife and shot to death. The first time, as the jet plane arrived at the Bucharest airport, I was watching the earth getting closer as it descended. Soon after it touched down, a vehicle ran parallel to the plane, adjusting its speed to match that of the plane. It took me a while to notice that it was an armored car with twin machine guns pointed at us. When it stopped and the door to the stairs opened, the two barrels of the guns were squarely aimed at this opening. What was the reason for this display? Was it just the act of a megalomaniac displaying his unfettered power? It left me with an odd feeling, shared by my fellow passengers whose faces reflected the helplessness of a situation they had no control over. Obviously, they were not going to shoot anybody, but still the implied menace was hard to ignore.

Although there is no comparison between then and now, in late September 2008, for the first time I had a bad feeling about the rumor of a new wave of layoffs that was spreading through the company like a brush fire in Southern California. Through the grapevine, we heard that our direct superior would not be involved in the selection of the potential victims. It was a good thing for him. Who likes to be involved in that kind of Russian roulette? On the other hand, this was bad news for some of us. It meant that the ax would be handled by individuals who did not know us as he did. In addition, the worst part of the rampant chitchat was that past appraisals would not be taken into account. That was the clincher for me. If past performances were not part of the evaluation, what criteria were left? Being non-union employees, seniority became a liability instead of a shield. The salary was another millstone. I was close to the maximum of the "career band range," as it was called. I had been through several rounds of layoffs already and survived each of them. This time my vulnerability was all too evident. I was in the bull's eye of the corporate machine guns aimed at me. I knew I would not survive the hail of bullets.

I had never told my wife of the past Reductions in Force (RIF). Why worry her for no reason when it was likely that I would make it through untouched? This time, however, the vibes were ominous. When I told her the possibility, she took it rather calmly, gave me a hug and just told me to wait and see, saying: "We'll worry about it when it happens." Being of Italian ancestry she smiled and added: *Que sera sera*, "Whatever will be will be." Her attitude was a great comfort.

The official confirmation of the rumor that Verizon's tectonic plates were shifting again came early in October. The unfortunate employees would be notified of their status by the end of the month, and it was understood that they would leave the company by the close of November.

A cloak of melancholy hovered over the office. Everybody felt vulnerable to the whims of the ax man. Rumors and gossip were spreading faster than in a sewing circle; some downright scary; some hopeful. A few of us were more despondent than others, but somehow, the work continued to be done.

The last two weeks were rife with hearsay. To my immediate superior's credit, he kept me abreast of what trickled down from higher levels, confirming that things did not look too good for me. I would have welcomed a word from our director, just a simple confirmation that pressures from above were weighing heavily on his shoulders; that he had to make decisions that he abhorred. We all want to believe that people do things for the correct reasons. Unfortunately, more often than not, they do what is appropriate for them, not what is right. In good times, it may be self-interest, in bad ones, self-preservation. Or he simply did not care. As Lincoln said, true leaders "Will summon their better angels"; they are in the minority.

Once again, I thought about the advice my father gave me: "Keep everything in writing; do not be afraid to say "I don't know" or "I need help"; if you did something wrong, admit it, don't try to shift the consequence of your mistakes on others." And, although he did not usually quoted the Bible, he added "And a man's foes shall be they of his own household." In other words, be careful of the people you think you know.

My own guardian angel must have been otherwise occupied, for this time, he left me unprotected. On Thursday night, the last week of October, Rick, gave me a call at home confirming the worst. Although the official notification was to be done the next day, I greatly appreciated the fact that he passed along the news as soon as he got it, sparing me a sleepless night filled by unanswered speculations. My respect for him, already quite high, increased a few more notches. Rather sheepishly I told my wife that my open-ended oral contract with Verizon had reached its expiration date. Although this twist of fate was beyond my control, there is a certain humiliation attached to being cast away like an empty oyster shell. After all, it meant the end of my professional career; not a milestone one can put aside lightly. She took it in stride and hugged me tightly for a while. I think my wife has more mettle than I do. Her understanding helped. I had a good night's sleep as it turned out.

The next day, Rick came to my Huntington office and

handed me the ominous envelope. Since he was not involved in the selection process, he did not have to give me a long-winded explanation about how it came to pass. He just said he was sorry and that he would miss having me on his team. I believed him. I took the envelope while my heart kept its steady pace. Oddly I felt at peace. An inner contentment, if you will, washed over me. This envelope had been expected but the wait was over. Rick and I chatted for a while and that was it.

Later on, I got a call from our director, not of his own volition, but prompted by Rick. Now, if I had bet you my severance pay I would be given the heartfelt but unconvincing "It was such a gut-wrenching process, Paul; you cannot imagine how painful it was to go through these calls," I would have lost. In fact, I do not remember much of this conversation, not because the telephone connection was bad. His words just did not register in my brain. In any case, he did not start with trite semi-apologies. What I recall clearly is his mentioning the name of a colleague who had passed away a few months before after a losing a long fight with cancer. While I did not exactly grasp what he was saying, I assume that his message was that it was better to be laid off than to be laid to rest for eternity. How could one argue with this logic, crass as it was? Still, this approach left me dumbfounded. His tone being utterly empty of emotional concern belied his words of "comfort", if it is what they were. Obviously, he was not wracked with guilt. I cut him off quickly with a retort I thought clever at the time - something like "I hope you sleep well at night." Lame last words, no? Yes, pathetic even, but it was yet another confirmation about me: I was not very good at thinking quickly on my feet.

In a way, it was ironic. I was being laid off by a colleague that had been hired after me, who I had protected during the "Zeckendorf" false invoice fiasco, and who had climbed through the ranks to become a director at a young age. I considered him, wrongly, to be a friend, to the extent that a colleague that you see episodically in the context of company's activities can be one.

This would qualify as a friendly lay off, but there was nothing sentimental about it. It was more akin to the paradoxically named "friendly fire", in which front line soldiers are mistakenly but tragically killed by their own brethren in arms. There was not even an indifferent grumble of thanks for all the years I spent with the company, no "remember when?"; no allusion to the awards that had peppered my career; no congratulations for my achievements, which were not inconsequential. As a matter of fact, he had acknowledged quite a few himself in writing several times.

Still, I wish he had been more honest and just told me that he had to reduce his head count because the company was going through hard times, and that he was ordered to do so. We all knew what was going on; it would have been a valid explanation for me, totally acceptable. I would said that I understood. Honestly, I did not envy him having to make this decision. After all, upending lives, even for a while, would leave scars in any sane individual.

It was not exactly how I had envisioned my ultimate separation from Verizon. I was nonetheless old enough to know that, when the time to lay people off would come, somebody's bad fortune would be somebody else's good luck. The end of my career was not so far off anyway; if I had been asked to volunteer to save the jobs of fathers of young children, I would gladly have taken a step forward. Actually, one of my fellow employees was the head of a large family. He had seven kids. I envied him greatly; what was life worth without kids? What in this world could replace the blessed "grandparents" moments, when they visit with their own kids?

I would have welcomed the opportunity to save him, had he been at risk. In a way, it would have given some deeper meaning to my early departure from Verizon. Although people were asked to volunteer in other departments, it had not yet happened in Real Estate. The leaders of this department appeared to be the type that would conveniently bend in a strong wind and, as in the fable the oak and the reed, survive the strongest storms. Who can blame them?

During the day, as the news spread, I received countless calls. Some were stunned by the news, all expressed sympathy; they were heartfelt in their comments and I appreciated all of them.

For me, this turn of events had not been unexpected. This was not the case of the colleague in our department who shared my fate. He was dazed at being thrown under the bus by somebody he had worked with very closely. His relationship with our director had been more pronounced and closer than mine. Among other undertakings, they had worked long hard hours together in the West Street central office in the aftermath of September 11 and had forged strong bonds with the alleged promise of permanent employment. He really felt betrayed when he was discarded without warning and felt, and still does, extremely bitter. But that is his story to tell.

For a while, this colleague and I toyed with the idea of suing the company for age discrimination. We were after all the two oldest members of the team. When it appeared that I would be part of the new wave of sacrificial lambs to the altar of the bottom line, I had approached a lawyer who confirmed that indeed a case could be made. I believe my colleague was even a little older than I was. We were both in our mid-sixties, not far away from a deserved retirement if we had been left alone. However, suing the company would have meant that we would have to forfeit the severance, which was nothing to sneeze at. So, in the honored tradition of "one in the hand is worth two in the bush", we took the money. Cowardice, greed, incertitude as to the outcome of a lawsuit? A little of each probably. So we signed the separation form with all it entailed.

To return to the way we were let go, let's quote Maya Angelou: "People will forget what you said, people will forget what you did, but people will never forget how you made them feel."

CHAPTER 39

Last Month

The purpose of the month of November was to allow the "riffed" employees to search for another job. In normal times, one would immediately contact friends in other departments inside Verizon to try to find a position. In fairness to Verizon, this was a nice gesture. In other companies, you were told to stop at HR, usually on a Friday afternoon, spend a few minutes signing forms and maybe be granted an exit interview. Then, with an earnest or insincere goodbye and "good luck", you were on your way home to contemplate the rest of your life. Since I knew exactly what I was going to do with my new found freedom, it made me feel better.

If all my appraisals were to be believed, even when they were deftly massaged to fit the bell curve, I had been constantly an above average employee. Don't get me wrong, I was never in danger of being nominated for the Nobel Prize for Engineering, but I had been a smart engineer nonetheless. I stuck to what I wanted to be since I was a boy, an engineer. Lucky for me, I never had to stray too far away from this dream. This allowed me to get up every morning with a spark of excitement that was never extinguished, even when the paperwork became more time-consuming than the technical challenges.

From what I heard from my fellow workers, I was in a privileged minority. I felt sorry for all those employees that hated what they were doing. I rarely did during my entire career. Of course, luck was involved. Somehow I had avoided the typical shuffling bullshit that permeates so many organizations - that is, taking an employee who is very good at what he does and shipping him somewhere else where he will not be as efficient and content.

It happened to me only once in my career. At the time, I was working for Michelin Tire in France. Due to an internal struggle between managers, I was transferred from what I liked and was good at, i.e. the Research and Development group, to a department involved in Methodology. One of the activities, based on Taylor's division of work theory[1], consisted of observing workers at their post, analyzing their movements, timing them with a stop watch and coming up with better and simpler ways for them to perform the same task. It had been decried as a scientific system of "sweating" more work from laborers. I hated this position and was equally loathed by the workers.

---

1 Frederick Winslow Taylor (1856-1915) was an American mechanical engineer who sought to improve industrial efficiency. He recorded his findings in his book *The Principles of Scientific Management.*

I felt like a huckster, a stalker, a spy, a male Mata Hari! I loathed that job and I hated myself for doing it. After a few weeks, I handed in a letter of resignation and my wife and I decided to take our lives to the New World. Nothing of the sort happened to me at the Telephone Company, for which I am deeply grateful.

I always tried not to be political, staying away from intrigue and the good old boys' clique. In retrospect, this might have been a shortcoming. There is an old adage among managers: "Contacts trump competence!" Another version being: "It's not what you know, but who you know." There is no doubt that, as you climb the rungs of the corporate ladder, it becomes too often true. Attending a few golf outings, leaving a humble trail of divots behind me, telling raunchy jokes in some bar, cursing like a fish monger, drinking beer until I became either boisterous or sick, may well have earned me a couple of more years on the payroll.

On the other hand, I also knew and accepted that the company could use me at will and spit me out like a piece of bubblegum that had lost its sugary taste. In the end, that is what happened. However, I did not leave with a sour taste in my mouth. A corporation is not the Salvation Army. Its only goal is to earn profits, share them among the officers, the shareholders, and lastly the employees if there are any crumbs left. Forget the "We are a family" one so often hears. Some employees may fall in love with a company, but this feeling will never be reciprocated. Employees are merely cannon fodder for capitalism's guns. Once you accept this simple principle, everything turns out all right. One common error is to think one is indispensable. I'll repeat my father's aphorism: "The cemeteries are full of irreplaceable people!"

So, my dilemma was: Shall I go back to the office and use the tools offered me to look for a job? What purpose would it serve? Unfortunately, none! Every department had sprouted more holes than a rusted sieve. Through each one, people were being dropped left and right. There were simply no opportunities anywhere. Outside, with the economy in a meltdown mode, the situation was not much better. I debated what to do. Should I stay home and pretend to look for a job that was not there to be found while watching TV and enjoying undeserved afternoon naps? Should I spend the last few days away from my office, visiting former colleagues and friends across Long Island's Verizon buildings, shooting the breeze, taking a trip down memory lane? Should I go down to the Florida Keys for a few days to work on my tan?

The idea of going to the office with the intent of doing nothing but sharpening my skills at "Minesweeper", "Solitaire" and "Blackjack" crossed my mind too. Honestly, I felt a little concerned about going back. News of "riffed" employees traveled at lightning speed and everybody would know by now, I had become one of them. I knew colleagues would feel sorry for me. Still, at the same time, they'd be quite happy that it was me that was let go rather than them. I did not want pity, furtive peeks the way one looks at an accident from another lane of the expressway, or false tokens of sympathy. Also, would this month seem like a sentence to be served?

In the end, I decided the right thing to do was to continue working. My immediate supervisor had always been extremely fair to me. Leaving him in a lurch was out of the question. I was managing more than thirty-six projects when the termination papers were handed to me. It would have been easy to say "the hell with it" and let my replacement pick up the pieces the way I had to do when I was transferred to Long Island and Rhode Island. However, that was not how I had been raised. Acting that way would have been an insult to my parents, who always taught me to take the high road, and my own code of ethics. Moreover, I was still being paid by Verizon until the end of November. I therefore owed the company my expertise until the hour of the last day of the last month.

So the next Monday morning, I was at my desk at about seven. As usual, I was the first one in. I contemplated what had been my main office for the last fifteen years. I took in my map of Long Island that adorned the back wall, along with paper clippings of the great victory of France in the 2000 soccer World Cup, as well as its heartbreaking loss to a sneaky Italy in the finale, four years later. I lingered over the shelves sagging under the array of three-ring binders that contained the work of a decade and a half. I took in the plaques, the hunks of etched glass and other trinkets I had been awarded. It was a bittersweet moment.
Then I pushed the voice mail button and listened to

genuinely earnest messages as my computer churned to life. All were sorry to have heard this news; with some people, it's just words, but I could feel the empathy in these messages. Then I read the e-mails; all were equally wholehearted and I felt comforted by these displays of support. As colleagues trickled in, my desk became surrounded by well-wishers. Some thought I was either too honest or crazy to be there, maybe both. "Screw them!" was one of the more often cited epithets. The expletive topping the list started with the sixth letter of the alphabet, ended with the eleventh and was followed by "them". Short and to the point, but not my style.

One thing was sure; trusted and dedicated employees were becoming an endangered species. At this depletion rate, the department would soon be able to hold a staff meeting in a phone booth on Sixth Avenue (should there be any left in these days of the advent of cell phones). The morale was terrible and company loyalty at an all-time low. If one were to try to pinpoint when this ill-fated shift had begun, one might attribute it to the moment the Personnel Department became Human Resources. When employees are treated as commodities that you can buy in a store; when they become ballast that can be tossed off the corporate balloon every time Wall Street coughs or when profits drop a tad, is it surprising that their professional commitment would weaken? Loyalty is a two-way street; why would the employees remain devoted to a company that did not return it?

At any rate, I worked with my successor, Justin, who happened to be a great guy. Besides, he was also a talented engineer, always on an even keel, with a dry sense of humor and a walking pace of about one mile an hour. He always reminded me of a joke I heard long ago:

> One fellah is walking down the street; all of a sudden, he turns around and stomps on a snail. "Why in God's name did you do that?" asked a shocked passerby. "It was getting on my nerves," replied the snail killer, "it had been following me for the last two miles!"

So I cued Justin in on the workings of Long Island, took him around. He thanked me for showing him the ropes. I paid bills; I closed projects; I packed my things.

Now, Verizon must again be given its due. A security guard was not posted behind my back to follow my every move, checking whether I was raiding the supply cabinet, stealing erasers, filching paper clips, rubber bands or felt markers.

Nobody in uniform escorted me to the exit like a pariah. I am deeply grateful for this. I do not think I could have survived the humiliation. The separation, as far as Verizon was concerned, was not cold-hearted. At times, corporations must practice some form of triage that may go beyond logic in its choice of victims, but that is a pragmatic move dictated by the economic conditions. It was ruthless, more so in small companies where you were told Friday around quitting time that there would be no point in showing up Monday morning, unless you wanted to work for free!

Verizon was more tactful and generous. I believe that it was, in no small part, due to a powerful union. Yes, managers were not unionized, but the union's presence had created a healthy oversight within the entire company over a long period of time with its concern for employee rights. Indeed, some of the union's victories had spread to the non-union employees.
Of course in this new penny-pinching era, the retirement parties that had enlivened my first days at the phone company some twenty years before had fallen by the wayside. The only celebrations were with friends at local restaurants and they always picked up the tab.

Another way to feel better about a wrong is to pretend that it did not happen. A few weeks following my forced removal, I received this letter signed by Verizon's President.

> Dear Colleague,
>
> Congratulations on reaching this milestone in your career and thank you for your contributions to Verizon's current success.
>
> In the time you've worked for Verizon, your dedication to putting customers first has helped us provide excellent service and great communications experiences. As we look to the future, it's important that every Verizon employee comes to work every day

focused on winning in the marketplace - and doing it in the right way - by putting customers first ... acting with integrity ... treating people with respect ... raising our standards of performance…and being accountable to our customers and teammates.

That's the kind of company you have helped build. And that's the philosophy that will help Verizon continue on our path to being one of the great companies in America.

Please select a gift in appreciation for your service.

Thanks again for your commitment to Verizon,

Ivan Seidenberg

How is that for historical revisionism! I was no longer a reject, but one of a long line of dedicated employees who had been instrumental in making Verizon one of the great companies in America. In a way, I was pleased by this recognition.

The icing on the cake was a beautiful set of cookware that my wife selected from the gift catalogue, and has since put to good use.

CHAPTER 40

Dignity

On May 15, 1891, Pope Leo XIII issued an encyclical which addressed the condition of the working classes. Entitled *Rerum Novarum* (Latin for Of New Things), it was prompted by the appalling exploitation of the workers in Europe and North America at the end of the nineteenth century. Section 3 covered it in a direct and honest manner: "Hence, by degrees it has come to pass that working men have been surrendered, isolated and helpless, to the hardheartedness of employers and the greed of unchecked competition. The mischief has been increased by rapacious usury, which, although more than once condemned by the Church, is nevertheless, under a different guise, but with like injustice, still practiced by covetous and grasping men. To this must be added that the hiring of labor and the conduct of trade are concentrated in the hands of comparatively few; so that a small number of very rich men have been able to lay upon the teeming masses of the laboring poor a yoke little better than that of slavery itself."

Rerum Novarum, in the section pertaining to the Rights and Duties of Workers and Employers, urged employers to uphold workers' dignity: "Work is not a simple merchandise. In work must be recognized the human dignity of the worker."

These principles were reiterated in *Centesimus Annus* (Latin for "hundredth year"), an encyclical written by Pope John Paul II in 1991, on the hundredth anniversary of *Rerum Novarum*. It revisited the themes of exploitation and preservation of the dignity of the workers.

But like so many teachings of the Church, or the Bible, or any other religion, or common human decency for that matter, few are followed. It is nothing new; John Adams said: "Power always thinks… that it is doing God's service when it is violating all His laws."

No one has ever believed a corporation is a democracy. At best, it is a benevolent or paternalistic dictatorship, sometimes an indifferent one, and at worst, an exploitive one. A company is only the sum of all its people, so they are the ones who make it what it is. As it happens, the majority are good employees. It is a mirror image of the world at large where most people are decent, and problems are created by a minority. The actions of these bad apples do not necessarily reflect the company's policies, but they sometimes manage to sully the entire barrel.

There are some acts that should not be permitted. One of them is to strip a worker of her/his dignity as a human being. Even if causes are present to justify discipline, it should be carried out with professionalism and a reasonable amount of empathy. Unfortunately, there are some employees who, when placed in a position of power, tend to work out their shortcomings on the backs of others. Life for most people is simple, ordinary. It is filled with enough misfortunes without having the bitterness of strangers added to it. It is sadly true that, too often, someone will make life even more difficult, just to prove right Sartre's assertion that "Hell is the other people".[1]

One beautiful morning, a dear friend of mine was called to HR in the new company complex in Basking Ridge, New Jersey. We had worked together for a couple of years when I had been transferred to Long Island. During that time, she performed well, always in a professional manner, courteous and polite if somewhat outspoken. Her good performance was reflected in her annual appraisals. Shortly after her arrival in the HR office, she was told that she had been terminated.

Let's listen to the account of the ordeal this African-American friend went through:

> "I had just returned from vacation and was in my office in the company's headquarters on Sixth Avenue

---

[1] Jean-Paul Sartre was a French philosopher, playwright, novelist, political activist, biographer, and literary critic. He was one of the key figures in the philosophy of existentialism.

when my phone rang. It was a woman from HR; she asked me where I was. I told her in 1095. She told me I needed to come to HR in Basking Ridge at 10:00 a.m. the next morning. What is it in reference to, I asked? Her answer: "It's something we'll discuss when you get here." I did not think anything of it because, you know, being in charge of furniture, maybe somebody complained about some chairs or desks. When I got there, somebody came to get me and took me to an office. There were two persons in it. The HR lady, who was an African-American like me and a white lady who, I was told, was from Corporate Security. It dawned on me then that this meeting might not be good after all. The lady from HR started asking me how long I had been with the company, about my pay and who I reported to. I told her almost thirty years, gave her my salary, the name of my supervisor and director. Then she told me she was asking me these questions in connection with a letter they had received stating that I had called somebody a "nigger." I said: Excuse me, why would I call somebody that? I come from that era in the 60s. I traveled with my family down South. I saw the signs "White people only" and "Colored people." I do not know who said this to you, but this is not my style. I would never say that about anyone. I know that this word is a hurting word. She just pursued the same line: "Are you sure you didn't say that?" "Yes I'm sure." Can you picture me saying that to another black person? Do you know where I come from? I would not say that to anybody. Then she changed the subject, saying "Oh, and I see you are close to *name withheld*." "Yes, I admitted, he's a VP in Real Estate, a friend of mine, but an on-the-job type of friend." "Well, it seems you called him babe, you called him hon." "I sure do," I replied, "I call a lot of people that way."

"Yes, I remember you called me that too," I interjected.
"Yeah, sure, Paulie, as a matter of fact, that comes from my mother growing up. That's what she used to say to people "Hi babe, hi hon, how are you, sweetie". You know, I call people by their name, but if I feel close to that person, I will use these words. That's the way I was raised. So the HR lady, she continued, telling me that I had hugged that VP. I said that every time I saw him I hugged him, we knew each other well and we would do that. Well she said: "Be that as it may, we have to terminate you because of the ethics of it." This is when I exploded. I told her: "Let me tell you something, if this is what you think that I am, that I said that word, you do what you feel is best, but I tell you this is not over." "What do you mean?", she asked. "Just what I said, if you can't tell me who said it, I'm gonna find out. When desegregation in schools came, I was the first black girl in the fourth grade to go into a white school because before that, there were no black children allowed."

"I apologize for this interruption, but schools in Hempstead, New York, were segregated in the 50s? I thought it was only in the South those things happened."

"Oh no, it was here too. I remember an African-American teacher always on my case: You're not going to embarrass me, are you? She was the first black teacher hired in that school and I was the first black girl in the same school. So when the HR lady came at me with that BS, about me calling somebody the "N" word, I lost it because I knew then and there that it was a lie, a bold face lie. Who would say something like that was beyond me."

"Did you ask her who said that? Did she show you the letter?"
"Yes I did! She would not tell me, nor did she show the letter. So I left. By the way, you know Paulie, the security person did not say a word during the entire session. You know, as I said before, I did not know why they had called me. If I had, I would have asked my supervisor to come along. And what's worse, she had not been told either that I was fired."

"But this is not right, your supervisor should have been made aware of the situation. I do not think HR followed the rules."
"That's right, my boss said that had she been made aware, she would have met me in Basking Ridge, but they never, ever called her and she was baffled when she heard about it. I felt like I had been set up. I came back to 1095. Dominique, he was director at the time, had just called me about the termination. He said: "I do not know where they got that crap from. Normally, Security would walk you out of the building."

Dominic said: "I'm not going to let them do that."

So I got my stuff and he walked out of the building with me. He said to me that if there's anything that I needed, I should call him because that's a bunch of junk. Then he hugged me and it felt good. He was nice. That HR person, she thought I was going to bow down to her but I was not going to, no way. So I called Johnnie Cochran's office. Johnny defended O.J. Simpson, you remember. He had an office nearby on Broadway. He had passed away by then, but I explained my situation to somebody. They did not call me right away, but in the meantime a friend gave me the name of another attorney. I phoned him, told him my story and he asked me to come right away. What the lawyer said to me first was: "You want to be exonerated, have your name cleared, then go after them hard and we'll ask for damages." My mom and I agreed. I had worked at the phone company too long to leave under such a cloud. I could not put on a résumé that I worked thirty years and was terminated for saying the "N" word, come on Paul. I could not accept that. The lawyer added that Verizon was a big 500 company and sometimes, you fear going against them, to which I replied I'm not going to fear them at all, I want to sue them. OK, then, hopefully we can get a settlement without going to trial. After a couple of months of preparations, he presented the suit to Verizon. In addition to unjust termination, age discrimination was also included. Meanwhile, I had been in touch with *name withheld*. He was an officer on the thirty-ninth floor."

"He came from Bell Atlantic, right? We had a meeting with him when he arrived here. How did you know him so well?"

"Because of furniture. When we were redoing the floor, I met him, and Ivan Seidenberg, Verizon's CEO and all of those cats. I knew them very well. I was always around during the refurbishing, showing them catalogs of chairs, desks, posters, paintings, and they liked me. I think that made some people become jealous of me. I don't know why because it did not change me. I did not go around and brag: "Yeah, yeah, I know Ivan. Yeah, yeah, I know so and so." No, I was always straight up, I had a very good rapport with them but did not take advantage. The officer from Bell Atlantic and I became friends because his mother was sick and he was taking care of her. My mother was also living with me and it created a connection that became stronger with time. I guess we were sharing similar stories, that's all. I met his wife, his children. I talked with all the officers and maybe, somebody got envious of me and resentful."

"That letter accusing you that HR had allegedly received. Did the lawyer see it?"

"No, it was like it did not exist. I'm not surprised because I never said that word. I remember, you know, Paulie, my mind is all over the place, I remember getting into a fight when I was in fifth grade. This white girl was on the playground and some friends and I went in. She said to me: "What are you yard niggers doing here?" And, Paul, I asked her: "What you said?" And I remember wrapping her golden hair around my hand and dragging her and she skinned her knees. The principal called my mother and I was suspended for two days. That's because of her saying that word to me; that's a very hurtful word and that's what I was trying to tell the HR person. But she did not want to understand. That was unfair to me and it hurt me terribly. But you know, they let you go too."

"Yes, but it was different."
"Why did they lay you off?"

"Well, the company was not doing well. The director had been told to cut down on staff and I was a good candidate."
"He should have fought for you."

"No, he should not have and I would not have asked him. I was close to retirement, probably one of the oldest and highest paid in the group. I'd rather go than somebody younger with kids. I don't blame the director for picking me, I just thought he should have been more honest about the reasons, that's all. Anyway, that's another story. So how did it go after?"
"At one point my attorney told me: I can't continue calling people at Verizon, they all tell me the same thing. You're a good-hearted person, you would never say anything like that. I had put your name down, Paulie, but he did not get to you because at this point,

he was trying to find somebody who would have said anything negative about me.

"How long was the case?"
"It lasted about two years. In the end, Verizon called the lawyer to settle. The wrongful termination was wiped out from my record and a cash settlement was reached. I kept Verizon health care too. The age discrimination suit did not go anywhere because I was only fifty-four at the time. The HR person was disciplined and eventually she left Verizon on her own or not, I did not care to find out."

"Did they propose your return to the company?"
"Yes, but I said no, I did not want to have anything to do with them at all. Can you imagine me going back there after what they did to me? Also, everybody I knew had retired, quit or been let go. At the time, they were chopping heads left and right. So no, I would not go back. My name was cleared, it's really all I wanted. I found a good job where I am liked. When my mother got sick, they allowed me to work three days a week to take care of her. They are nice people. So I'm fine now."

An injustice had been perpetrated and I was glad that, in the end, this person who I am proud to call a friend was thoroughly vindicated. I never believed that she ever said that word. Her expressing ethnic slurs was about as credible as Martin Luther King exchanging Christmas cards with the grand wizard of the Klu Klux Klan.

This sad affair reminded me of a curious episode. On October 3, 1995, I was in the lobby of the Pearl Street Verizon Building. Located near the entrance to the Brooklyn Bridge, City Hall and Police Plaza, it was built in 1975. The stark and severe thirty-two story structure appears to be windowless but has three-foot-wide slits cut at regular intervals, some of which feature windows, running up the entire height of the building on the limestone façade. If its color had been black instead of white, it would look like a sinister dungeon. It has the dubious merit of having appeared on a *Daily Telegraph* list where it ranked 20th in a survey of "the ugliest buildings in the world."[2]

The reason for my presence was to retrofit some of the chillers to meet the new refrigerant codes required by the Montreal Protocol. That afternoon, a large group of employees was gathered in the lobby, watching a television mounted on a wall. They were waiting for the outcome of the O.J. Simpson trial. I did not really care. The verdict seemed to be a foregone conclusion. Still there was an anticipatory hush that had settled as the moment approached, so I joined the crowd. There was probably an equal number of white and African-American employees.

When the verdict was announced, Simpson was found,

---

[2] In September 2007 the building was sold. Verizon leased back floors 8 through 10 for its equipment. In late 2016, the building was renovated. The limestone walls on the upper stories were removed and replaced with plate glass panels to improve the building's appearance.

against all odds in my opinion, not guilty. Cries of joy erupted. It took me a while to discover they came exclusively from the African-American crowd. I thought why are they cheering a murderer going free? It was a strange scene, surreal in a way: One ethnic group was applauding the verdict in a jubilant manner, while the other, crestfallen, was confused by this display; I could not fathom what was happening. The racial lines were so clear it left me mystified. But should it have? Once the secretary of the department, an African-American, said to me, when I asked her if she thought Simpson was guilty of killing his wife, "She probably deserved it!"

Later, after some soul searching, this reaction became clear. This was their "Walk a mile in my shoes" moment. Their happy shouts translated into "Now you know how it feels to witness a miscarriage of justice". But was it a miscarriage of justice for them? Many believed that it was likely that Simpson was innocent and was framed-up by racist cops. In any case, for once, it was a black man involved in a notorious trial who was not convicted for alledgedly killing white people. Theirs was a reaction to four centuries of white men exonerated for murdering black people against all the evidence of their guilt. Who could blame them? Who has not seen pictures of lynchings treated as Saturday night entertainment, with white families cheering as they were munching on food sold by an opportunistic profiteer? A print I had seen came to mind. It depicts such a scene. A white mother is holding her daughter between her arms raised so that the young girl can see above a crowd. Unseen on this

print by the artist Reginald Marsh[3], one can imagine on the left a mob flinging a rope over a tree limb in the glow of torch lights; aren't the more depraved and cowardly deeds done in the cover of night?
This mother is proudly telling her neighbors: "This is her first lynching".

For African-Americans, decades of injustice and resentment had been erased. They had sustained appalling damages and it was difficult to bear them ill will while they celebrated, at last, a few glorious hours.

---

3   Reginald Marsh was an American printmaker and painter. He studied at the Arts Students League in New York under John Sloan and George Luks, both members of the Ashcan artistic movement.

CHAPTER 41

Some Final Numbers

The precarious state of employment of the first decade of the new century had not abated. The reduction-in-personnel occurrences had become as predictable as devastating hurricanes, and happened almost as often. In 2007, Verizon had 235,000 employees. In 2017, the number dropped to 155,400, a loss of almost 80,000 employees; the greatest plunges happening in 2010 and 2016.*[1] With an equivalent attrition rate, by 2027, the number of employees will hover around 80,000.

In ancient Greece, a hecatomb[2] was the sacrifice of one hundred bulls to the gods to celebrate some long forgotten event. Nowadays, in an ironic and poignant twist of fate, it is workers who are sacrificial victims to the caprices of

---

1   Source: https://www.statista.com/statistics/257304/number-of-employees-at-verizon
2   Hecatomb: hekaton = one hundred, bous = bull

the bull of Wall Street. According to rumors, the bloodshed may get much worse. Numbers are being thrown around, the goal of the company being eventually to distribute its workforce as 20 percent Verizon employees and 80 percent contractors.

This ratio is skewed even further in the Real Estate department. The Design and Construction department, which counted close to fifty engineers or architects when I was hired, is presently down to less than ten, the slack having been picked up by consultants. The property management department has been eradicated, and is now outsourced to various companies. Luckily, most Verizon property managers have been hired by these firms. By some accounts, they are being well treated.

Meanwhile, as the number of employees being let go escalated in most companies, a less overt phenomenon occurred to the CEO's brains. Apparently, the intelligence and expertise indispensable to run a company underwent a rate of evolution that would have astonished Darwin himself. There is no scientific evidence to back up this kind of miracle, only an economic one which is corroborated by their remuneration. From 1978 to 2013, the CEO compensation, inflation-adjusted, increased 937 percent. Over the same period of time, the average worker's salary increased only an embarrassingly low 10.2 percent.

The CEO to worker compensation ratio was 20 to 1 in 1965 and close to 30 to 1 in 1978. It grew to 122.6 to 1 in 1995 and reached 296 to 1 in 2013.[3]

---

[3] https://www.epi.org/publication/ceo-pay-continues-to-rise

Even more upsetting, the *New York Times* gave a few examples that will make you, if they do not leave you tongue-tied, ask: "How, in God's name did we get to this point?" One of the instances illustrated in the paper was about Time Warner, the famous media and entertainment conglomerate. In 2017, the average compensation for salaried employees was a little higher than $75,000 a year. Now, brace yourself: an employee earning that salary would have to work 651 years to receive the same compensation the CEO was awarded in 2017 which is a staggering $49 million.[4]

Some may take solace in James 5:1-3: "Go to now, ye rich men, weep and howl for your miseries that shall come upon you. Your riches are corrupted, and your garments are moth-eaten. Your gold and silver is cankered; and the rust of them shall be a witness against you, and shall eat your flesh as it were fire. Ye have heaped treasure together for the last days."

What drives these individuals to ask for such obscene and unprincipled amounts of money, far more than they can ever possibly spend in their lifetime? They are smart enough to know they are not going to take it to the great beyond. Greed is the most aggressive way to blur moral boundaries and overcome beliefs.

Yet, is it the only motive? Probably not. One reason often

---

4   The *New York Times*, Sunday, May 27, 2018.

advanced is that the compensation packages are competitive with that of other companies in Verizon's industry. In other words, "I want it because he has it."

But this tantrum-like behavior does not explain everything. Having it is not enough; in the rarefied atmosphere of their clannish group, one CEO needs more than the other. His/her ego or some kind of perverse peer pressure demands it. These captains of industry are caught up in a lofty competition with each other; their Olympic games if you will, where the gold medal is awarded to the recipient of the highest compensation. Unfortunately, these financial awards too often are not commensurate with accomplishments. Let's give the original robber barons their due: They were self-made men and their fortunes were tightly linked to their competence.

This is not the case for these diminished robber baronets. How much money, and land do they need? Tolstoy had the answer for one of them: *Six feet from his head to his heels was all he needed, that is enough to be buried in.* This is where they all end up and none will take his riches with him.

About some dubious accomplishment, Warren E. Buffett, the chief executive of Berkshire Hathaway, commented:

"Too often, executive compensation in the U.S. is ridiculously out of line with performance. The upshot is that a mediocre-or-worse CEO, aided by his handpicked VP of human relations and a consultant from the ever-accommodating firm of Ratchet, Ratchet & Bingo, all too often receives gobs of money from an ill-designed compensation arrangement." These compensations, as grandiose as they are indecent, have led others to comment on their impact on society.

Frederick E. Rowe Jr., Chairman of the Texas Pension Review Board said: "Everybody should have an interest in controlling this explosion in executive pay. The wealth of America has been built through the returns of our public corporations, and if those returns are being redirected to company management, then the people who get the short end of the stick are the people who hope to retire some day."[5]

---

5   Source: https://www.nytimes.com/2006/04/10

Epilogue

Now, the end of this story has been reached. It would be a lie if I said I had not had twenty very good years at Verizon, aka Bell Atlantic, aka NYNEX, aka New York Telephone. They were challenging, enriching, fulfilling. If at times, some were bordering on the absurd, they were nonetheless rewarding years. I never considered myself a genius, but by all accounts I had been a good engineer. I knew my worth. It had been written in black on white on all those yearly appraisals. As the years passed, I got better at my chosen career. I applied myself fully to the tasks that came my way, sometimes with an independent streak, bending some rules, not breaking them, just to spice things up and make them more interesting. Also, because when you reach a certain age, the sourest of all feelings is regret: "Why did I not do this when I had the chance?" This allowed me to get up every morning with a spark of excitement that was never extinguished. Like for too many, my professional life had not been as irrelevant as a flag on a windless day. I had avoided the concern of Thoreau, that "The mass of men lead lives of quiet desperation, and go to the grave with the song still in them."

All in all, I am proud of those years. My job was to protect the interests of the company. I achieved that and, if in the end, I was not exactly rewarded for it, the company had been very good to me until it was not. What remains true is that one bad day does not erase more than seven thousand mostly satisfying ones.

I also left with the respect of the people who mattered most. It was shown by the attitude of my colleagues, designers and contractors who had worked with me through countless projects. One way to know if you have been a good person is to count how many individuals will be present to thank you when you leave and are no longer of any use to them. I received many testimonials of the esteem in which I was held during several celebrations. At one of these farewell parties, I was offered the rare pleasure of sipping on a heavenly old Cognac worth $180 a glass. Just warming it in the palm of my hand, sniffing its heady and rich bouquet was enough to make me half tipsy. It would have been a waste to drink it in one sitting. This was the first and last time I asked for a "doggy bag" for a glass of brandy.

My last day was a Friday. The following Monday, I was ready to start my new life. When I met my future wife, Dorothy, my world went from black and white to magnificent technicolor. Not to the same extent, mind you, the same feeling of unfettered possibilities now washed over me.

Regrets? None! The Greeks had two words for time. The first was "chronos", the personification of linear and measured time that can be associated with a work schedule. The second was "kairos" and it applies to a special time that is chosen rather than imposed. I had entered my "kairos" phase. I was born again, free to do things that gave me as much pleasure as engineering work had, without the constraints associated with it. It would become more gratifying because there would be no living wage attached, no schedule to meet, and no boss to report to.

My exit strategy from my professional life had been planned for a long time. First it was getting a dog. It is unfair to leave a dog alone all day, so I waited until I retired to get one. At *Little Shelter*, an adoption center in Huntington, I looked at all these rescued caged animals. They were well treated, clean. Most of them looked at you with hope in their eyes: "Please take me, I'll be good" they implored. I would have taken half of them, but of course, it was not possible. Also, I had to convince my wife. A dog had bitten her when she was a child; she had not forgotten. So for her, one was already too much. Thankfully she relented. I wandered through the beautifully kept shelter and set my eyes on a Beagle who looked fairly happy in a cage he shared with a smaller one. His story was simple: Homer, around eight or nine years old, had been a hunting dog somewhere in West Virginia. He was discarded when he became half blind. *Little Shelter* had saved him from a kill center before his planned execution. He had been at the center for months, ready to be sent to a farm upstate where he would spend the rest of his life. Nobody wanted to adopt him because he was too old. "Come with me," I told him, "we'll get old together."

I have an immense respect for the written word and believe that without books, we would still be living in caves or huts. As Pablo Neruda wrote: "Dies slowly he or she who does not read a book." My love of books began when I was a boy. It never wavered. Once, in Paris, I did not know what to do in the evening (yes, I know, really in Paris!) so I took a course in bookbinding. It is a dying art in America where, all too often, working with your hands is wrongly seen as a lowly activity reserved for underachievers. I have more respect for a good plumber than a hedge fund manager.

My skills have become known, and I have been restoring and binding books for quite a while. Together, with a computer savvy friend, I developed a website that provides me with a stream of just enough work not to get bored.

I always wanted to teach. Maybe "teach" is not the right word. What I really aspired to was to pass along what I myself had learned. When I was working as a consulting engineer in New York before joining the phone company, I had taken a young technician under my wing. I became his mentor. When I left the firm, the usual platitudes, such as "it was a pleasure to work with you", "you're an all right guy" and so on were uttered. Most were just words, but this young man asked, "Who's going to teach me now?" I found myself more touched by his honest plea than by any of those clichéd expressions. It stayed with me like an unfulfilled promise.

I gave several talks on the subject of bookbinding and restoration at Long Island University's Brookville campus and at other universities in Brooklyn and Stonybrook. For a while, I taught book restoration at LIU Post.

It was a great kick to be addressed as "Professor." I also started writing. The first books were memoirs, then I moved on to fiction, art books and a photographic biography of Elvis Presley's career. I now have five books published in France and eleven in the United States.

My greatest achievement though is having become a real teacher. On December 6, 2014, as part of a segment called "Act 2", *Newsday* published a three-page feature about my craft, with color photos. A few days later, I got a call from Linda Dickman, the librarian at Norwood Avenue Elementary School in Northport. She is a dedicated teacher and an inspiration to many of her young students.

A group of enterprising youngsters had banded together to create "The Book Doctors". Their aim was to fix damaged books in their library. She asked me if I would be willing to come to give them a little presentation. I went. I love libraries. They are secular cathedrals of knowledge. Learning is venerated there. In this beautiful room, I met a group of ten-year-old kids. They believed in education, erudition and the unlimited power of reading. Answering their pointed questions was an experience I had never quite faced before. Their enthusiasm, eagerness to discover and absorb was amazing, and I must admit, contagious. Their first attempts were tentative, but they displayed them with unconcealed pride. They were like explorers relying on imprecise maps but determined to reach their elusive goal. From the moment I met them, I wanted to be a part of their undertaking, become a kind of guide.

Since their skills relied a little too much on *Scotch* tape, I volunteered my services. The school accepted. For the past five years, I have passed along parts of my craft as a book restorer to these motivated kids. The hours I spend there with them are by far the best ones of the week. Really, what is not to like? Their unaffected enthusiasm, their genuine trust, their uncomplicated happiness, their down-to-earth questions, the way their eyes light up when they have brought a book back to life, their laughs and giggles as pure as the tinkling of the bells of a sauntering flock of lambs. Is there a more beautiful sound on earth than a child's laughter?

I have found Thoreau's song. These wonderful kids, without even knowing it, give us the impossible gifts, a little bit of our own youth and the precious opportunity to leave something behind. Lord, how I cherish these moments. When asked why they want to become a book doctor, they say:

- I don't like to see a book hurt!
- No book shall ever die!
- It's fun to help a book in need.
- I do not want books to go to waste.

It makes it all worthwhile.

Acknowledgements

In my first book in English, I mentioned that at the end of the play *Cyrano de Bergerac*, the hero confesses: "I did not climb too high, maybe, but I did it all by myself." Was he entirely right? Wasn't he raised by parents? Wasn't he educated by teachers? Wasn't he helped by friends?
Who can claim to have reached his goals without any help while not stretching the truth? I certainly cannot.
Without the help of many, this book would be but an idea. I want to thank those who made it a reality.

First and foremost, my wife Dorothy, who read, corrected, suggested, re-read; in brief, my most trusted advisor.

A *très grand merci* goes to Jackie Marks, a friend who gave much of her time to review the book.

To all my friends and colleagues at Verizon who refreshed my sometimes hazy memory and contributed their own experiences.

Appendix I.

ENERGY USER NEWS
NEWS FOR BUILDING MANAGERS AND ENGINEERS
Vol. 19, No. 1. January 1994.

N. Y. Phone Company's Energy Program Focuses on Employee Behavior
By PAUL BELARD, P.E.

Paul Belard is a project manager at New York Telephone, where he is responsible for implementing design and construction activities. He is also a member of New York Telephone's energy team, which was created to reduce the company's energy consumption.

Since 1991 New York Telephone has embarked on an aggressive energy conservation program to reduce its energy expenses, which presently exceed $100 million per year. The energy crisis of the 1970's raised the company's energy consciousness, but energy conservation somehow had a poor image. The key word at the time was "conservation." It connoted sacrifice: lower the thermostat in winter and put a sweater on; raise the thermostat in the summer and sweat a little; de-lamp light fixtures at the expense of lighting levels. Savings were very often made at the expense of quality. In the 1980's, energy conservation efforts fell by the wayside.

However, the attitude of upper management toward energy issues has changed dramatically in the past two years. Under the leadership of John Colarco, director of operations, a special group called Product Management was created; its responsibilities include energy and environmental issues. This represents a sweeping commitment to save energy and improve the environment.

With top management's support, a full-scale program has been put in place to change employees behavior. This group acts as a think tank to define strategies and guidelines, set objectives, and educate and lend support to technical groups that implement energy management programs.

The Green Lights Program

A good illustration of the group's activities is its implementation of the U. S. Environmental Protection Agency's (EPA) Green Lights program, which encourages users to adopt energy efficient lighting as means of reducing energy costs and preventing air pollution. The program has clearly shown that energy efficiency inside a building has important consequences for the quality of the air outside the building.

In 1991 New York Telephone and its parent company, NYNEX, signed an agreement with the EPA to retrofit 90 percent of its building square footage with efficient lighting. Since New York Telephone owns or lease approximately 20 million square feet, replacing the lights was a major project. Under the direction of a Product Management group member, a team of engineers was put together. Each engineer was responsible for a geographical area and determined which buildings were candidates for retrofits, established costs and schedules for implementation, contacted the local utilities for rebate, and estimated potential savings.

In the course of this project 355 buildings will be retrofitted. Estimated savings amount to $3 million a year, with an average payback of less than three years.

Building Systems

In addition to the Green Lights implementation group there is a building system group that looks at other ways to save energy. It considers a wide array of well-known energy savings measures, such as replacing existing motors with high efficiency units, installing low leakage outside air dampers, and tightening operations and maintenance measures.

In addition to these traditional measures, new technologies are also evaluated and incorporated in building systems. For example, gas-fired chillers are now installed at several locations; an added benefit of these units is the absence of CFC's in the refrigeration process.

Variable air volume and variable speed systems are also incorporated in new designs. Liquid pressure amplification technology is presently evaluated to measure its effect on the efficiency of refrigeration systems. All these energy-efficient systems are eligible for utility rebates.

In 1994 each building will be allocated an annual energy budget. For example, an equipment building operating 24 hours per day, seven days a week, will have an annual energy budget of 125,000 BTU per square foot. It will be the responsibility of the building manager to ensure that all energy conservation measures are taken to meet this goal.

Economic pressures to reduce building operating expenses are also challenging the traditional control systems of HVAC systems. The advent of solid state electronic control devices and powerful personal computers have led to dramatic advances in energy management and control systems. By incorporating direct digital control, the capacity and flexibility of energy management and control systems have been greatly enhanced , particularly in the area of remote operation.

With this in mind, a centralized control center is being deployed. It will be configured as a 24 hours per day, seven days a week operation that provides New York Telephone with a means of constant surveillance of key buildings and helps make effective use of plant systems and personnel.

Through direct digital control technology, energy management and control systems can be programmed for customized control of HVAC, lighting, fire protection, and security systems. They can also optimize energy management routines such as electrical peak demand limiting, chilled water and hot water reset, economizer cycles, duty cycling, and night setback. by using direct digital control, an energy management and control system can integrate automatic temperature control functions with energy management functions to ensure that HVAC systems operate in tandem for greater energy savings.

The Product Management group is actively involved with field engineers in developing the implementation strategies. Since it can be difficult to justify removing an existing functioning control system to replace it with direct digital control equipment solely for energy conservation purposes, the group is closely looking at which buildings should be retrofitted first for the maximum savings.

Since the hardware configuration varies from manufacturers to manufacturers, the Product Management group is also evaluating this aspect, trying to retain a flexible and efficient system while maintaining competitive bidding.

By 1997, the current plan calls for approximately 100 buildings to be monitored and anticipated savings in the range of 5 millions.

During the last quarter of 1991, an energy awareness campaign was developed. Technical personnel involved in the operation of buildings attended seminars that left them with a better understanding of energy management and with an added knowledge that has them better prepared to implement energy-savings measures.

All employees were informed of the campaign via company publications. Energy saving tips were listed to allow each employee to participate. Cornell University was also involved in several seminars given to employees.

A new and wider campaign is now underway. It will include video highlighting the benefits of energy conservation and illustrate how personal contributions make a difference; a media campaign to publicize the importance of conserving energy; and the creation of local interdepartmental energy teams trained to perform energy audits.

A continuing increase in both demand and price of energy is projected and energy costs will become a larger part of the costs of doing business. Those who can manage their energy consumption will gain a competitive advantage. The New York Telephone energy management program is already yielding financial and environmental results. This can be attributed to a clear sense of purpose and direction that may have been lacking in the 1970s. New York Telephone will continue to take a proactive attitude to reduce costs on a permanent basis It will be one of the necessities of doing business.

Appendix II.

Date: 9/29/94
To: Paul Belard
From: Rose Andrews

Here is the copy submitted for NYNEX NEWS. Regards, Rose.

Putting Long Island on the Map

Paul Belard says that painting is in his blood. His father, a native Frenchman, painted landscapes in the Auvergne country side of France. His sisters continue to paint in France. Now, this NYNEX project engineer in Brooklyn, NY, does watercolor painting in his basement art studio. Belard also enjoys living on Long Island, which has been his home since he left France 16 years ago. So when an opportunity arose to merge Belard's passion for art with his love of Long Island, well you get the picture of what happened.

"About a year ago I was visiting a local framing shop I use in Northport, when the shop owner pulled me aside and showed me a pictorial map of Long Island. I was amazed to learn it was created in 1935, and that no other one had been made since then," recalled Belard.

As it turned out, creating a pictorial map was the ideal assigment for Belard, whose engineering background provided the drafting skills necessary for designing the map. Belard said the project also gave him the opportunity to learn more about Long Island, both in terms of its resources, its history, and its landmarks. "I borrowed stacks of books on Long Island from the library," he said. "My wife and I did a lot of driving around Long Island, and she took plenty of photos."

In addition to determining which land mark to include on the map, Belard was challenged in simply fitting it all in. "I painted the map true to scale, rather than painting each section separately and photographically fitting them together for the final version," he explained. "Particularly towards the end, it got a little tricky trying to find space for everything and having only one shot to paint it correctly."

But correct it is. Belard's creation, a 22" x 30" poster, is a soulful refreshing rendition of Long Island, with colorful inset paintings of such landmarks as Sagamore Hill, Old Westbury Gardens, the fishing boats at anchor on the South Shore at Freeport and the Burial Headstone for the last Matinecock Indian in Douglaston. The map offers a wealth of information about Long Island's history, both in words and in pictures, and is framed by the official seals of Long Island's towns and counties. "The dea for adding the seals originates from France," Belard noted. "In France the coats of arms of the provinces are often included on maps." Of course artists get to be a bit parochial too. Only one high school seal is included on the map: Harborfields High School. "My son goes there," Belard explained with a smile.

In addition to his gift of painting, Belard brought with him from France a skill rarely found in the U.S.: He is an experienced book binder. "I take old books that are worn badly and broken down, and I revive them," he explained. "In fact, the worse condition the book is, the more of a challenge, and I like challenges." Using special tools and a time intensive manual process, Belard repairs old leather-bound books, Bibles and albums. Author Pat Conroy praised Belard for rebinding his first edition copy of his best-seller "The Prince of Tides." Belard also created a special binding for an anthology, prepared by a group of Long Island poets, commemorating President Clinton' inauguration. The book now rests in the Presidential Library in Washington D.C.

Whether it's a painting, a pictorial map, or a restored book, Belard said he relishes his role as a creator. Said Belard, " For me the thrill is knowing that somewhere out there, perhaps hanging in someone's living room - even if I don't know them - rests a piece of my art. That means that I've touched them. As an artist that brings real satisfaction."

Appendix III.

Farewell Gary

Date: 8/8/2017
To: All
From: Paul Belard

I met Gary sometime around 1992 in the Brooklyn Livingston Street office, both of us working for the phone company. Occasionally, we would walk back to the LIRR together to catch a train at Flatbush Avenue. We exchanged a few words, but it did not go much beyond that. In 1994 one of the offers to leave the company that popped up with too much regularity appeared again. He took it, and went to work for WFC. I was transferred to Long Island in 1996, and this is when we went from colleagues to friends.

Never in my career have I met somebody that was as dedicated to his work as he was. To say he was a workaholic does not diminish him in any way, and his stamina was certainly a plus for WFC and the phone company. You could call his office as late as 8:00 p.m. on week nights or on Saturday mornings, and he would always pick up the phone. He was the exemplary employee, with no personal agenda; his only ambition to do what he did best better.

When we started to work together, WFC had but a small nucleus of employees working on company projects: I recall W. Collins, Patti Shimkus, Nick Demaso (another former telephone company employee) and Gary. Gary, by his dedication, his long hours, his professionalism, put WFC on the phone company map. When I was asked why my projects were always on schedule and with a minimum of change orders, my explanation was brief: Gary Shumway handled them! Little by little, his reputation spread. Selfishly, I had to share him with my NYC colleagues. Though his workload expanded, he never let me down. There was a time of crisis during the frantic collocation years when we had to provide space for competitors in our central offices. Despite the somewhat unrealistic schedules, once again, no deadlines were missed. A large part of the credit rested on Gary's shoulders. Without him, my work would have been much, much harder. Without him, WFC would not have grown as it did. Almost every employee of WFC and its offshoot companies owes an enormous debt of gratitude to him. He was indeed a creator of jobs, and in his own way, left the world a better place. His allegiance to the phone company never wavered. In fact, to say that he was more loyal to the company than the company is now to itself, is not an overstatement.

He will be missed. I miss him. We had lunch occasionally these past few years. I told him about my retirement activities. He told me about his family and his latest projects. Retirement was not a word that was part of his vocabulary! However, it was not hard to see his frustration with the changes that were taking place at the phone company.

I can still picture him arriving at meetings with his attaché-case in one hand and a roll of drawings under one arm. I still see him grab a bundle of pencil stubs held by a rubber band, and that thought endears him to me again. I too like to use a pencil until you can barely hold it in your fingers. Call us thrifty, but waste not, want not! This was reflected in his work; no padding in his projects, no gold plating to increase the fees, just an efficient approach devoid of greed. Never did I hear him say a bad word about anyone. He was a gentleman in the purest sense of the word. He will always remain an example to me and I consider myself a better person for having known him.

It is not stating a lie to say that at times we live in an unfair world. None of us is immune to its wrongs. Gary left too soon, and in a way that should have been more in tune with his life. He should have left us working at his desk on the CAD or doing a punch list.

Farewell Gary.

Appendix IV.

000000
JOHN SAMPLE
1234 MAIN ST.
ANYTOWN USA 56789

October, 2012

Dear Mr. SAMPLE:

I am writing to inform you about a change we are making regarding the funding and payment of your monthly pension benefit from the Verizon Management Pension Plan. This change will not affect the amount of your monthly pension benefit or the amount of any benefits that may be available to your beneficiaries. Beginning with the transfer of about $8 billion in cash and pension assets to The Prudential Insurance Company of America ("Prudential") in December, 2012, Prudential will assume the responsibility for your pension benefit.

Today, your monthly pension benefit is being paid out of the assets in the Verizon pension trust. In December 2012, responsibility for your monthly pension benefit will transfer to Prudential and payments will no longer be made from the Verizon pension trust. Your payments will continue to be processed by Wells Fargo Bank until June 30, 2013. Beginning July 1, 2013, Prudential will be issuing your monthly pension benefit payments.

Key Facts About the Transfer of Your Verizon Pension

- **The amount of your monthly pension benefit does not change.**
- Your monthly pension benefit continues to be paid on the same dates each month as it is now.
- The pension transfer does not affect your eligibility for and participation in any other Verizon retiree benefits.
- The amount of survivor benefits you selected when you began receiving payments does not change.
- On July 1, 2013, the issuer of your check or direct deposit will change from Wells Fargo Bank to Prudential. You will be notified in advance of this change taking place.
- When Prudential takes over responsibility from Verizon, your pension will be protected by the state guaranty fund within your state (as described in the enclosed document titled **Special Information Regarding Annuity**).
- The pension transfer will happen automatically – you do not need to take any action.

You may be wondering why Verizon has made this decision. Over the years, Verizon has become a money-manager for about $24 billion in funds to pay our pension holders. Managing the pension trust is a complex and expensive obligation that Verizon believes can best be managed outside of Verizon to ensure future obligations are met. Ensuring the timely and safe payment of monthly annuities is the core business of Prudential. This move will allow Verizon to ensure that the pension obligation remains in safe and trusted hands, while allowing Verizon to better focus on its core mission of providing the best communications network around the world.

Let me assure you that this decision was made after careful consideration and a thorough review of both our funding obligations and what is legally permissible under the terms of the Plan. Moreover, Verizon has determined that Prudential is well-positioned, based on its expertise, asset base and overall credit worthiness, to assume this financial responsibility. You will have the full financial backing of Prudential and over $250 billion in assets and capital. In addition, your monthly pension benefit will have the backing of state guaranty insurance funds. Prudential has a well-established and strong reputation for providing pension plan services to 3.7 million active workers and retirees.

In the next few months, Prudential will mail you additional information, including an annuity certificate describing your right to continued monthly benefit payments from Prudential.

Enclosed is a **Pension Benefit Statement** that provides information about your current monthly pension benefit amount. In addition, enclosed is a list of frequently asked questions about this pension transfer. For more details on the pension transfer, please go to **www.vzpensiontransfer.com** (password: pension2013).

If you believe any information on the enclosed **Pension Benefit Statement** is incorrect, or if you have questions, please call the Pension Transfer Information Center at **1-800-340-1139**.

Sincerely,

Marc C. Reed
Chief Administrative Officer

Appendix V.

November 29, 2012 13:46 ET

Verizon Retirees Sue to Halt Verizon's $7.5 Billion Sell-Off of 41,000 Pensions

Federal Court Action Seeks to Reverse Spin-Off to Prudential Insurance Annuity Plan

COLD SPRING HARBOR, NY--(Marketwire - Nov 29, 2012) - Management retirees of Verizon Communications Inc. (NYSE: VZ) have filed a federal lawsuit to halt their former employer's plan to sell off 41,000 Employee Retirement Income Security Act (ERISA) protected pensions to the Prudential Insurance Company of America (NYSE: PRU) in exchange for providing Prudential with $7.5 billion in Verizon retirees' pension assets. If the pension spinoff, which was expected to close in December, is not halted, beginning in January 2013, Prudential will replace retirees' pensions with insurance annuities that are not ERISA-protected.

Attorneys Curtis L. Kennedy of Denver and Bob Goodman of Dallas representing retirees in conjunction with the 128,000 member non-profit Association of BellTel Retirees Inc. (www.BellTel-Retirees.org) have filed for a request for an immediate temporary restraining order to be followed by a hearing to consider a preliminary injunction in the United States District Court, Northern District of Texas, Dallas Division charging that Verizon's plan to transfer the retirees' pensions from the Verizon Management Pension Plan into Prudential issued insurance annuities violates federal ERISA law.

On October 17 Verizon surprised 41,000 pre-January 1, 2010 company management retirees when it disclosed the transaction. Retirees claim the conversion to an annuity wipes out the federally insured pension safety net provided by the Pension Benefit Guaranty Corporation (PBGC) and is an effort to sever retirees ERISA protections, as well as the company's fiduciary responsibilities to the very retirees who built their company. The Verizon Management Pension Plan currently has approximately 100,000 participants, including plaintiffs.

Retiree association President C. William Jones said, "On behalf of 41,000 Verizon retirees scattered across the country, who are being given no choice, no voice and no protection in the transfer of their pension assets, we are calling upon the company to reverse this action and halt this predatory business transaction that will impact many retired Americans, who labored a lifetime to fund their earned pension benefits."

Retirees note that Prudential could also sell or transfer all or part of its ownership of the annuity asset to another company. While Prudential looks and sounds like a solid insurance company, the retirees say America's history is littered with the carcasses of many once-great and too-big-to-fail financial powerhouses such as: AIG, Kentucky Central Life Insurance Co, Executive Life, The Equitable Life Assurance Society (Equitable Life), Lehman Brothers and Bear Stearns.

Should the insurer experience a default or asset shortfall, the PBGC would be replaced with a patchwork network of state guaranty associations, many of which are underfunded.

Corporate retirees, like Verizon's who are at least 65 years of age, are insured by the PBGC, up to the limit of $55,800 per year, per retiree for an unlimited number of years. By spinning off the 41,000 pensions to an annuity provider, Verizon retirees' PBGC protections are replaced by insufficient and varying coverage -- generally determined by state of residence at the time of impairment -- from $100,000 - $500,000 (lifetime per person cap).

Eight states and one U.S. territory -- AK, AZ, IN, MA, MS, MO,

NH, NV and Puerto Rico -- limit total lifetime coverage for annuity holders in case of a default or shortfall to a lifetime maximum of $100,000;

28 others -- CA, CO, DE, HI, ID, IL, IA, KS, LA, ME, MD, MI, MN, MT, NE, NM, ND, OH, RI, SD, TN, TX, UT, VT, VA, WV, WY - go up to $250,000 lifetime coverage;

10 states and District of Columbia use a $300,000 top end -- AL, AR, FL, GA, NC, OK, OR, PA, SC, WI;

Just 4 -- CT, NJ, NY, WA -- go up a ceiling of $500,000;

Mr. Jones said, "Retirees and their spouses, especially in states with the lowest protection levels, will be seriously harmed and left with as little as two years pension replacement in case of insurer default. Verizon's pension spin-off and conversion to a non-PBGC insurance annuity offers zero protection or upside for tens of thousands of Ma Bell's orphans."

The case is: William Lee and Joanne McPartlin and Plan Beneficiaries of the Verizon Management Pension Plan vs Verizon Communications Inc. in the United States District Court, Northern District of Texas, Dallas Division (Case No: 3:12-CV-04834-D).

Source: http://www.marketwired.com/press-release/verizon-retirees-sue-to-halt-verizons-75-billion-sell-off-of-41000-pensions-nyse-vz-1731941.htm

Appendix VI.

From:
Living Our Values
Verizon Corporate Responsibility Report 2005

Improving Through Innovation

Fuels Cells

In 2005, we launched a major trial of an environmental friendly technology at our switching center and office building in Garden City, N.Y.

Paul Belard (foreground) with Jon Chesnut (right), spearheaded the largest trial of alternative use in America at Verizon's Garden City, N.Y., switching center and offices.

The project - the largest of its kind in the country - consists of seven fuel cells, each of which is capable of generating 200 kilowatts of electrical power per hour, enough to supply the energy needs of about 400 single-family households.

By using electricity generated by the fuel cells and reclaiming the heat and water they produce to help heat and cool the building, Verizon will eliminate annually approximately 11.1 million pounds of CO_2 that would have been emitted into the atmosphere by a fossil-fuel based power plant of similar size.

Verizon's Garden City project is unique because the existing commercial power grid, the new fuel cells and existing Verizon back-up power generators work together to meet any set of operational needs required. They include electrical backup for commercial power outages, natural disasters and periods of peak commercial power demands.